Prefaces to
SHAKESPEARE

Harley Granville-Barker

Hamlet

B. T. BATSFORD LTD
LONDON

FIRST PUBLISHED 1930
FIRST PUBLISHED IN THIS FORMAT 1968
SECOND IMPRESSION 1971
THIRD IMPRESSION 1977

*For copyright reasons this book may not be issued
to the public on loan or otherwise,
except in its original soft cover.*

ISBN 0 7134 2050 2

REPRODUCED AND PRINTED IN GREAT BRITAIN BY
BILLING & SONS LTD, GUILDFORD, LONDON AND WORCESTER
FOR THE PUBLISHERS
B. T. BATSFORD LTD.
4 FITZHARDINGE STREET, LONDON W1H 0AH

Introduction

WE have still much to learn about Shakespeare the playwright. Strange that it should be so, after three centuries of commentary and performance, but explicable. For the Procrustean methods of a changed theater deformed the plays, and put the art of them to confusion; and scholars, with this much excuse, have been apt to divorce their Shakespeare from the theater altogether, to think him a poet whose use of the stage was quite incidental, whose glory had small relation to it, for whose lapses it was to blame.

The Study and the Stage

THIS much is to be said for Garrick and his predecessors and successors in the practice of reshaping Shakespeare's work to the theater of their time. The essence of it was living drama to them, and they meant to keep it alive for their public. They wanted to avoid whatever would provoke question and so check that spontaneity of response upon which acted drama depends. Garrick saw the plays, with their lack of "art," through the spectacles of contemporary culture; and the bare Elizabethan stage, if it met his mind's eye at all, doubtless as a barbarous makeshift. Shakespeare was for him a problem; he tackled it, from our point of view, misguidedly and with an overplus of enthusiasm. His was a positive world; too near in time, moreover, as well as too opposed in taste to Shakespeare's to treat it perspectively. The romantic movement might have brought a more concordant outlook. But by then the scholars were off their own way; while the theater began to think of its Shakespeare from the point of view of the picturesque, and, later, in terms of upholstery. Nineteenth century drama developed along the lines of realistic illusion, and the staging of Shakespeare was further subdued to this, with inevitably disastrous effect on the speaking of his verse; there was less perversion of text perhaps, but actually more wrenching of the construction of the plays for the convenience of the stage carpenter. The public appetite for this sort of thing having been gorged, producers then turned to newer—and older—contrivances, leaving "realism" (so called) to the modern comedy that had fathered it. Amid much vaporous theorizing—but let us humbly own how hard it is not to write nonsense about art, which seems ever pleading to be enjoyed and not written about at all—the surprising discovery had been made that varieties of stagecraft and stage were not historical accidents but artistic obligations, that Greek drama belonged in a Greek theater, that Elizabethan plays, therefore, would, presumably, do best upon an Elizabethan stage, that there was nothing sacrosanct about scenery, footlights, drop-curtain or any of their belongings. This brings us to the present situation.

There are few enough Greek theaters in which Greek tragedy can be played; few enough people want to see it, and they will applaud it encouragingly however it is done. Some acknowledgment is due to the altruism of the doers! Shakespeare is another matter. The English theater, doubtful of its destiny, of necessity venal, opening its doors to all comers, seems yet, as by some instinct, to seek renewal of strength in him. An actor, unless success has made him cynical, or his talent be merely trivial, may take some pride in the hall mark of Shakespearean achievement. So may a manager if he thinks he can afford it. The public (or their spokesmen) seem to consider Shakespeare and his genius a sort of national property, which, truly, they do nothing to conserve, but in which they have moral rights not lightly to be flouted. The production of the plays is thus still apt to be marked by a timid respect for "the usual thing"; their acting is crippled by pseudo-traditions, which are inert because they are not Shakespearean at all. They are the accumulation of two centuries of progressive misconception and distortion of his playwright's art. On the other hand, England has been spared production of Shakespeare according to this or that even more irrelevant theory of presentationalism,

symbolism, constructivism or what not. There is the breach in the
wall of "realism," but we have not yet made up our minds to pass
through, taking our Shakespeare with us.

Incidentally, we owe the beginning of the breach to Mr. William Poel, who, with fanatical courage, when "realism" was at the
tottering height of its triumph in the later revivals of Sir Henry
Irving, and the yet more richly upholstered revelations of Sir
Herbert Tree, thrust the Elizabethan stage in all its apparent
eccentricity upon our unwilling notice.[1] Mr. Poel shook complacency. He could not expect to do much more; for he was a
logical reformer. He showed us the Elizabethan stage, with Antony and Cleopatra, Troilus and Cressida, in their ruffs and farthingales as for Shakespeare's audiences they lived. Q.E.D. There,
however, as far as the popular theater was concerned, the matter
seemed to rest for twenty years or so. But it was just such a demonstration that was needed; anything less drastic and provocative
might have been passed over with mild approval.

To get the balance true, let us admit that while Shakespeare
was an Elizabethan playwright he was—and now is to us—predominantly something much more. Therefore we had better not
too unquestioningly thrust him back within the confines his
genius has escaped, nor presume him to have felt the pettier circumstances of his theater sacrosanct. Nor can we turn Elizabethans as we watch the plays; and every mental effort to do so will
subtract from our enjoyment of them. This is the case against the
circumstantial reproduction of Shakespeare's staging. But Mr.
Poel's achievement remains; he cleared for us from Shakespeare's
stagecraft the scenic rubbish by which it had been so long encumbered and disguised. And we could now, if we would, make a
promising fresh start. For the scholars, on their side, have lately—
the scholarly among them—cut clear of the transcendental fog
(scenic illusion of another sort) in which their nineteenth century
peers loved to lose themselves, and they too are beginning again
at the beginning. A text acquires virtue now by its claim to be a
prompt book, and the most comprehensive work of our time upon
the Elizabethan stage is an elaborate sorting-out of plays, com-

---

[1] But it should not be forgotten that Sir Herbert Tree, happy in the orthodoxy
of public favor, welcomed the heretic Mr. Poel more than once to a share in his
Shakespeare Festivals.

panies and theaters. On Dr. Pollard's treatment of the texts and on the foundations of fact laid by Sir Edmund Chambers a new scholarship is rising, aiming first to see Shakespeare in the theater for which he wrote. It is a scholarship, therefore, by which the theater of today can profit, to which, by its acting of Shakespeare, it could contribute, one would hope. Nor should the scholars disdain the help; for criticism cannot live upon criticism, it needs refreshment from the living art. Besides, what is all the criticism and scholarship finally for if not to keep Shakespeare alive? And he must always be most alive—even if roughly and rudely alive—in the theater. Let the scholars force a way in there, if need be. Its fervid atmosphere will do them good; the benefit will be mutual.

These Prefaces are an attempt to profit by this new scholarship and to contribute to it some research into Shakespeare's stagecraft, by examining the plays, one after another, in the light of the interpretation he designed for them, so far as this can be deduced; to discover, if possible, the production he would have desired for them, all merely incidental circumstances apart. They might profit more written a generation hence, for the ground they build upon is still far from clear. And this Introduction is by no means a conspectus of the subject; that can only come as a sequel. There has been, in this branch of Shakespearean study, too much generalization and far too little analysis of material.[2]

Shakespeare's Stagecraft

SHAKESPEARE's own career was not a long one. The whole history of the theater he wrote for does not cover a century. Between Marlowe and Massinger, from the first blaze to the glowing of the embers, it is but fifty years. Yet even while Shakespeare was at work, the stage to which he fitted his plays underwent constant and perhaps radical change. From Burbage's first theater to the Globe, then to Blackfriars, not to mention excursions to Court and into the great halls—change of audiences and their behavior, of their taste, development of the art of acting, change of the stage itself and its resources were all involved in the progress, and are all, we may be sure, reflected to some degree in the plays them-

---

[2] I do not deal in general therefore with certain vexed questions, such as act-division, which still need to be looked at, I think, in the light of the particular play.

selves. We guess at the conditions of each sort of stage and theater, but there is often the teasing question to which of them had a play, as we have it now, been adapted. And of the "private" theater, most in vogue for the ten years preceding the printing of the First Folio, so far we know least. The dating of texts and their ascription to the usages of a particular theater may often be a searchlight upon their stagecraft. Here is much work for the new scholarship.

Conversely, the watchful working-out of the plays in action upon this stage or that would be of use to the scholars, who otherwise must reconstruct their theaters and gloss their texts as in a vacuum. The play was once fitted to the stage; it is by no means impossible to rebuild that stage now, with its doors, balconies, curtains and machines, by measuring the needs of the play. It is idle, for instance, to imagine scenes upon inner or upper stage without evidence that they will be audible or visible there; and editing is still vitiated by lack of this simple knowledge. Here, if nowhere else, this present research must fall short, for its method should rightly be experimental; more than one mind should be at work on it, moreover.

The text of a play is a score waiting performance, and the performance and its preparation are, almost from the beginning, a work of collaboration. A producer may direct the preparation, certainly. But if he only knows how to give orders, he has mistaken his vocation; he had better be a drill-sergeant. He might talk to his company when they all met together for the first time to study *Love's Labour's Lost*, *Julius Cæsar* or *King Lear*, on some such lines as these Prefaces pursue, giving a considered opinion of the play, drawing a picture of it in action, providing, in fact, a hypothesis which mutual study would prove—and might partly disprove. No sort of study of a play can better the preparation of its performance if this is rightly done. The matured art of the playwright lies in giving life to characters in action, and the secret of it in giving each character a due chance in the battle, the action of a play becoming literally the fighting of a battle of character. So the greater the playwright, the wider and deeper his sympathies, the more genuine this opposition will be and the less easily will a single mind grasp it, as it must be grasped, in the fullness of its emotion. The dialogue of a play runs—and often intricately—

upon lines of reason, but it is charged besides with an emotion which speech releases, yet only releases fully when the speaker is —as an actor is—identified with the character. There is further the incidental action, implicit in the dialogue, which springs to life only when a scene is in being. A play, in fact, as we find it written, is a magic spell; and even the magician cannot always foresee the full effect of it.

Not every play, it must be owned, will respond to such intensive study. Many, ambitiously conceived, would collapse under the strain. Many are mere occasions for display of their actors' wit or eloquence, good looks or nice behavior, and meant to be no more; and if they are skillfully contrived the parts fit together and the whole machine should go like clockwork. Nor, in fact, are even the greatest plays often so studied. There is hardly a theater in the world where masterpiece and trumpery alike are not rushed through rehearsals to an arbitrarily effective performance, little more learned of them than the words, gaps in the understanding of them filled up with "business"—effect without cause, the demand for this being the curse of the theater as of other arts, as of other things than art. Not to such treatment will the greater plays of Shakespeare yield their secrets. But working upon a stage which reproduced the essential conditions of his, working as students, not as showmen merely, a company of actors might well find many of the riddles of the library answering themselves unasked. And these Prefaces could best be a record of such work, if such work were to be done.

We cannot, on the other hand, begin our research by postulating the principles of the Elizabethan stage. One is tempted to say it had none, was too much a child of nature to bother about such things. Principles were doubtless imposed upon it when it reached respectability, and heads would be bowed to the yoke. Shakespeare's among them? He had served a most practical apprenticeship to his trade. If he did not hold horses at the door, he sat behind the curtains, we may be sure, and held the prompt book on occasion. He acted, he cobbled other men's plays, he could write his own to order. Such a one may stay a journeyman if he is not a genius, but he will not become a doctrinaire. Shakespeare's work shows such principles as the growth of a tree shows. It is not haphazard merely because it is not formal; it is shaped by inner strength. The theater, as he found it, allowed him and encouraged him to great freedom of development. Because the material resources of a stage are simple, it does not follow that the technique of its playwriting will stay so. Crude work may show up more crudely, when there are none of the fal-lals of illusion to disguise it that the modern theater provides. But, if he has it in him, a dramatist can, so unfettered, develop the essentials of his art more boldly and more subtly too. The Elizabethan drama made an amazingly quick advance from crudity to an excellence which was often technically most elaborate. The advance and the not less amazing gulf which divides its best from its worst may be ascribed to the simplicity of the machinery it employed. That its decadence was precipitated by the influence of the Masque and the shifting of its center of interest from the barer public stage to the candle-lit private theater, where the machinery of the Masque became effective, it would be rash to assert; but the occurrences are suspiciously related. Man and machine (here at any rate is a postulate, if a platitude!) are false allies in the theater, secretly at odds; and when man gets the worst of it, drama is impoverished; and the struggle, we may add, is perennial. No great drama depends upon pageantry. All great drama tends to concentrate upon character; and, even so, not upon picturing men as they show themselves to the world like figures on a stage—though that is how it must ostensibly show them—but on the hidden man. And the progress of Shakespeare's art from *Love's Labour's Lost* to *Hamlet*, and thereafter with a difference, lies in the simplifying of this paradox and the solving of the problem it presents; and the process involves the developing of a very subtle sort of stagecraft indeed.

For one result we have what we may call a very self-contained drama. Its chief values, as we know, have not changed with the fashions of the theater. It relies much on the music of the spoken word, and a company of schoolchildren with pleasant voices, and an ear for rhythm, may vociferate through a play to some effect. It is as much to be enjoyed in the reading, if we hear it in imagination as we read, as drama meant to be acted can be. As with its simplicities then, so it should be, we presume, with its complexities. The subtly emotional use of verse and the interplay of motive and character, can these not be appreciated apart from the bare boards of their original setting? It does not follow. It neither follows that the advantages of the Elizabethan stage were wholly negative nor that, with our present knowledge, we can imagine the full effect of a play in action upon it. The imagining of a play in action is, under no circumstances, an easy thing.[3] What would one not give to go backward through the centuries to see the first performance of *Hamlet*, played as Shakespeare had it played![4] In default, if we could but make ourselves read it as if it were a manuscript fresh from its author's hands! There is much to be said for turning one's back on the editors, even, when possible, upon the First Folio with its demarcation of acts and scenes, in favor of the Quartos—Dr. Pollard's "good" Quartos—in their yet greater simplicity.

The Convention of Place

It is, for instance, hard to discount the impression made merely by reading: *Scene i—Elsinore. A platform before the Castle*; and most of us have, to boot, early memories of painted battlements and tenth century castles (of aging Hamlets and their portly mothers for that matter) very difficult to dismiss. No great harm, one protests; it was a help, perhaps, to the unimaginative. But it is a first step to the certain misunderstanding of Shakespeare's stagecraft. The "if, how and when" of the presenting of localities on the Elizabethan stage is, of course, a complex question. Shakespeare himself seems to have followed, consciously, no principles in the matter, nor was his practice very logical, nor at all consistent. It may vary with the play he is writing and the particular stage he is writing for; it will best be studied in relation to each play. We can, however, free ourselves from one general misconception which belongs to our own overlogical standpoint. When we learn with a shock of surprise—having begun in the school-

---

[3] I remember a most intelligent reader of a modern play missing the whole point of a scene through which the chief character was to sit conspicuously and eloquently silent. He counted only with the written dialogue. I remember, when I thought I knew *King Lear* well enough, being amazed at the effect, all dialogue apart, of the mere meeting, when I saw it, of blind Gloucester and mad Lear.

[4] Though, in a sense, there was no first performance of *Hamlet*. And doubtless many of the audience for Shakespeare's new version of the old play only thought he had spoiled a good story of murder and revenge by adding too much talk to it.

room upon the Shakespeare of the editors, it comes as belated
news to us—that neither battlements, throne rooms nor picturesque churchyards were to be seen at the Globe, and that *Elsinore.
A platform before the Castle* is not Shakespeare at all, we yet
imagine ourselves among the audience there busily conjuring
these things up before the eye of faith. The Elizabethan audience
was at no such pains. Nor was this their alternative to seeing the
actors undisguisedly concerned with the doors, curtains and balconies which, by the play's requirements, should have been anything but what they were. As we, when a play has no hold on us,
may fall to thinking about the scenery, so to a Globe audience,
unmoved, the stage might be an obvious bare stage. But are we conscious of the scenery behind the actor when the play really moves
us? If we are, there is something very wrong with the scenery,
which should know its place as a background. The audience was
not conscious of curtain and balcony when Burbage played Hamlet to them. They were conscious of Hamlet. That conventional
background faded as does our painted illusion, and they certainly
did not deliberately conjure up in its place mental pictures of
Elsinore. The genus audience is passive, if expectant, imagina-
tively lazy till roused, never, one may be sure, at pains to make any
effort that is generally *un*necessary to enjoyment.

With Shakespeare the locality of a scene has dramatic importance, or it has none; and this is as true of his early plays as his
late ones. Both in *Richard II* and *Antony and Cleopatra*, scene after
scene passes with no exact indication of where we may be. With
Cleopatra we are surely in Egypt, with Cæsar in Rome. Pompey
appears, and the talk tells us that both Egypt and Rome are elsewhere; but positively where Pompey is at the moment we never
learn.[5] Indoors or outdoors? The action of the scene or the cloth-
ing of the characters will tell us this if we need to know. But,
suddenly transported to the Parthian war, our whereabouts is
made amply plain. It is, however, made plain by allusion. The
information peeps out through talk of kindred things; we are
hardly aware we are being told, and, again, we learn no more than
we need to learn. This, truly, is a striking development from the
plump and plain

---

[5] Unless it may be said that we learn in the scene after whereabouts he *was*.

Barkloughly Castle call they this at hand?

of *Richard II*, even from the more descriptive

> I am a stranger here in Gloucestershire:
> These high wild hills and rough, uneven ways
> Draw out our miles. . . .

by which Shakespeare pictures and localizes the maneuvers of Richard and Bolingbroke when he wants to. But the purpose is the same, and the method essentially the same.[6] Towards the end of the later play come scene after scene of the marching and countermarching of armies, of fighting, of truce, all the happenings of a three days' battle. Acts III and IV contain twenty-eight scenes long and short; some of them are very short; three of them have but four lines apiece. The editors conscientiously ticket them *A plain near Actium, Another part of the plain, Another part of the plain* and so on, and conclude that Shakespeare is really going too far and too fast, is indeed (I quote Sir Edmund Chambers) "in some danger of outrunning the apprehensions of his auditory." Indeed he might be if this cinematographic view of his intentions were the right one! But it utterly falsifies them. Show an audience such a succession of painted scenes—if you could at the pace required—and they would give attention to nothing else whatever; the drama would pass unnoticed. Had Shakespeare tried to define the whereabouts of every scene in any but the baldest phrases—the protesting editors seem not to see that he makes no attempt to; only *they* do!—he would have had to lengthen and complicate them; had he written only a labeling line or two he would still have distracted his audience from the essential drama. Ignoring whereabouts, letting it at most transpire when it naturally will, the characters capture all attention. This is the true gain of the bare stage; unless to some dramatic end no precious words need be spent, in complying with the undramatic demands of space and time; incarnation of character can be all in all. Given such a crisis as this the gain is yet greater. We are carried through the phases of the three days' battle; and what other stage convention would allow us so varied a view of it, could so

---

[6] And in *Coriolanus*, which probably postdates *Antony and Cleopatra*, with Marcius' "A goodly city is this Antium," we are back to the barely informative. It serves Shakespeare's purpose; he asks no more.

isolate the true drama of it? For do we not pass through such a crisis in reality with just that indifference to time and place? These scenes, in their kind, show Shakespeare's stagecraft, not at its most reckless, but at its very best, and exemplify perfectly the freedom he enjoyed that the stage of visual illusion has inevitably lost. His drama is attached solely to its actors and their acting; that, perhaps, puts it in a phrase. They carry place and time with them as they move. The modern theater still accepts the convention that measures time more or less by a play's convenience; a half-hour stands for an hour or more, and we never question the vagary. It was no more strange to an Elizabethan audience to see a street in Rome turned, in the use made of it, to the Senate House by the drawing of a curtain and the disclosure of Cæsar's state, to find Cleopatra's Monument now on the upper stage because Antony had to be drawn up to it, later on the lower because Cleopatra's death-scene could best be played there; it would seem that they were not too astonished even when Juliet, having taken leave of Romeo on the balcony of her bedroom and watched him descend to the lower stage, the scene continuing, came down, a few lines later, to the lower stage herself, bringing, so to speak, her bedroom with her—since this apparently is what she must have done.[7] For neither Senate House, Monument nor balcony had rights and reality of their own. They existed for the convenience of the actors, whose touch gave them life, a shadowy life at most; neglected, they existed no longer.[8]

Shakespeare's stagecraft concentrates, and inevitably, upon opportunity for the actor. We think now of the plays themselves; their first public knew them by their acting; and the development of the actor's art from the agilities and funniments of the clown, and from round-mouthed rhetoric to imaginative interpreting of character by such standards as Hamlet set up for his players, was a factor in the drama's triumph that we now too often ignore. Shakespeare himself, intent more and more upon plucking out

[7] I fancy, though, that the later Shakespeare would have thought this a clumsy device.

[8] How far this is true of other dramatists than Shakespeare I do not pretend to say; nor how far, with him, the influence of the private theater, making undoubtedly towards the scenic stage and (much later) for illusion, did not modify his practice, when he had that stage to consider. A question, again, for the bibliographers and historians.

the heart of the human mystery, stimulated his actors to a poignancy and intimacy of emotional expression—still can stimulate them to it—as no other playwright has quite learned to do.

The Speaking of the Verse

His verse was, of course, his chief means to this emotional expression; and when it comes to staging the plays, the speaking of the verse must be the foundation of all study. The changes of three hundred years have of themselves put difficulties in our way here; though there are some besides—as one imagines—of Shakespeare's own making. Surely his syntax must now and then have puzzled even his contemporaries. Could they have made much more than we can of Leontes'

> Affection! thy intention stabs the centre;
> Thou dost make possible things not so held,
> Communicat'st with dreams;—How can this be?
> With what's unreal thou coactive art,
> And fellow'st nothing; then, 'tis very credent
> Thou may'st co-join with something; and thou dost;
> And that beyond commission; and I find it,
> And that to the infection of my brains,
> And hardening of my brows.

The confusion of thought and intricacy of language is dramatically justified. Shakespeare is picturing a genuinely jealous man (the sort of man that Othello was *not*) in the grip of a mental epilepsy. We parse the passage and dispute its sense; spoken, as it was meant to be, in a choking torrent of passion, probably a modicum of sense slipped through, and its first hearers did not find it a mere rigmarole. But we are apt to miss even that much. Other passages, of early and late writing, may always have had as much sound as sense to them; but now, to the casual hearer, they will convey more sound than sense by far. Nor do puns mean to us what they meant to the Elizabethans, delighting in their language for its own sake. Juliet's tragic fantasia upon "Aye" and "I" sounds all but ridiculous, and one sympathizes with an actress hesitating to venture on it. How far, apart from the shifting of accents and the recoloring of vowels, has not the whole habit of English speech changed in these three hundred years? In the theater it was slowing down, one fancies, throughout the eighteenth century; and in the nineteenth, as far as Shakespeare was concerned, it grew slower and slower, till on occasions one thought—even hoped—that shortly the actor would stop altogether. There may have been more than one cause; imitation of the French Augustans, the effort to make antiquated phrases understood, the increasing size of the theaters themselves would all contribute to it. The result, in any case, is disastrous. Elizabethan drama was built upon vigor and beauty of speech. The groundlings may often have deserved Shakespeare's strictures, but they would stand in discomfort for an hour or so to be stirred by the sound of verse. Some of the actors no doubt were robustious periwig-pated fellows, but, equally, it was no empty ideal of acting he put into Hamlet's mouth—and Burbage's. We may suppose that at its best the mere speaking of the plays was a very brilliant thing, comparable to *bel canto*, or to a pianist's virtuosity. The emotional appeal of our modern music was in it, and it could be tested by ears trained to the rich and delicate fretwork of the music of that day. Most Hamlets—not being playwrights—make a mild joke of telling us they'd as lief the town-crier spoke their lines, but we may hear in it the echo of some of Shakespeare's sorest trials.

The speaking of his verse must be studied, of course, in relation to the verse's own development. The actor must not attack its supple complexities in *Antony and Cleopatra* and *Cymbeline*, the mysterious dynamics of *Macbeth*, the nobilities of *Othello*, its final pastoral simplicities in *A Winter's Tale* and *The Tempest* without preliminary training in the lyricism, the swift brilliance and the masculine clarity of the earlier plays. A modern actor, alas, thinks it simple enough to make his way, splayfooted, through

> The cloud-capped towers, the gorgeous palaces . . .

though Berowne's

> I, forsooth, in love . . .

or one of Oberon's apostrophes will defeat him utterly. And, without an ear trained to the delicacy of the earlier work, his hearers, for their part, will never know how shamefully he is betraying the superb ease of the later. If we are to make Shakespeare our own again we must all be put to a little trouble about it. We must recapture as far as may be his lost meanings; and the sense of a phrase we *can* recapture, though instinctive emotional response to it may be a loss forever. The tunes that he writes to, the whole great art of his music-making, we can master. Actors can train their ears and tongues and can train our ears to it. We talk of lost arts. No art is ever lost while the means to it survive. Our faculties rust by disuse and by misuse are coarsened, but they quickly recover delight in a beautiful thing. Here, at any rate, is the touchstone by which all interpreting of Shakespeare the playwright must first—and last—be tried.

The Boy-Actress

More than one of the conditions of his theater made this medium of accomplished speech of such worth to him. Boys played the women parts; and what could a boy bring to Juliet, Rosalind or Cleopatra beyond grace of manner and charm of speech? We have been used to women on the stage for two hundred and fifty years or more, and a boy Juliet—if the name on the program revealed one, for nothing else might—would seem an odd fish to us; no one would risk a squeaking Cleopatra; though, as for Rosalind, through three-parts of the play a boy would have the best of it. But the parts were written for boys; not, therefore, without consideration of how boys could act them most convincingly. Hence, of course, the popularity of the heroine so disguised. The disguise was perfect; the make-believe one degree more complex, certainly, than it needs to be with us; but once you start make-believe it matters little how far you go with it; there is, indeed, some enjoyment in the make-believe itself. But, further, it is Shakespeare's constant care to demand nothing of a boy-actress that might turn to unseemliness or ridicule. He had not much taste for what is called "domestic drama," nor does he dose us very heavily with Doll Tearsheet, Mistress Overdone and their like. Constance mourns Arthur's loss, Lady Macduff has her little son, but no mother croons over the child in her arms. Paulina brings Hermione's baby to Leontes, it is true; but see with what tact, from this point of view, the episode is managed. And love-scenes are most carefully contrived. Romeo and Juliet are seldom alone together; never for long, but in the balcony-scene; and in this, the

most famous of love-scenes, they are kept from all contact with
each other. Consider *Antony and Cleopatra*. Here is a tragedy of
sex without one single scene of sexual appeal. That aspect of
Cleopatra is reflected for us in talk about her; mainly by Enobar-
bus, who is not mealymouthed; but his famed description of her
voluptuousness is given us when she has been out of our sight for
several scenes. The play opens with her parting from Antony, and
in their two short encounters we see her swaying him by wit,
malice and with the moods of her mind. Not till the story takes
its tragic plunge and sex is drowned in deeper passion are they
ever intimately together; till he is brought to her dying there has
been occasion for but one embrace. Contrast this with a possible
Cleopatra planned to the advantage of the actress of today.

Shakespeare, artist that he was, turned this limitation to account,
made loss into a gain.[9] Feminine charm—of which the modern
stage makes such capital—was a medium denied him. So his men
and women encounter upon a plane where their relation is made
rarer and intenser by poetry, or enfranchised in a humor which
surpasses more primitive love-making. And thus, perhaps, he was
helped to discover that the true stuff of tragedy and of the liveliest
comedy lies beyond sensual bounds. His studies of women seem
often to be begun from some spiritual paces beyond the point at
which a modern dramatist leaves off. Curious that not a little of
the praise lavished upon the beauty and truth of them—mainly
by women—may be due to their having been written to be played
by boys!

Much could be said for the restoring of the celibate stage; but
the argument, one fears, would be academic. Here, though, is
practical counsel. Let the usurping actress remember that her sex
is a liability, not an asset. The dramatist of today may refuse to
exploit its allurements, but may legitimately allow for the sympa-
thetic effect of it; though the less he does so, perhaps, the better
for his play and the more gratitude the better sort of actress will
show him. But Shakespeare makes no such demands, has left no

---

[9] There is no evidence, of course, that he felt it a loss, no such reference to the
insufficiency of the boy-actress as there is to the overself-sufficiency of the clown.
Women did appear in the Masques, if only to dance, so the gulf to be bridged was
not a broad one. But the Elizabethan was as shocked by the notion of women
appearing upon the public stage as the Chinese playgoer is today.

blank spaces for her to fill with her charm. He asks instead for
self-forgetful clarity of perception, and for a sensitive, spirited,
athletic beauty of speech and conduct, which will leave prettiness
and its lures at a loss, and the crudities of more Circean appeal
looking very crude indeed.

The Soliloquy

THIS convention of the boy-actress may be said to give a certain
remoteness to a play's acting. The soliloquy brings a compensating
intimacy, and its use was an important part of Shakespeare's
stagecraft. Its recognized usefulness was for the disclosing of the
plot, but he soon improved upon this Soliloquy becomes the means
by which he brings us not only to a knowledge of the more secret
thoughts of his characters, but into the closest emotional touch
with them too. Here the platform stage helped him, as the stage
of scenic illusion now defeats his purpose. But it is not altogether
a question of "realism" and the supposed obligation this lays upon
a real man in a real-looking room to do nothing he would not do
if the whole affair were real.

There is no escape from convention in the theater, and all conventions can be made acceptable, though they cannot all be used
indiscriminately, for they are founded in the physical conditions
of the stage of their origin and are often interdependent one with
another. Together they form a code, and they are as a treaty made
with the audience. No article of it is to be abrogated unless we can
be persuaded to consent, and upon its basis we surrender our imag-
inations to the playwright.

With the soliloquy upon the platform stage it is a case—as so
often where convention is concerned—of extremes meeting. There
is no illusion, so there is every illusion. Nothing very strange about
this man, not even the dress he wears, leaning forward a little we
could touch him; we are as intimate and familiar with him as it
is possible to be. We agree to call him "Hamlet," to suppose that
he is where he says he is, we admit that he thinks aloud and in
blank verse too. It is possible that the more we are asked to
imagine the easier we find it to do. It is certain that, once our
imagination is working, visual illusion will count for little in the

stimulating of emotion beside this intimacy that allows the magnetism of personality full play.

There is no more important task for the producer of Shakespeare than to restore to the soliloquy its rightful place in a play's economy, and in particular to regain for it full emotional effect. We now accept the convention frigidly, the actor maneuvers with it timidly. Banished behind footlights into that other world of illusion, the solitary self-communing figure rouses our curiosity at best. Yet further adapted to the self-contained methods of modern acting, the soliloquy has quite inevitably become a slack link in the play's action, when it should be a recurring reinforcement to its strength. Shakespeare never pinned so many dramatic fortunes to a merely utilitarian device. Time and again he may be feeling his way through a scene for a grip on his audience, and it is the soliloquy ending it that will give him—and his actor—the stranglehold. When he wishes to quicken the pulse of the action, to screw up its tension in a second or so, the soliloquy serves him well. For a parallel to its full effectiveness on Shakespeare's stage we should really look to the modern music-hall comedian getting on terms with his audience. We may measure the response to Burbage's

> O, that this too too solid flesh would melt . . .

by recalling—those of us that happily can—Dan Leno as a washerwoman, confiding domestic troubles to a theater full of friends, and taken unhindered to their hearts. The problem is not really a difficult one. If we solve the physical side of it by restoring, in essentials, the relation between actor and audience that the intimacy of the platform stage provided, the rest should soon solve itself.

Costume

THE problem of costume, when it arises, is a subtler one; nor probably is it capable of any logical solution. Half the plays can be quite appropriately dressed in the costume of Shakespeare's own time. It is a false logic which suggests that to match their first staging we should dress them in the costume of ours. For with costume goes custom and manners—or the lack of them. It may be both a purge and a tonic to the sluggish-fancied spectator to be

shown a Prince of Denmark in coat and trousers and a Gravedigger in a bowler hat, for reminder that here is a play, not a
collection of ritualized quotations. But physic is for the sick; also,
there may be less drastic cures. When archaeology took hold upon
the nineteenth century mind it became a matter of moment to
lodge Hamlet in historic surroundings; and withers were wrung
by the anachronisms of ducats and a murder of Gonzago, French
rapiers and the rest. A needlessly teasing difficulty; why reproduce
it in terms of a young man in a dinner jacket searching for a
sword—a thing not likely to be lying about in his modern mother's sitting room—with which to kill Polonius, who certainly has
window curtains to hide behind instead of arras? This gain of
intimacy—with a Hamlet we might find sitting opposite at a
dinner party—may well be a gain in sympathy. It was originally
a great gain, a gift to Shakespeare's audience. But we pay too high
a price for it.

What was the actual Elizabethan practice in this matter of costuming is not comprehensively known. We can only say safely
that, as with other matters, it was neither constant, consistent, nor,
from our present point of view, rational. It was based upon the
use of the clothes of the time; but these might be freely and fantastically adapted to suit a particular play or advantage some character in it. Dramatic effect was probably the first consideration
and the last. There were such fancy dresses as Oberon or Puck or
Caliban might wear; there was always the symbolizing of royalty,
and a king would wear a crown whenever he could; there was
the utility of knowing Romans from Britons by sight in *Cymbeline*, the martial Roman from the effete Egyptian in *Antony and
Cleopatra*, and a Scottish lord when you saw him in *Macbeth*, if
we may judge by Malcolm's comment upon Rosse's appearance:

> My countryman; and yet I know him not.

Our difficulty, of course, arises mainly over the historical plays.
Not over the English Histories, even so; we can dress Richard III
or Henry V by the light of our own superior knowledge of what
they wore, and never find it clash violently with anything Shakespeare has put on their backs or in their mouths. But when we
come to Julius Cæsar plucking open his doublet, to the con-

spirators against him with their hats about their ears, and to Cleopatra's

> Cut my lace, Charmian.

not to mention British Imogen in her doublet and hose, we must stop and consider.

The common practice is, in these instances, to ignore the details of Shakespeare's text altogether; to dress Cæsar in his toga, Cleopatra in her habit as she lived, with never a stay-lace about her (though, truly, the costumier, let alone, will tend to get his fashion a few thousand years wrong and turn her out more like the wife of Tutankhamen); and as to Imogen and her surroundings, we do our best to compromise with skins and woad. This may be a lesser evil than presenting a Cæsar recalling Sir Walter Raleigh and a Cleopatra who would make us think of Mary Queen of Scots, but it is no solution of the problem. For the actors have to speak these lines, and if action and appearance contradict them, credibility is destroyed. And the constant credibility of the actor must be a producer's first care. Nor is this all, nor is it, perhaps, the most important thing to consider. The plays are full of reference, direct and indirect, to Elizabethan custom. They are, further, impregnated with what we call "Renaissance feeling," some more, some less, but all to a degree. Now of this last we have a sense which is likelier to be a better help to their appreciation than any newfangled knowledge of the correct cut of Cleopatra's clothes will be! We know Iago for a Machiavellian figure (so called), and miss none of Shakespeare's intention. But if ever two men breathed the air of a sixteenth century Court, Hamlet and Claudius of Denmark do, and to relate them in habit and behavior to the twilight figures of Saxo Grammaticus is as much a misinterpretation as any mauling of the text can be. They exist essentially doubtless—as do all the major characters of the plays—in their perennial humanity. But never let us forget the means by which this deeper truth of them is made vivid and actual. There have been better intellects than Shakespeare's, and poetry as good as his. He holds his supreme place by his dramatist's necessary power of bringing thought and vague emotion to the terms of action and convincing speech; further, and far more than is often allowed, by his peculiar gift of bringing into contribution the commonplace traffic of life. However wide the spoken word may range, there must be the actor, anchored to the stage. However high, then, with Shakespeare, the thought or emotion may soar, we shall always find the transcendental set in the familiar. He keeps this balance constantly adjusted; and, at his play's greatest moments, when he must make most sure of our response, he will employ the simplest means. The higher arguments of the plays are thus kept always within range, and their rooted humanity blossoms in a fertile upspringing of expressive little things. Neglect or misinterpret these, the inner wealth of Shakespeare will remain, no doubt, and we may mine for it, but we shall have leveled his landscape bare.

Shakespeare's own attitude in this matter of costume and customs was as inconsistent as his practice was casual. He knew what *his* Cæsar or Cleopatra would be wearing and would casually drop in a reference to it. Yet the great Romans themselves were aliens to him. The great idea of Rome fired his imagination. Brutus, Cassius and Antony do not turn typical Elizabethan gentlemen; and to the end of that play he is striving to translate Plutarch. Whenever, on the other hand, even for a moment he has made a character all his own, he cannot but clothe it in lively familiar detail. Cleopatra's are the coquetries of a great lady of his own time, in their phrasing, in their savor. When the heights of the tragedy have to be scaled, manners will not so much matter. But if we make her, at the play's beginning, a pseudo-classic, languishing Oriental, we must do it in spite of Shakespeare, not by his help. What then is the solution of this problem, if the sight of the serpent of old Nile in a farthingale will too dreadfully offend us? We can compromise. Look at Tintoretto's and Paolo Veronese's paintings of "classic" subjects. We accept them readily enough.

Sometimes, within the boundaries of a play, the centuries seem all at odds. *Cymbeline* need not trouble us, its Roman Britain is pure "once upon a time." But in *King Lear*, for instance, Shakespeare is at unwonted pains to throw us back into some heathen past. Yet Edmund is another Iago, Edgar might have been at Wittenberg with Hamlet, and Oswald steps straight from the seventeenth century London streets. Here, though, the dominant barbarism is the important thing; the setting for Goneril and

Regan, Lear's tyranny and madness, and Gloucester's blinding. To
a seventeenth century audience Oswald was so identifiable a
figure that it would not matter greatly how he dressed; the modern designer of costume must show him up as best he may. Each
play, in fine, if it presents a problem at all, presents its own.

The Integrity of the Text

THE text, one says at first blush, can present no problem at all.
The plays should be acted as Shakespeare wrote them—how dispute it? They should be; and it is as well, before we discuss hard
cases, to have the principle freely admitted. Lip service enough is
done it nowadays, and Colley Cibber's *Richard III*, Tate's *Lear*
and Garrick's improvements are at the back of our bookshelves,
but we still find Messrs. John Doe and Richard Roe slicing out
lines by the dozen and even a scene or so, or chopping and changing them to suit their scenery. This will not do. Shakespeare was
not a perfect playwright; there can be no such thing. Nor did he
aim at a mechanical perfection, but at vitality, and this he
achieved. At best then, we cut and carve the body of a play to its
peril. It may be robustly, but it may be very delicately organized.
And we still know little enough of the laws of its existence, and
some of us, perhaps, are not such very skillful surgeons; nor is
any surgeon to be recommended who operates for his own convenience.

This good rule laid down, what are the exceptions that go to
prove it? There is the pornographic difficulty. This is not such a
stumbling block to us as it was to Bowdler, to some bright young
eyes nowadays it is quite imperceptible, in fact. Yet, saving their
presence, it exists; for it exists aesthetically. Shakespeare's characters often make obscene jokes. The manners of his time permitted
it. The public manners of ours still do not. Now the dramatic
value of a joke is to be measured by its effect upon an audience,
and each is meant to make its own sort of effect. If then, instead
of giving them a passing moment's amusement, it makes a thousand people uncomfortable and for the next five minutes very
self-conscious, it fails of its true effect. This argument must not be
stretched to cover the silliness of turning "God" into "Heaven"
and of making Othello call Desdemona a "wanton" (the practice,

as I recollect, of the eighteen-nineties), nor to such deodorizing of *Measure for Measure* that it becomes hard to discover what all the fuss is about. If an audience cannot think of Angelo and the Duke, Pompey and Lucio, Isabella and Mistress Overdone, and themselves to boot, as fellow-creatures all, the play is not for them. Othello must call Desdemona a "whore," and let those that do not like it leave the theater; what have such queasy minds to do with the pity and terror of her murder and his death? Again, to make Beatrice so mealymouthed that she may not tell us how the devil is to meet her at the gates of hell, "like an old cuckold with horns on his head," is to dress her in a crinoline, not a farthingale. But suppression of a few of the more scabrous jokes will not leave a play much the poorer; nor, one may add, will the average playgoer be much the wiser or merrier for hearing them, since they are often quite hard to understand.

Topical passages are a similar difficulty. With their savor, if not their very meaning lost, they show like dead wood in the living tree of the dialogue and are better, one would suppose, cut away. But no hard and fast rule will apply. Macbeth's porter's farmer and equivocator will never win spontaneous laughter again. But we cannot away with them, or nothing is left of the porter. Still the baffled low comedian must not, as his wont is, obscure the lines with bibulous antics. There will be that little dead spot in the play, and nothing can be done about it. Rosencrantz' reference to the "eyrie of children" is meaningless except to the student. Is the play the poorer for the loss of it? But the logic that will take this out had better not rob us of

> Dead shepherd, now I find thy saw of might;
> Who ever loved that loved not at first sight?

And there is the strange case of

> The lady of the Strachy married the yeoman of the wardrobe.

Nobody knows what it means, but everybody finds it funny when it is spoken in its place. And this has its parallels.

In general, however, better play the plays as we find them. The blue pencil is a dangerous weapon; and its use grows on a man, for it solves too many little difficulties far too easily.

Lastly, for a golden rule, whether staging or costuming or cutting is in question, and a comprehensive creed, a producer might well pin this on his wall: Gain Shakespeare's effects by Shakespeare's means when you can; for, plainly, this will be the better way. But gain Shakespeare's effects; and it is your business to discern them.

1927

Hamlet

The Nature of the Play

THE GENIUS OF THE WORKSHOP

FEW things throw more light on the nature of Shakespeare's art than does the fact that his masterpiece—not his greatest piece of work, perhaps, but the one in which he attains to a freedom and fullness of dramatic impression unknown before—should be the recasting, in all probability, of a ready-made play. Hamlet himself, it may be said, the most lifelike and "original" of his creations, was a ready-made character too; the conventional Elizabethan "melancholy man." His achievement was in the reconciling of these seeming contradictions.

But he "wanted art," said Jonson; and Milton implied it; and Dryden, despite his admiration for him, felt bound to confess it And if we mean, as Jonson and Dryden will have meant, a scheme of consistent principles and a studied method of expressing them, the Shakespeare of the greater plays lacks that most decidedly. There is an aspect of him which turns towards pure beauty of form, and the discipline and the limitations involved. It shows in the poems and in the earlier plays—in the exceptional homogeneity of *Richard II* and the graces of *A Midsummer Night's Dream*—and we may divine it in his instructed love for the music of his time. Had he begun by writing plays to please himself, it is possible that the lyric poet in him would have prevailed. We can imagine him in Lyly's place, with schoolboys for his actors, delicate, docile instruments, to be taught their parts line by line; the result an etherealized semiclassic drama, of which Jonson could have approved without cavil. But he found himself instead learning his playwright's trade amid the comradely give-and-take of the common theater workshop; and the result was very different. Let us cheerfully admit that he "wanted art"; he was the genius of the workshop.

What he learned there was to think directly in terms of the medium in which he worked; in the movement of the scene, in the humanity of the actors and their acting. Heroic acting, as Shakespeare found it, left the actor's identity with the character still not quite complete. It was comparable to those Japanese puppet-shows, in which the puppet, life-size and gorgeous, is handled by its black-suited showman in full view of the audience, who take pleasure in the patent skill of the handling. Tamburlaine was very much such a puppet. Alleyne himself wore the finery and went through the motions; but Marlowe had made the character something rather to be exhibited than acted. The trick of speech by which Tamburlaine and Zenocrate—Barabas, Hieronimo, Alphonsus and the rest—so often address themselves by name has its significance.

But the instinct of the actor is to identify himself with the character he plays, and this instinct Shakespeare the actor would naturally encourage Shakespeare the dramatist to gratify. The progress here is rapid. Richard III is still somewhat the magnificent puppet, yet the effect already will be less that of Burbage exhibiting the character than of Richard himself "showing off." The gain is great. With the actors forgetting themselves in their characters the spectators the more easily forget their own world for the world of the play. The illusion so created, we should note, is lodged in the actors and characters alone. Shakespeare's theater does not lend itself to the visual illusion, which, by the aid of realistic scenery and lighting, seems physically to isolate them in that other world. But he can, helped by the ubiquity of his platform stage, preserve the intimacy which this sacrifices. His aim is to keep the actor, now identified with the character, in as close a relation to the spectators—as that by which the clown, in his own right, exercises sway over them. It is not merely or mainly by being funny that the clown captures and holds his audience, but by personal appeal, the intimacy set up, the persuading them that what he has to say is his own concern—and theirs. It is with the comic and semicomic characters—from Angelica and Shylock to Falstaff—that we are first brought into this fellowship; and whatever conventions Shakespeare may discard, it will not be the revealing soliloquy and aside. A large part of the technical achievement of Hamlet lies in the bringing home his intimate griefs so directly to us. In whatever actor's guise we see him he is Hamlet, yet the appeal is as genuine as if the man before us were making it in his own person. But the actor does not lose himself in the character he plays. On the contrary, He not only presents it under his own aspect, he lends it his own emotions too, and he must repass the thought of which it is built through the sieve of his own mind. He dissects it and then reconstructs it in terms of his own personality. He realizes himself in Hamlet. And if he did not his performance would be lifeless. The thing is as true of a Falstaff. If the humor is no more a part of the actor than the padding is, our laughter will be empty.

Shakespeare learned the secret of this intimate and fruitful collaboration in the workshop of the theater. And it is the dramatist's master-secret. He has to learn, for his part, just what sort of material to give to the actors of his characters; the nature, the quality, also the effective quantity of it, neither more nor less. If it is dialogue of little more substance than have the skeleton scenes of the *Commedia dell' Arte*—for a dramatist may have his characters fully imagined, and still leave them as inexpressive as they might be in real life—that will allow the actor too much initiative. Actors who are in themselves interesting, lively and resourceful can make a passingly brilliant effect with such material. But, like other fairy gold, it will be dead leaves in the morning. The records of the theater are choked with such empty, perished plays. The dramatist must not, on the other hand, try to do for the actor what the actor can do as well, and better, for himself. It is waste of time—and nothing in the theater is more precious—to construct a character complete in every detail, to dictate personal appearance (unless, as with Falstaff, there is dramatic capital in this), to elaborate habits and tricks and minor traits. A hint or so will suffice. The actor takes these things in his stride. It is even better to leave him to devise the incidentals of a character for himself. They will fit his personal presentment of it the more closely; there will be a gain in spontaneity and increase of illusion. Nor must the actor be burdened with matter, however fine, which does not give the character life, which he cannot convert to its self-expression. It was here that the University poets, with their contempt for the actor, were blind; and here "literary dramatists," in their ignorance of his art, are still likeliest to fail. The actor, to them, is a mouthpiece—the written word made more eloquent—for their poetry, their ideas. That they must put consideration of the character itself and the actor of it before this, that the character acquires a certain freedom, and the actor even a certain property in it, is a thing they find hard to understand, harder still to profit by. Yet actually to profit by this self-abnegation is what the dramatist must cunningly learn to do. To provide raw material for acting; is there something undignified about it? Shakespeare, in the theater workshop, and an actor himself, will soon have been cured of that notion if ever he had it. The play as it leaves his hands is not a finished product, only its performance makes it that. Nor is it finished even then. Good actors never stereotype the playing of their parts, they keep them alive by continual little changes and developments. Shakespeare, in the same spirit, would retouch and recast his plays. Had he not retouched and recast other men's? That was the custom of the workshop. It could hardly result in perfection of form. But it made, both with dramatist and actor, for resourcefulness and flexibility, those needs of a crescent art. And the give-and-take of this continuing collaboration, the united force and the never-checked flow of it, did give free play to that sheer vitality, which, when all else is done, is the making of the drama, without which nothing avails.

Shakespeare learns to work in the living medium of the actors and their acting, the thing that is peculiar to the theater; if the dramatist cannot work in it, clearly he is no dramatist at all. He soon sees, moreover, that it is the essential thing, which no pageantry must be let overshadow, nor mechanical tricks degrade. His progress is marked by a discarding of the artifices—presenters, dumb shows, Latin tags, elaborate formulas of speech—which constrict its humanity; and, positively, by an ever-increasing enrichment of the human character it is to paint for him. But there is no drastic change of method. The economy of the workshop forbids this. Also the human medium is not a passive one; actors will only do well what they know how to do and like to do. Shake-

speare may add what he can to the dramatic commonwealth; he must
see that he loses nothing of account, nor leaves any of his fellows
in it impoverished. When he has provided the clown with a
Touchstone or a Feste, then—but only then—can he insist on his
speaking no more than is set down for him. I doubt if the
exiguous Peter of *Romeo and Juliet* could be so controlled; nor, it
would seem, was it to the advantage of the entertainment that he
should be. *Romeo and Juliet* abounds in artifices which are quite
soon to be discarded; antiphonies, Euphuisms, volleys of puns.
They stand incongruous now beside its vital dramatic poetry and
forthright prose. But if the actors can make these inherited, still
recognized conventions effective, and his own invention has momentarily failed him, the dramatist does well to furnish them. For
the sustained effect upon the audience; that is the thing. And very
certainly, here or elsewhere, he must sacrifice none of the power
of the magnificent rhetoric, by which it is that Marlowe and those
others have recreated this theater he works for, by which the actors
can so stir their audience, until he has found some means to that
same end of even greater power.

He comes to need this. There comes a time when the life in
his poetry flags; when, beside Falstaff's humor, King Henry's
rhetoric sounds hollow, when he turns to prose for Benedick and
Beatrice, Rosalind and Orlando, and, with a tributary sigh for the
"dead shepherd," can allow Jaques his gibe of

Nay, God be wi' you, and you talk in blank verse. . . .

What has happened? He is now a masterly creator of character.
But the old rhetoric robs these creatures of flesh and blood of their
reality. Yet while prose may suffice for comedy, for pathos and the
poignancy of tragedy it will not. Nor can he think of impoverish-
ing the theater and its actors by depriving them altogether of the
enhancing magic of poetic speech. Moreover he is a poet, predominantly that; and poetry will out. What he needs is a poetic
method by which to realize character.

The development to come is, in some kind, inevitable. It follows
from the identifying of actor and character, from the dramatist's
sense that he is collaborating with the actor, and from the fact
that the dramatist, in this case, was a poet who had learned to
think in terms of drama. He will keep the rhetoric for rhetorical

purposes; his captains and kings will always have occasion for it. But, once the actor is realizing the character, eloquent self-description becomes superfluous. With what, then, can his collaborator the dramatist best provide him, apart from what is called for by the sheer action of the play?—and this will be little; for the thing to be done in drama is better done than talked of, if the talk has no other end. With what can he best provide him for self-expression? It follows, if the actor can fulfill in himself the greater part of what we may call the "physics" of the character, that the dramatist will devote himself more and more to its "metaphysics." And when the dramatist is such a poet as was Shakespeare, these "metaphysics" will be of the kind with which poetry is most concerned, the world of the imagination and the things of the spirit; they will, it is not too fantastic to say, begin to give the character something very like an immortal soul. This is the development which leads him to Hamlet.

It involves no fresh departure. He has realized character in poetry before now; in old Angelica, in Hotspur very notably. But there was little of the metaphysical in either of them; abounding unself-consciously in a perfect conceit of themselves, as boldly self-expressive as two children. It involves no drastic changes of poetic form. He is too skilled a craftsman now to be fettered by rule. When his verse is alive it is such a natural language to him that it seems spontaneously to fall into form. Much enrichment of its substance, that there will be; a fresh vocabulary needed, a dramatic syntax, a dynamic use both of the sense and sound of words. And there will be a devising of action and situations which carry their poetry in them, with, at most, an illuminating touch or so to replace the direct description of the earlier plays. For dramatic poetry is not primarily a matter of words, but of the poetic conception of character and action. Where, before *Hamlet*, can we find such a "setting" contrived as that for the first scene on the battlements? Compare it, for method and effect, with the tomb-scene in *Romeo and Juliet*, or the storm in *Julius Cæsar*, and this again with the storm-scenes in *King Lear*.

The development may not affect the whole play. We do not need to know minor characters intimately. Some are simply the functionaries of the story. Shakespeare will not be calling upon the minor actors to do more than they know how to do, nor anything very different from what they have done so far. He must, on the other hand, see that these "metaphysics" do not so rarefy a dominant character as to rob it of the reality it has gained; he must not exchange the rhetorical for the merely abstract. His task now, in fact, is to give—the actor aiding him—to these creatures of his imagination, by a single means, both actuality and the larger and profounder life with which poetry can endow them. His plays never lack the actualities of action; and the practice of his theater provides for its continuous flow. But the sublimer the poetry, the more intimate now, we shall find, may be its images; and he will salt the greatest dramatic occasions with familiar little touches. There is the balance secured. Why is *King Lear* so full of them? Because he must take particular care to make that primitive colossus humanly real to us.

THE DEVELOPMENT OF HAMLET

There is more than one tentative at Hamlet in earlier work. Facets of him show already in Romeo and Richard II; Jaques is the "melancholy man" derided; and in Brutus, the sensitive philosopher misgivingly impelled to action, the likeness is distinct. Shakespeare could not have his way with Brutus. He had too much respect for Plutarch, and those stoic Romans are spiritual strangers to him. But here, clearly seen, if not yet fully felt, is the man whose tragedy is within him—and where else, if it can but be shown, does true tragedy lie? What he now needs is suppler material to work upon; and this he finds in the story and play of *Hamlet*. We can only guess at the changes he made, and how much of the Hamlet we have he found there. But, with the character already half-ripe in his mind, we can, I think, detect him developing it further out of the very obligations of the borrowed story. And a very remarkable process this is; a masterpiece in workshop economy, did nothing more masterly come out of it.

In the older play there was apparently much ado about Hamlet's shamming madness. This was his protection while he plotted against the King; and it may have furnished incidents enough to fill up the time between the Ghost's first crying "Revenge" and the final catastrophe, if there were "whole . . . handfulls of tragical speeches" to be delivered besides. Shakespeare takes over this device. He could hardly have done otherwise. Hamlet without his madness would not have been Hamlet at all. But though it allows for an amusing passage or so with Polonius, some oracular talk with Rosencrantz and Guildenstern, and remains an effective ambush against the King, beyond this—if it is to be simple shamming —it must prove more hindrance than help. For how can he develop Hamlet's character if the man is to be continually behind a mask? There can be revealing soliloquies, of course; and the candor of the friendship with Horatio will be useful. But with the Queen, and with Ophelia; here also a Hamlet feelingly himself is needed. Nor can an artificially antic disposition support scenes of crisis, nor carry a tragedy of character to its consummation. So Shakespeare's Hamlet is impelled beyond simple shamming. Yet it cannot be into sheer inconsequent lunacy, for there is no making that dominate a play either. Is not this the origin of the alloy of sanity and insanity, pretense and reality, which we vainly try to resolve into its elements again?

Shakespeare does marvels with this Hamlet who is neither mad nor sane, both "mad in craft" and "punished with sore distraction"; the victim—as we all at some time feel we are—of the world's "sane" view of his "insane" perplexities; the man—as which of us has not been?—at war within himself; and a traveler, with that passport, into strange twilight regions of the soul. But he cannot, for all his skill, so assimilate character and story that no incongruities appear. For the two are of a different dramatic nature. To do this he would have had to recast the play's whole scheme. He will not let his Hamlet suffer; but the other characters and their share in the action inevitably must.

He never, I think, made this mistake again. In *Measure for Measure* he rather takes the opposite course; the characters, one and all, are constricted to the borrowed story. But since the Moor of Cinthio's excellent tale (a far likelier tale than Shakespeare's version of it) has none of the nobility with which he means to dower Othello, since in Leir and the old chronicle behind him there is none of the catastrophic grandeur which is to be the making of Lear, in each case the story is first remolded to the man, and the other characters are fitted to his support or opposing. This effective opposition of character to character is the strength of drama. It composes the structure in which Shakespeare's sense of form came, in the maturity of his art, chiefly to lie; for his theater's freedom in space and time encourages him to maneuver the mere action as he will, to be an opportunist in that. This opposition and structure and strength is certainly lacking in *Hamlet*.

But the character of Hamlet suffers too. Is it not odd, when we are studying it, how many of its details will, without the keenest watchfulness, escape us, and that students should still dispute the significance of some of the most salient things about it? Ought we to be able to ask so many—quite intelligent—questions? It is partly, of course, that Hamlet himself is struggling amid obscurities and contradictions; and here is our genius of the workshop, as usual, not only adapting means to end, but end to means, and making capital out of shortcomings. And the result stands the test of performance, which was all he had to care about. But put the play—as the student has a right to—on the dissecting table, and the flaw, and I think the cause of it, are apparent. Shakespeare has not—paradox though this may seem—finally *dramatized* Hamlet. Here is the character, at which he has had more than one imma-ture and fragmentary try, fully and vividly imagined at last—what character was ever more so? But he does not submit it to the final discipline which would make it an integral part of the play. He could do so by reducing it to an equality with the rest. Such limitation would bring clarity. But this is just what he now will not do. The play, when he has finished with it, may be a masterpiece of the workshop, but with Hamlet himself he is pioneering a new world of drama. Later he will learn how to shape and economize that to his theater's needs. Meanwhile—and we may be thankful for it—no lesser considerations turn him back.

The Nature of the Action

THE FIVE ACTS OF THE EDITORS

THE long-accepted division of the play into five acts is not, of course, authentic. Here, as with other plays, the editors of the Folio were bent upon giving their author this classic dignity; and it may be, besides, that by 1623 theatrical practice had itself im-posed this division upon such of his plays as were still being acted. In the private theaters it had commonly been the custom to divide plays into acts and to provide music for intervals. The practice of the public theaters is a matter of dispute. If they did observe act divisions—four of them—they are hardly likely to have done so more than formally unless or until they also had some entertaining means of filling the gaps.[1] It is possible that their practice changed, and this during Shakespeare's own lifetime. He certainly did not (except for one instance) think out his plays in five-act form; whatever the exigencies of its performance are to be, the play itself is an indivisible whole. It was the telling of a story; its shape would be dictated by the nature of the story and the need to make this dramatically effective. And that meant, among other things, that if there were to be breaks in its progress, one generally did better to minimize than to accentuate them; for the attention of an audience, once captured, must be held.

In the dividing-up of *Hamlet* the Folio editors for some reason get no further than *Actus Secundus*[2]; and not till the "Players' Quarto" of 1676, do we find an end made of their Act II, and a III, IV and V. That almost certainly represents the theatrical practice of the Restoration; but quite possibly it has an earlier origin in the performance of the play in private theaters about the date of the printing of the Folio. Rowe (who, for text, picks and chooses between Q2 and F1) adopts it, and later editors follow him.[3]

But, whatever its origin, it illustrates no consistent dramatic purpose on Shakespeare's part. It cannot but to some extent thwart his technique; and at one point—in the contriving of the

---

[1] Or unless the strain upon the audience became too great. That might entail a definite pause or so for recovery; but hardly four pauses. The Elizabethans, moreover, could apparently support sieges from which their modern descendants shrink. Their sermons ran notably to length. While the plays could be acted through in two hours or a little longer, there would be no physical need for a pause.

[2] To be quite accurate, they mark it *Scaena Secunda* and stop there. But scene-division is another matter. This is implicit in the text; for it depends, customarily, upon the incidence of a cleared stage.

[3] It the more certainly represents Restoration theatrical practice that this Quarto (of Davenant's editing, presumably) marks passages "to be omitted in representation," which are not included in the Folio's abbreviation of Q2. It will still be a homage to classical tradition; but there is no doubt, I think, that, whatever had been done earlier, the Restoration theater did observe the five-act division, either by formal or appreciable pauses in the performance.

end of a third act and a beginning for a fourth—the offense is patent and the cobbling of the clumsiest.[4]

A unit of dramatic action for a first act—if there had to be one —was not hard to find; for the story, as Shakespeare tells it, carries us at a sustained stretch and upon a plainly indicated time-scheme to the Ghost's revelation and Hamlet's heartsick acceptance of his task. So definite an "act" is this, on both counts, that an editor is tempted to set down as definitely at the end of it: *Some weeks pass.*[5] Now Shakespeare certainly suggests in the next scene that time has been passing; a remark of Ophelia's several scenes later makes it, in fact, a calculable two months. But, to realize this, we should need, as the line is spoken, to connect it mentally with another line spoken by Hamlet almost as long before, and do a small sum in subtraction—which we certainly shall not do at that moment. No such exact impression, therefore, is meant to be made on us.

The divider ends his second act upon Hamlet's resolution to put Claudius to the test of the play. This is an important milestone in the story; the scene is sure to gain applause; and in the following scene, if we are listening carefully, we shall gather that between the two a night has passed. So here, for the act-divider, are excuses enough for a few minutes' halt. Hamlet will have wrought us to share in his excitement; we shall relieve our feelings by applauding; we shall be given time to adjust our recollection of what has passed and prepare for what is promised. It may well be that Shakespeare's own actors found they had to give their audience an occasional rest from the strain of attention to such a play as *Hamlet;* it would be a greater mental-plus-emotional strain than any earlier play had exacted. It may even be that, Shakespeare consenting, they picked on this juncture as the likeliest for the purpose hereabouts; he might even pick on it himself. Never-

---

[4] Dr. Johnson comments severely on it, and other editors may note its ineptitude. But Dowden (for instance) only says in the introduction to the *Hamlet* volume of the Arden Shakespeare that "the received division between III. and IV. is unfortunate," taking for granted, apparently, that for some sort of five-act form Shakespeare himself was responsible. And while he records the pertinent variants in his *apparatus criticus,* he leaves them without comment. Of so little importance did this aspect of Shakespeare's stagecraft seem even to him.

[5] Dover Wilson does so in the new Cambridge Shakespeare. In *What Happens in Hamlet* (p. 94, note), however, he modifies the statement; and I find myself in agreement with him.

theless, since he did not so plan the play, the halt and the pause
betray his stagecraft. He is not apt to check the impulse of his
action at an emotional crisis which only anticipates a sharper
crisis still, but rather to find means to relax the tension, yet without so loosening it as to lose hold on his audience. And his dramatic intention here is plain. It is to carry us straight from the
deadly intent of Hamlet's

> The play 's the thing
> Wherein I'll catch the conscience of the King.

to the sight of the puzzled King and Queen questioning the still
equally puzzled Rosencrantz and Guildenstern, but learning with
relief—that the harmless pastime of a play is in hand!

> it doth much content me
> To hear him so inclin'd.
> Good gentlemen, give him a further edge,
> And drive his purpose on to these delights.

says the unsuspecting Claudius. With the loss of the quick
sequence of the scenes, the irony of this will be largely lost.

Further, not five minutes should elapse (there are fifty-five lines
to speak) between that passionate soliloquy with its ringing and
resolute end (the sound of it will be still in our ears) and the
pessimism of

> To be or not to be . . .

This is one of a series of such contrasts, a capital feature in the
presenting of the character. Here, too, the full effect will be lost if
the continuity of the action is broken.

As to the passing of a night between the scenes; at a guess,
Shakespeare did not think about the matter at all till he came to
write the sentence in the second scene indicating that a night has
passed. (Nor, even so, is this a certain sign that it has; the performance may have been impatiently hurried forward.) It was
natural in the earlier scene for Hamlet to set the play for "tomorrow night," since he had to write the "speech of some dozen
or sixteen lines" to be inserted in it. But after the passionate

> O, what a rogue and peasant slave am I! . . .

what concerns Shakespeare is to see that the unavoidable anticlimax is at least given some antidote. Rosencrantz's reply to the Queen, the

> certain players
> . . . have already order
> *This night* to play before him.

provides this. It restimulates our interest. The exciting event we are expecting is already nearer. That is the dramatic worth of the statement; the chronology is incidental to it.

For a halt and a pause at the end of what is known as the closet-scene there can, as we said, be no excuse whatever. By a very usual turn of Elizabethan technique one scene simply evolves into another when the characters pass from the inner stage (the closet) to the outer (some antechamber or lobby).[6] And a change in the Folio—made by whatever hand—does but better Shakespeare's main intention, which plainly is to carry forward the action here with as little slackening as possible. It is the King who is driving it ahead; for his purpose is to rid himself of his enemy without delay. And the pulse of the play has never been more feverish, nor Hamlet more beside himself; and he knows he "must to England." If somehow or other hereabouts this now lengthy third act must be brought to an end, the act-divider has but to let pass another hundred and fifty lines. Hamlet by then will be gone, and Claudius gain a breathing-space, and we can be allowed one too.

To complete the customary tale one has now only to find an end for the fourth and as likely a beginning for a fifth act. Our act-divider could hardly have done much better than he does. We hear of Ophelia's death; there is finality in that. The ensnaring of Hamlet has been prepared against his promised return, so that the pause intervening will be an expectant one. And—since the last act is to begin with the Gravediggers—it will give the stage carpenters a good chance to open the grave-trap and make all ready.

------

[6]   Hamlet in madness hath Polonius slain,
          And from his mother's closet hath he dragged him. . . .
—the King tells Rosencrantz and Guildenstern; *i.e.* from some place other than this in which he now stands speaking. The Elizabethan imagination will have responded the more readily to this changing of place by passing from inner stage to outer since it answered to the disposition of the Elizabethan house, in which one passed, as a rule, directly from room to room, not by a corridor.
The various alternatives offered at this point by Q2 and the Folio are more fully discussed in the footnote to p. 108.

But, once again, Shakespeare's intentions (though here they may not be grossly thwarted) are falsified. The suspense between the news of Hamlet's return (brought first to Horatio, then to the King) and his actual appearance is fully provided for by the scenes which intervene. And a break in the action here can only weaken the effect of the apposition of the tragic fantasy of Ophelia's madness, the warped cunning of the King's plotting with Laertes, the lyric beauty of the tale of the girl's death on the one hand, and on the other the wholesome prose humor of the Clowns. Hamlet, when he arrives, is, by that colloquy in the graveyard, to point this contrast for us. The simple and the clever, the innocent and the guilty alike all come to the grave—to the plain prose of the grave. But how much more effective the pointing will be if we have also let Shakespeare realize the contrast for us, as he has planned to!

For our own convenience we may make pauses in the performance of the plays. Shakespeare himself had doubtless sometimes to show his audiences that consideration. If he did not at first, the growing length of his maturer work will surely have compelled him to. It would be both a sturdy and a spellbound crowd, indeed, that could—literally, as to about half of them—stand up to an uninterrupted performance of *Hamlet, King Lear* or *Antony and Cleopatra*. But he never ceased to conceive a play as a single organic whole, nor its action as a continuous progress—which a never-halted performance of the shorter *Comedy of Errors, Love's Labour's Lost* or *The Merchant of Venice* could quite well show it to be.[7] And to learn how to minimize our dramatic loss, if we

---

[7] I believe this to be essentially true, but subject—as with so much else to be said about his work—to qualification and exception. Among the earlier plays, the exceptional length of *Richard III* is puzzling; among the later, one seems to detect a positive effort to keep *Measure for Measure* and *Othello* within bounds. *Henry V* is definitely divided into acts. *Romeo and Juliet* shows some rudiments of a division by choruses. *A Winter's Tale* is dramatically divided into two parts. It may be hazarded, perhaps, that Shakespeare was indifferent to external form, though as willing to experiment in it—as he was to take a popular subject for the making of a play, or to pay a passing compliment to Elizabeth or James. But he did most eagerly experiment in the expression of the dramatic *ideas* which possessed him.

Another point. In estimating the acting-time of a play one must always consider the nature of the subject and the method of the writing; mere line measurement can be deceptive. *A Comedy of Errors* and *Love's Labour's Lost* will move far more swiftly than *As You Like It* or *Twelfth Night*. *Hamlet* moves at very varying

must interrupt a performance here and there, the Procrustean
editors should first be forgotten; then the play's natural structure
will appear, and divisions can at least be made to conform, as far
as possible, to that.[8]

PLACE-STRUCTURE AND TIME-STRUCTURE

There is both a place-structure and a time-structure in *Hamlet*.
The place-structure depends upon no exact localization of scenes.
The time-structure answers to no scheme of act-division. But each
has its dramatic import.

The action of *Hamlet* is concentrated at Elsinore; and this
though there is much external interest, and the story abounds in
journeys. As a rule in such a case, unless they are mere messengers, we travel with the travelers. But we do not see Laertes in
Paris, nor, more surprisingly, Hamlet among the pirates; and the
Norwegian affair is dealt with by hearsay till the play is two-
thirds over. This is not done to economize time, or to leave space
for more capital events. Scenes in Norway or Paris or aboard ship
need be no longer than the talk of them, and Hamlet's discovery
of the King's plot against him is a capital event. Shakespeare is
deliberately concentrating his action at Elsinore. When he does at
last introduce Fortinbras he stretches probability to bring him and
his army seemingly to its very suburbs; and, sooner than that
Hamlet should carry the action abroad with him, Horatio is left

speeds; averaged out, the pace both of *Measure for Measure* and *Coriolanus* will
probably be slower. It is likely, again, that any play would then have been acted
at a quicker pace than it commonly is today. The verse, and even the prose, would
be spoken quicker; first, because the art of speaking was the actor's primary
achievement; secondly, because in that age of little reading and much public
discourse audiences would be better listeners too.

Yet another. The quickest shifting of the simplest scenes will add, say, half an
hour to a quite straightforward "platform" performance of *Antony and Cleopatra*.

[8] It is hard to wipe the five-act division clean from one's consciousness. Most
modern editions insist on retaining it, with a bare reference, if that, to its unau-
thenticity. Dover Wilson, in the new Cambridge Shakespeare, relegates it to the
margin. That is a gain; and it is no doubt hard to go further, since some system of
reference from text to notes and from one edition to another is needed, and this is
on all counts the most convenient. The thing is to remember, when one is consider-
ing the play aesthetically, that these acts—and sometimes the scenes—have no true
existence. The student must constantly have this in mind, or he will find himself
still thinking of the play in acts and scenes—and thinking wrong. And it is for
this reason that I have—with some difficulty for myself; I hope less for my
readers—avoided all reference to acts and numbered scenes in this Preface.

behind there to keep him in our minds. On the other hand he
still, by allusion, makes the most of this movement abroad which
he does not represent; he even adds to our sense of it by such
seemingly superfluous touches as tell us that Horatio has journeyed from Wittenberg, that Rosencrantz and Guildenstern have
been "sent for"—and even the Players are traveling.

The double dramatic purpose is plain. Here is a tragedy of
inaction; the center of it is Hamlet, who is physically inactive too,
has "foregone all custom of exercises," will not "walk out of the
air," but only, book in hand, for "four hours together, here in the
lobby." The concentration at Elsinore of all that happens en-
hances the impression of this inactivity, which is enhanced again
by the sense also given us of the constant coming and going
around Hamlet of the busier world without. The place itself,
moreover, thus acquires a personality, and even develops a sort of
sinister power; so that when at last Hamlet does depart from it
(his duty still unfulfilled) and we are left with the conscience-sick
Gertrude and the guilty King, the mad Ophelia, a Laertes set on
his own revenge, among a

people muddied,

Thick and unwholesome in their thoughts and whispers . . .

we almost seem to feel it, and the unpurged sin of it, summoning
him back to his duty and his doom. Shakespeare has, in fact, here
adopted something very like unity of place; upon no principle, but
to gain a specific dramatic end.

He turns time to dramatic use also, ignores or remarks its
passing, and uses clock or calendar or falsifies or neglects them
just as it suits him.

The play opens upon the stroke of midnight, an ominous and
"dramatic" hour. The first scene is measured out to dawn and
gains importance by that. In the second Hamlet's "not two months
dead" and "within a month . . ." give past events convincing
definition, and his "tonight . . . tonight . . . upon the platform
'twixt eleven and twelve" a specific imminence to what is to come.
The second scene upon the platform is also definitely measured
out from midnight to near dawn. This framing of the exordium
to the tragedy within a precise two nights and a day gives a

convincing lifelikeness to the action, and sets its pulse beating rhythmically and arrestingly.[9]

But now the conduct of the action changes, and with this the treatment of time. Hamlet's resolution—we shall soon gather—has paled, his purpose has slackened. He passes hour upon hour pacing the lobbies, reading or lost in thought, oblivious apparently to time's passing, lapsed—he himself supplies the phrase later—"lapsed in time." So Shakespeare also for a while tacitly ignores the calendar. When Polonius dispatches Reynaldo we are not told whether Laertes has already reached Paris. Presumably he has, but the point is left vague. The Ambassadors return from their mission to Norway. They must, one would suppose, have been absent for some weeks; but again, we are not told. Why not insist at once that Hamlet has let a solid two months pass and made no move, instead of letting us learn it quite incidentally later? There is more than one reason for not doing so. If the fact is explicitly stated that two months separate this scene from the last, that breaks our sense of a continuity in the action; a thing not to be done if it can be avoided, for this sense of continuity helps to sustain illusion, and so to hold us attentive. An alternative would be to insert a scene or more dealing with occurrences during these two months, and thus bridge the gap in time. But a surplusage of incidental matter is also and always to be avoided. Polonius' talk to Reynaldo, Shakespeare feels, is relaxation and distraction enough; for with that scene only halfway through he returns to his main theme.

He could, however, circumvent such difficulties if he would. His capital reason for ignoring time hereabouts is that Hamlet is ignoring it, and he wants to attune the whole action—and us—to

---

[9] It is perhaps worth remarking that, while the first scene upon the platform closes with Horatio's cheerfully beautiful

> But look, the morn, in russet mantle clad,
> Walks o'er the dew of yon high eastern hill. . . .

in the second, when the Ghost scents the morning air, we have:

> The glow-worm shows the matin to be near,
> And 'gins to pale his uneffectual fire. . . .

—and then no more, nothing of hopeful dawn or cheerful day at all. An audience may not consciously observe the difference. Shakespeare evidently did not attach much importance to it, and he had, of course, no means of giving it scenic effect. But the producer of today, with light at his command, may do well to indicate it.

Hamlet's mood. He takes advantage of this passivity; we learn to know our man, as it were, at leisure. Facet after facet of him is turned to us. Polonius and Rosencrantz and Guildenstern are mirrors surrounding and reflecting him. His silence as he sits listening to the Players—and we, as we listen, watch him—admits us to closer touch with him. And when, lest the tension of the action slacken too much in this atmosphere of timelessness, the clock must be restarted, a simple, incidental, phrase or two is made to serve.

It is not until later that Shakespeare, by a cunning little stroke, puts himself right—so to speak—with the past. *The Murder of Gonzago* is about to begin when Hamlet says to Ophelia:

> look you, how cheerfully my mother looks, and my father died within's two hours.

—to be answered

> Nay, 'tis twice two months, my lord.

There is the calendar reestablished; unostentatiously, and therefore with no forfeiting of illusion. Yet at that moment we are expectantly attentive, so every word will tell. And it is a stroke of character too. For here is Hamlet, himself so lately roused from his obliviousness, gibing at his mother for hers.

But the use of time for current effect has begun again, and very appropriately, with Hamlet's fresh impulse to action, and his decision, reached while he listens abstractedly to the Player's speech, to test the King's guilt:

> we'll hear a play to-morrow. Dost thou hear me, old friend;
> can you play the Murder of Gonzago? ... We'll ha't to-mor-
> row night.

We do not yet know what is in his mind. But from this moment the pressure and pace of the play's action are to increase; and the brisk "tomorrow" and "tomorrow night" help give the initial impulse. The increase is progressive. In the next scene the play is no longer to be "tomorrow" but "tonight." The King, a little later, adds to the pressure. When he has overheard Hamlet with Ophelia:

> I have in quick determination
> Thus set it down; he shall with speed to England. ...

And this—still progressively—becomes, after the play-scene and the killing of Polonius:

> The sun no sooner shall the mountains touch
> But we will ship him hence. . . .

After the spell of timelessness, then, we have an exciting stretch of the action carried through in a demonstrated day and a night. But the time-measure is not in itself the important thing. It is only used to validate the dramatic speed, even as was timelessness to help slow the action down.

After this comes more ignoring of the calendar, though the dramatic purpose in doing so is somewhat different. The scene which follows Hamlet's departure opens with the news of Ophelia's madness. We are not told how much time has elapsed. For the moment the incidental signs are against any pronounced gap. Polonius has already been buried, but "in hugger-mugger"; and Ophelia, whom we last saw smiling and suffering under Hamlet's torture, might well have lost her wits at the very news that her father had been killed, and that the man she loved had killed him. But suddenly Laertes appears in full-blown rebellion. With this it is clear why the calendar has been ignored. Shakespeare has had to face the same sort of difficulty as before. Let him admit a definite gap in time, realistically required for the return of Laertes and the raising of the rebellion, and he must either break the seeming continuity of the action, or build a bridge of superfluous matter and slacken a tension already sufficiently slackened by the passing of the Fortinbras army and Hamlet's "How all occasions . . ." soliloquy. So he takes a similar way out, ignoring incongruities, merely putting in the King's mouth the passing excuse that Laertes

> is *in secret* come from France . . .
> And wants not buzzers to infect his ear
> With pestilent speeches of his father's death . . .

—an excuse which would hardly bear consideration if we were allowed to consider it; but it is at this very instant that the tumult begins. And once again the technical maneuvering is turned to dramatic account. The surprise of Laertes' appearance, the very inadequacy and confusion of its explanation, and his prompt success, are in pertinent contrast to Hamlet's elaborate preparations —and his failure.[10]

Only with news of Hamlet do we revert to the calendar, and then with good reason. By setting a certain time for his return, the tension of the action is automatically increased. First, in the letter to Horatio, the past is built up:

> Ere we were *two days* old at sea, a pirate of very warlike appointment gave us chase.

Then, in a letter to the King:

> *To-morrow* shall I beg leave to see your kingly eyes. . . .[11]

---

[10] Does this contriving, however, stand the test of performance? Personally I have always felt so far that it did not, that Laertes' appearance was a little too surprising, that the King's excuse only made the matter worse, that Shakespeare has, for once, been too slapdash, in fact that the flawed illusion of the action is not restored till Ophelia reappears, and in the pathos of the sight of her the rebellion is forgotten both by us and by Laertes. But this is perhaps to be overnice of apprehension; and such a performance as Shakespeare would stage might cover the weakness.

[11] There is another but not very noticeable piece of upbuilding of the past in the King's line to Laertes:

> Two months since
> Here was a gentleman of Normandy. . . .

This with what follows implies that Laertes has been absent from Denmark for an appreciably longer time—and incidentally it falsifies the play's calculable calendar. But that is, of course—since, as listeners, we go by impressions, not calculation—no great matter; and the dramatic intention clearly is to give, by this passing touch, an added sense of solidity to the time-structure.

There is yet another to come, a more subtle and a far more effective one, in Hamlet's talk to the Gravediggers, in the passage about Yorick. Why does Shakespeare take the trouble, thus late in the day, to establish Hamlet's age so exactly? To counteract the impression of the youthful prince, which circumstances—his studentship at Wittenberg, Gertrude still in the heyday of her blood, and, as played by a boy, her youthful appearance—will have made on us; and thus late in the day, because, with the great central mass of the play's thought and passion behind him, Hamlet is inevitably a maturer figure than was the morbid young rebel of its beginning.

But the immediate effect, though we probably receive it unconsciously, is more dramatically valuable even than this. The play is nearing its end, and it must be, we feel, a tragic end; we know of the plot against Hamlet, which he can hardly escape. And the casting-back of his thoughts to his birth, to his childhood, gives us the sense of a life approaching its term. He stands with the skull in his hands; it is thirty years since he was born, three and twenty since the dead jester used to carry him laughing on his back. To this complexion must he also come—how soon? The picture, and the tale of the years, will set flowing some such undercurrent of imagination in us; nothing more explicit, for we travel with Hamlet, not ahead of him. But this is typical of the true use that Shakespeare makes of time.

—the resumption of the war between them is made imminent. The scene in the graveyard thus takes place on the morrow; and this is verified for us as it ends, by the King's whisper to Laertes:

Strengthen your patience in our *last night's* speech. . . .

The general effect produced—not, and it need not be, a very marked one—is of events moving steadily now, unhurriedly, according to plan; the deliberation of Hamlet's returning talk to the Gravediggers suggests this, and it accords with the King's cold-blooded plot and Laertes' resolution.

The calendar must again be ignored after the angry parting of Hamlet and Laertes over Ophelia's grave. If it were not, Shakespeare would either have to bring in superfluous matter and most probably slacken tension (which he will certainly not want to do so near the end of his play) or explain and excuse an indecently swift passing from a funeral to a fencing match. He inserts instead a solid wedge of the history of the King's treachery and the trick played on the wretched Rosencrantz and Guildenstern. This sufficiently absorbs our attention, and dramatically separates the two incongruous events. It incidentally builds up the past still more solidly; and there is again a falsifying hint of time elapsed in Horatio's comment that

It must be shortly known to him [Claudius] from England
What is the issue of the business there.

—which is to be justified when all is over by the actual arrival of the English ambassadors to announce that the

commandment is fulfilled,
That Rosencrantz and Guildenstern are dead.

But this will simply be to give a sense of completeness to the action. Nothing is said or done to check its steady progress from the graveyard scene to the end; for that is the capital consideration involved.

It comes to this, I think. Shakespeare's true concern is with *tempo*, not time. He uses time as an auxiliary, and makes free with it, and with the calendar to make his use of it convincing.[12]

---

[12] Exceptionally the story itself (as with *The Merchant of Venice*) or a part of it (as in *Romeo and Juliet*) may depend upon a question of time. He must then give it attention for its own sake; but he will manage to keep it fairly malleable, and to make something of his habitual use of it, even so.

When he came to playwriting, time, it is true enough to say, was commonly being put to no dramatic use at all. A few passing references to "tonight," "tomorrow" or "the other day" there might be; for the rest, a play's end would leave a vague impression that so many events must have asked a fair amount of time for their enacting. This was not freedom—though it might seem to be —but anarchy; and he soon saw that some scheme of time would strengthen a play's action and add to the illusion.[13] For the unlikeliest story can be made more convincing by supplying it with a date or so.

An accurately realistic time-scheme, with the clock of the action going tick by tick with the watches in our pockets—that the theater can hardly be brought to accommodate. Few good stories can be made to pass in the two or three hours allowed for the acting of a play, still fewer if they must include striking and varied events. There are three main ways of dealing with the matter. Each belongs to a different sort of theater and a different type of drama. There is the so-called "classic" way. This may involve rather the ignoring than any plain falsifying of time. The drama accommodating it is apt to concentrate upon one capital event, the approaches to it elaborately prepared; and—with a master dramatist at work—motive after motive, trait after trait of character, will be unfolded like petals, till the heart of the matter is disclosed and the inevitable conclusion reached. There is the normal modern method of a suggested realism in "time," appropriate to a scenic theater's realism of place.[14] This commonly goes with a selecting of various events to be presented, one (or it may be more) to an act, the gaps in time between them accounted for by the act-divisions, the rest of the story relegated to hearsay and a sort of no man's land between the acts. Each act then becomes something of a play in itself as well as a part of one, the resulting whole a solid multiple structure, the economy of its technique akin to that of sound building, as thrifty and precise.

Lastly there is Shakespeare's freedom in time, which is the natural product of his stage's freedom in space, and which—

---

[13] Which is not to say that he was the only dramatist who saw this.

[14] The ratio will not be exact; but, generally speaking, the less realism in scenic place the less sense of realism shall we expect in time.

coupled with this—permits him a panoramic display of his entire story if need be, and uninterrupted action. And, having brought time out of anarchy, he is not concerned to regulate his use of it very strictly. He adds it to his other freedoms. Moreover he may take the greater liberties with it, because, for his audience, in their own actual world, the sense of time is so uncertain.

In nothing are we more open to illusion and suggestion than in our sense of time. We live imaginative lives of our own to quite another measure than the calendar's; a year ago might be yesterday; tomorrow will be days in coming, and gone in an hour. The Elizabethan convention of freedom in space, which depended upon the planning of the theater, shrank with each restrictive change in this and at last disappeared; but the dramatist may still exercise—in the most realistic surroundings—a discreet freedom in time. We readily welcome that fiction.[15]

Study of Shakespeare's stagecraft has shown us how we wrong it by depriving the plays when we present them of their freedom in space, by obstructing those swift, frictionless passages from here to there, or by defining whereabouts when he knew better than to define it. This freedom in time is also a part of his imaginative privilege. He makes his play a thing of movement, even as music is, and obedient to much the same laws; and the clock and the calendar are merely among the means by which this movement is made expressive.

For our convenience in performing the play, one or two stopping places can be found; there are two, at least, where the check and the pause will do little harm. For the purpose of this study, then, and as a hint to producers, I divide the play into three parts. But, as a reminder, "movements" will perhaps be the better word to use for them. The first will carry us from the beginning to Hamlet's acceptance of his mission (it coincides with the first act of the editors); the second from Reynaldo's dispatch to Hamlet's departure for England; the third from the news of Ophelia's madness to the end.

---

[15] Shakespeare's treatment of time is most notable in *Othello*. There is the undisguised freedom of the scene of the landing at Cyprus, when three separate vessels come into sight, ride out the storm, make harbor and disembark their passengers within the undivided speaking-space of 180 lines. There is the complex latent use of time throughout the rest of the play.

A First Movement

In the play's first four scenes[1] (which by the compactness of their
time-scheme and the synthesis of their events lend themselves
besides to definition as an "act") its action is fully set in train; the
main current of it which Hamlet is to dominate, and the auxiliary
action which Laertes will vitalize when, the play three parts
through and Hamlet absent for a while, he returns from France
—that also is prepared for now.

*Horatio is brought to encounter the Ghost and we hear of the
dangers that threaten Denmark.*

The first scene of the four gives us the appearance and reappearance of the Ghost, the talk in the interval between Horatio, Marcellus and Bernardo about the already troubled times, and their
final resolve to tell young Hamlet of the matter. For an opening
and purely preparatory scene it is lengthy; but its contents are of
unusual import. It lasts in imagined time, as we are definitely
reminded, from midnight to dawn; and the sense of this adds to
its importance. The passing of these hours is suggested when,
after the quick give-and-take of the dialogue about the Ghost,
Marcellus says:

> Good now, sit down and tell me, he that knows . . .

and they, all three, do sit down and relax; and there follows the
smooth flow of Horatio's long narrative. But note how the danger
(attendant upon all narrative in drama) of too great a slackening
of the tension is avoided. Nothing is said to show that the three
men expect the Ghost's return, but *we* inevitably do. So while we
listen we are also alert for this, and rather the more alert because
the characters in the scene seem not to be. Incidentally, the narrative adds stature to the Ghost. It is the spirit not only of a King
but of a renowned King that we have seen:

> our valiant Hamlet—
> For so this side of our known world esteem'd him . . .

Note besides that the Ghost's obstinate silence is a dramatic promise of speech later; and Horatio's last important line—that we
may be left expectant of the scene to come—so interprets it:

---

[1] Four scenes, not five. See p. 57.

This spirit, dumb to us, will speak to him.

—to Hamlet. Also that Horatio and Bernardo are on a wrong
scent in their explanations of the portent and are meant to set us
on one too; so that when in the next scene Hamlet immediately
fastens on the right one—not danger from abroad but some foul
deed done here—that will be a surprise, a thing of some dramatic
value always, and of double value in this case since the swift
prevision will enhance him in our eyes.[2] Also that the tale of
preparation for war, the sight of

this same strict and most observant watch . . .

while the spirit of the warrior king passes among the sentries, and
even "honest" Francisco, who has seen nothing, is "sick at heart"
—all this, so emphatically pictured, gives us a grim first impression
of a Denmark demoralized and in danger, its tried leader gone.
Shakespeare cannot allow much space to the political background
of his story; the more reason, then, that he should impress it upon
us while our attention is fresh, and in its sternest reality. This
picture will be quickly succeeded by its contrast and complement,
a sight of the Court under King Claudius, the man of words, the
diplomatist, the voluptuary, surrounded by acquiescent councilors;
in which setting the greater part of the action is to pass.[8] But the
play begins martially, and so ends, with

The soldiers' music and the rites of war . . .

and there is the half-removed passing of Fortinbras and his army
rather more than halfway through it; another setoff to the continuing picture of the brilliant and debased Court.

---

[2] An effect now lost by too great familiarity with the play.

[8] The train of the play's "foreign policy," though we have but occasional
glimpses of it, is very consistently developed. Claudius' diplomacy diverts Fortinbras
and his "lawless resolutes" towards Poland for the time being. But having done
well there, the young conqueror calls, all uninvited, at Elsinore on his way back.
Hamlet, he says,

was likely, had he been put on,
To have proved most royally.

But as to King Claudius, though he did not lack personal courage, the inference
throughout the play is that he was nothing of a fighter. And it looks—and the
actor can make it look—as if, had Fortinbras found him alive, the

I have some rights of memory in this kingdom,
Which now to claim my vantage doth invite me.

might still have been spoken, but to more truculent purpose.

Finally, the scene's lengthiness is counteracted by the simple fact that

'Tis bitter cold.

—for thus it must be briskly played.

Claudius, the new King, and Queen Gertrude hold their first Council. Laertes is granted leave to return to France, Hamlet refused it for his return to Wittenberg. We learn of the shame and grief with which his mother's remarriage fills him; he learns of the appearance of the Ghost.

THE second scene is launched upon a veritable shock of contrast. A flourish of trumpets; and the King and Queen come in state to preside at Council.[4] The King makes a brilliant figure—the "very, very peacock" of Hamlet's later gibe—and the courtiers, happily released from their recent mourning, would respectfully ape his fashion. In every aspect he is a contrast to that gaunt apparition of armored royalty which we have just seen stalking the night.

There is but one blot on the splendor; Hamlet himself in his "nighted colour." But we do not yet know who this is that so jars upon the general contentment. We are to listen to the King, addressing his Council, dispatching one piece of business after another; and only by degrees will the significance of the incongruous, recalcitrant figure be made clear. The business flows smoothly on; and there could surely be no better judged conclusion to the mourning for our dear brother's death than appears in that "wisest sorrow," in discretion's victory over nature, nor seal more tactfully set upon the ambiguous business of his marriage (an

---

[4] Q2's stage direction definitely gives us "Counsaile," and the proceedings are like those of a Privy Council meeting; and there should be no need to argue the matter except that the Folio stage direction adds Ophelia, and that theatrical practice has long falsified both the surroundings and dramatic purpose of the scene, has made vague and ineffective what Shakespeare made definite and significant. It is true that the Queen is there; but she is—and as if in explanation—referred to within the first ten lines as

The imperial jointress of this warlike state. . .

This may not precisely mean that she is the Queen Mary to Claudius' King William, but the impression conveyed is certainly that she has a right to be present. Dover Wilson strongly insists on this reading of the matter, and puts the case, I think, quite unanswerably.

affair of state, however, after all) than the avowal that he has
contracted it

> as 'twere with a defeated joy,
> With one auspicious and one dropping eye,
> With mirth in funeral and with dirge in marriage,
> In equal scale weighing delight and dole . . .

—unless perhaps it may all sound a little too elaborate, smack too
much of an apology. He becomes succinct enough about Fortinbras and with the Ambassadors, and then quite affectionately
gracious upon

> And now, Laertes, what's the news with you?
> You told us of some suit; what is't, Laertes?
> You cannot speak of reason to the Dane,
> And lose your voice. What would'st thou beg, Laertes,
> That shall not be my offer, not thy asking? . . .

—the repeated name is almost a caress.[5]

Finally—our curiosity having been well aroused by the delay—
Claudius provides an answer to the question we have been asking,
and joins the play's great issue by turning to that cryptic figure
with a quiet

> But now, my cousin Hamlet, and my son.

From the first—and the actor of Claudius can easily show it—he
will have resentfully noted this defiant mourning brought to a
Council called for the attesting of his marriage: it is little short
of an insult. The Prince's fellow-councilors will note it too, and
be awaiting the inevitable royal rebuke. The subtle Claudius,
however, first belittles the matter by ignoring it. And even now—
though there is added provocation in the muttered

> A little more than kin, and less than kind.

(it is not mannerly when your sovereign addresses you at the
council table to indulge in obscure comment)—he contents himself with a mild, if slightly ironic

> How is it that the clouds still hang on you?

He is repaid by the tart

---

[5] A point made by Mr. Harold Child.
There is no stage direction to tell us that Laertes retires after his suit has been
granted. But he is not a member of the Council, so he probably should.

> Not so, my lord; I am too much i' the sun.

—King, Queen and Court, the whole gaudy gathering lashed alike by the bitter jest. It is time for Gertrude to intervene:

> Good Hamlet, cast thy nighted colour off,
> And let thine eye look like a friend on Denmark. . . .

But the best she can do is to drive her son into a defensive argument—which serves, incidentally, to give us our first glimpse of his metaphysical mind. And it is ironically significant that he who is so soon to be ravaged by doubt should begin with that scornfully positive

> Seems, madam? Nay, it is. I know not 'seems.'

Claudius, expert himself at an argument, and still admirably calm and kindly, then delivers a veritable sermon, which both sets us questioning what sort of nature can be hidden beneath such banal piety, and shows—this is at once plain—that, clever as he may be, he quite misconstrues Hamlet, or he would not, surely, treat him in his sorrow to such frigidities as

> For what we know must be, and is as common
> As any the most vulgar thing to sense,
> Why should we, in our peevish opposition,
> Take it to heart? Fie, 'tis a fault to heaven,
> A fault against the dead, a fault to nature,
> To reason most absurd; whose common theme
> Is death of fathers. . . .

or, very certainly, ask him for consolation to

> think of us
> As of a father; for let the world take note,
> You are the most immediate to our throne. . . .

Hamlet indeed, the sermon ended, makes no response at all, stays obstinately silent. Gertrude intervenes again, to beg him at the least to

> stay with us; go not to Wittenberg.

She wins only a cold

> I shall in all my best obey you, madam. *all false*

Claudius promptly and diplomatically seizes upon this as

> a loving and a fair reply . . .

(which obviously it is not), declares that

> This gentle and unforced accord of Hamlet . . .

(it is as obviously neither: he is a prisoner)

> Sits smiling to my heart . . .

(his own so ready smile a trifle forced as he says it), and, with a little jovial bombast, breaks up the Council lest worse befall.

This accounts for only 128 lines of the scene—and I have written as many more about them. But it is important to note how categorically, for a start, Shakespeare establishes the triangle of false relations, within which the action is framed. Claudius, presented to us at the height of his good fortune, married to his mistress (that scandalous specter laid unrevealed) and confirmed in this as in his assumption of the crown by a complaisant Council, is naturally content that Hamlet should be his heir, genuinely ready, no doubt, to play the loving father to him. But his tactless tact, the mellifluous excess of speech, the smiling kindness overdone—such falseness shows that he feels his position to be false. By his concluding emphasis on the question of the succession, he implies— he will prefer it to be thought—that there is the secret, the "is" as against the "seems" of Hamlet's recalcitrance. Gertrude, as we learn later, knows better. It is, besides his father's death, her "o'er-hasty marriage" that is the trouble; not that Claudius is on the throne, but that she sits there beside him; and the constraint of her intervention tells us that, with her son, she too feels her position to be false. The pair still have their secret—the adultery— to guard from Hamlet and the rest, and Claudius keeps a deadlier one from her. As to Hamlet; that incongruous sequence of the long silence, the curt phrases, and the lucid and elaborate apology will leave us wondering what can be to come from him.[6]

---

[6] Why—since relations are inevitably so strained between them—did Claudius not let Hamlet go back to Wittenberg? I think no modern audience asks the question (if only they *would* ask questions about this play they think they know so well, how much more they would enjoy it!), but we, as students, may; since here perhaps is one of those points which, as Dover Wilson says, Shakespeare left unstressed because he knew that his own audience would instinctively grasp them. No one, of course, could leave England to travel abroad without permission; and in Shakespeare's Denmark the same laws apply. Laertes, having his father's leave, may return to Paris, for he is a person of no political importance (though in that, as it turns out, Claudius is to prove wrong). But one does not let a discontented

We have not long to wait. The Council over and the Court gone, the ash-grey surface of his calm breaks and seethes, on the instant, into the convulsive

> O, that this too too solid flesh would melt,
> Thaw, and resolve itself into a dew! . . .[7]

This is the first of the seven soliloquies by which we are brought into unimpeded contact with Hamlet's mind; an exceptional number, but Shakespeare has need of them all if he is to keep the secret instabilities of that mind an effective center of the action.[8] This one is turned to manifold use. It explains that oddly ambiguous attitude each toward other of King, Queen and Prince. It dates for us this marriage, made not a month since and within a month of the brother's, husband's, father's death.[9] It gives us, in its explosive mixture of anger and disgust, Hamlet's true mood of the moment. But beneath this shows something of the pith of his character too; a sensitive reverence for the beautiful and good (so, to him, was his father's marriage, and even as much as he yet

revolting
sufferings

---

heir to the throne go abroad and out of reach; and the Elizabethan audience would well appreciate that behind the King's smiling

> And we beseech you, bend you to remain
> Here in the cheer and comfort of our eye. . . .

there lay a grave consideration.

[7] Dover Wilson is all for "sullied," and he finds a more extended dramatic value in it than I fear I can. But the tripled emphasis of

> . . . melt,
> Thaw, and resolve itself into a dew!

does turn "solid" flesh into almost too explicit an image, whereas it both clarifies and enriches "sullied." On that ground (for one) the innovation may be counted dramatically preferable.

[8]   My father's spirit in arms . . .

would make eight; but this is no more than a flourish for the finishing of an important scene. On the other hand, while he is not alone on the stage for

> Now might I do it pat . . .

that is a true soliloquy.

[9] It can be assumed that the marriage has only just taken place; "within a month," that is to say, of the funeral, which was itself delayed a little less than a month. But I think the intention is clearly otherwise. "Within a month . . . she married": the past definite tense does not properly apply to yesterday or the day before. The importance of the point is that Hamlet is not here presented as a man suffering under a quite recent shock (we shall see the immediate effect upon him of a severer one later). He has been brooding over the miserable business for the best part of a month.

knows of his mother's treason to it is treason to an ideal); his
consciousness of his own weakness, in the casual

> no more like my father
> Than I to Hercules.

and in that final declension to

> But break, my heart, for I must hold my tongue.

And in the trick of iteration of thought and phrase there is already
something of that flogging of the will which is to be so manifest
later.

The dramatist's business is with action and character in action;
and it is not easy to indicate other traits of character than those
which the action immediately quickens without resorting to
reminiscence and description and similar enfeebling and dilatory
devices. Yet it is important to do this; we need to know something
of what a man would be under other circumstances if we are to
appreciate his conduct under present ones. It is the more important with Hamlet, swayed as he is to be this way and that, to make
what is constant in his disposition clear; and to do this too before
the shock comes which will set him, in mind and emotions both,
violently swaying, so that we may not lay even more to its account
than should be laid.[10]

By contrast with the orderly business of the Council and the
King's silky urbanities, this uprush of self-devouring, self-exhaust-
ing, purposeless passion is the more eloquent of Hamlet's helplessness and loneliness. And he has come, he feels, to the end of
things. Claudius is on the throne; the Council has "freely" set a
seal both on this and on the horrible business of his mother's
marriage; affairs of state are going their wonted way again.

> It is not nor it cannot come to good. . . .

—yet what can he do? At which zero point it is (we guessing
already that here is not an end of things but the beginning) that
he looks up to find those three sober figures standing waiting his
pleasure.[11]

---

[10] But Shakespeare finds later some other less direct means of doing this: cf.
pp. 244 et seq.

[11] Dover Wilson says that he does not recognize Horatio for the moment through
the mist of his tears, and I feel sure this is right. Shakespeare's men fairly fre-
quently break into passionate tears, "unmanly drops" though they may be called.

The march of the action is resumed. From here to its finish the pulse of the scene will beat quicker and quicker and ever more strongly. But it is to finish only upon suspense of purpose, expectation still, the incline of the climax not mounted very far; so the first steps must be restrained.

Shakespeare manages this by letting Hamlet draw Horatio from the others (who stay respectfully by the door) to stroll or stand with him, friendly arm through arm, while he questions and confides; and Horatio must await an opening to say what he has come to say.[12] But there is no undue slackening of tension or loss of tone; for Hamlet has gladdened at the sight of his friend, and the pulse of our own expectancy will be beating quickly enough while we wait for Horatio to begin. When, at last—with that deft

> My lord, I think I saw him yesternight.
> Saw! Who?
> My lord, the King your father.

—he does, there follows a stretch of verse dialogue, swift, vivid, simple, and close-knit, combining the actuality of prose with all that is needed of poetic power, done with a superlative ease, the finest thing, indeed, of its sort in the play, and perhaps in all Shakespeare. A four-voiced interchange; Horatio's exact and calm, Hamlet's ever tenser and keener, Marcellus' and Bernardo's ballast to the mounting excitement. This is let mount no higher than to

> I will watch to-night;
> Perchance 'twill walk again.
> I warrant it will.
> If it assume my noble father's person
> I'll speak to it, though hell itself should gape
> And bid me hold my peace. . . .[13]

Then the three are dismissed, and the scene is wound up with

So did the Elizabethans in real life. So do Frenchmen still, without being ashamed of it. I am not sure about Italians and Spaniards. And I do not know when it first became "the thing" for Englishmen not to cry.

[12] It is unthinkable that Hamlet would speak as he does of his mother's wedding in the hearing of Marcellus and Bernardo. But the conventional distances of the platform stage leave the two friends, if they are at the front of it, in perfect privacy. The two others do not approach till Horatio turns to them with

> Upon the witness of these gentlemen. . .

[13] This piece of dialogue is more minutely analyzed on pp. 191 *et seq.*

four swift lines, which will suffice to keep the enkindled Hamlet
vividly in our minds, and which give us (if we do not—as we
should not—already know the play's story) the first hint of the
truth:

> I doubt some foul play.... *Hor.*

He is quick at a surmise; we shall find him later preternaturally
so. And in the iterated "foul deeds . . ." there is even a touch of
gratifying anticipation.

Laertes departs after warning his sister against Hamlet, and Polo-
nius orders her to see no more of him.

BETWEEN the resolve to confront the Ghost and the encounter itself
comes a scene for Laertes, Ophelia and Polonius. Some scene in-
terposed there must be, if the interval of time is to be bridged
while the sense of continuity of action is sustained. But this is of
capital use also. Laertes is to be long absent from the action, and
his loving care for his sister should keep memory of him alive for
us till his return. Nor could our first sight of her come at a more
significant—a more ironically significant—juncture.

> For Hamlet and the trifling of his favour,
> Hold it a fashion and a toy in blood,
> A violet in the youth of primy nature,
> Forward, not permanent, sweet, not lasting. . . .
>   Perhaps he loves you now;
> And now no soil nor cautel doth besmirch
> The virtue of his will; but you must fear,
> His greatness weigh'd, his will is not his own. . . .
> Then weigh what loss your honour may sustain
> If with too credent ear you list his songs,
> Or lose your heart, or your chaste treasure open
> To his unmastered importunity.
> Fear it, Ophelia, fear it, my dear sister. . . .

This is how Laertes sees the danger; Polonius too. Ophelia herself, wistfully protesting, only knows of the Hamlet—melancholy
of late, it is true, since his father died—who is courtier, scholar,
soldier, and has importuned her "with love in honourable fashion." But *we* have just seen into a man's mind, poisoned already
by brooding on his mother's shame, and have left him prepared to
learn worse things still. What will such as he have to do with love-

doesnot confidein her.

making, honorable or other? He is to wreck her life indeed, but in far other fashion than father and brother fear. Here is the dramatic value of the scene; of its sententious talk, of the cheerful picture of the three, so secure in fortune as they seem—only a little worldly wisdom needed to carry them still prosperously ahead. They lavish good advice on each other; but the dark machine is already moving, in which they are, all three, to be caught and broken.

Hamlet himself encounters the Ghost, learns of his mother's adultery with his uncle, and of how his father died.

Now follows the discovery of the murder.

We have here, of course, one scene, not two. The Folio (though its scene- and act-division extend to beyond this point) marks no division after Horatio and Marcellus have followed Hamlet and the Ghost, even though there is the technical excuse of a cleared stage; nor does the Players' Quarto, nor did Rowe.[14]

What is involved? At such a critical juncture Shakespeare will not want the impetus of the action to be checked, as it will be if the integrity of the scene is broken even by a moment's clearing of the stage. But he must have Hamlet and the Ghost alone together; and Horatio and Marcellus can hardly be ordered off— like children told to leave the room. The ghostly mystery will be heightened by that silently repeated beckoning, the terror increased by the disappearance of the Ghost, and Hamlet's disappearance after it. The conventional vagueness of place allows them to pass out, through (say) the doorway on the main stage to the right. This leaves Horatio and Marcellus to sustain the ten-

[14] It filters in with Pope, Theobald and Warburton. But Pope is dividing his scenes "classically," not by location. Dover Wilson thinks that to this point the scene was meant to be played upon the upper stage (and that the first ghost-scene should be played there too), the Ghost and Hamlet re-entering upon the lower stage as Horatio and Marcellus disappear above. I see several objections to this. The scenes are long and the space is cramped. The Ghost—unless he was to be hidden from the groundlings—would have to be "on the top of" his interlocutors. In the first scene, moreover, Horatio and the others would themselves not be very visible when they sit down to talk politics unless they were to sit close to the balustrade; and from that position, though it is possible, it would not be effectively easy to see the Ghost. Generally speaking, I think the first scene is both too long and too important for the upper stage. Play this upon the lower, and it would be inappropriate to begin the second scene above.

sion by their five swift lines; then, as they follow into the imagined darkness, the Ghost will re-enter (I think) upon the inner
stage, Hamlet still following. And so both the integrity and intensity of the scene will be preserved. The technique of the matter
is no more complex than that.

The scene is begun (as was the first scene) by a brisk, picturesque exchange, which sets us again (this time the more easily)
in the midnight darkness and cold. Then Shakespeare unexpectedly changes the subject. We have in Q2

A florish of trumpets and 2. peeces goes of.

and, for explanation, the verbal picture of the oblivious King,
keeping wassail, drinking deep, reeling the "swaggering upspring" in comfortable warmth and light; a contrast heightening
the effect of the cloaked, close-standing, nervously expectant three.
But Q2 gives us, besides this, twenty-four lines from Hamlet
about drunkenness in Denmark (or England) and the one inborn
defect—

some vicious mole of nature . . .

or

the o'ergrowth of some complexion
Oft breaking down the pales and forts of reason . . .

—which may damn a man's whole reputation.

One might think this superfluous stuff, and the Folio cuts it
out.[15] But it has a definite dramatic purpose. Once again we are
given a glimpse of the intrinsic Hamlet. Of whom is he thinking
when he speaks of "the o'ergrowth of some complexion" which
can even break down "the pales and forts of reason," and of the
one defect—

Being nature's livery, or fortune's star . . .

—which may vitiate all other qualities in a man? Not of Claudius,
certainly. Of whom but himself?—and the actor can show this
well enough. As significant is the complex of parenthetical dia-
lectic itself. Here already is the Hamlet who will think, not so
"precisely" as dispersedly, upon whatever event. Here he is also,
at this expectant moment, taking refuge, so to say, from its emo-

---

15 Possibly, however, only because it would have offended Anne of Denmark,
and because James's Court was none too sober a place.

tions in the labyrinth of his mind. What is to come will shake his sanity to its base; but already (we are thus shown) the fine nature is perilously overwrought.

There is, besides, the effect gained by the abstracting, with this detached talk, of all immediate emotion from the scene. Upon the dry vacuum thus created the Ghost's advent tells profoundly; and the impression made on Hamlet by the simple sight of his dead father, can, in the sudden silence that falls, be felt.

His mind's immediate response is one of self-defensive doubt:

> Angels and ministers of grace defend us!
> Be thou a spirit of health, or goblin damned,
> Bring with thee airs from heaven, or blasts from hell,
> Be thy intents wicked or charitable. . . .

—for long not to be wholly cleared away. But in the increasingly poignant music of the lines that follow sounds the response of Hamlet's heart; devoted surrender. Here also is something of the intrinsic man.

Throughout the play Shakespeare makes much use of suspense. The story is, it might be said, one long essay in it; the single deed to be done, and to the last minute the doubt that it ever will be. And its incidental use is continual and various. We have had the suspense between the Ghost's first two appearances, the delay between the telling of the tale of them and this midnight; and now that the moment has come, we have this still obstinate silence. And when it is not suspense incidental to the action and imposed on him, there will be the checks, the delays, the zigzags of thought and intention in Hamlet himself to hold us in suspense.

Here it culminates in the deadlock of a physical struggle:

> It waves me still.
> Go on; I'll follow thee.
> You shall not go, my lord.
> Hold off your hands!
> Be ruled; you shall not go.
> My fate cries out,
> And makes each petty artery in this body
> As hardy as the Nemean lion's nerve.
> Still am I called! Unhand me, gentlemen;
> By heaven, I'll make a ghost of him that lets me!

And (for a piece of technical skill) note how the coming short interval of absence has a bridge built for it in the continuity between the

> Go on, I'll follow thee.

with which Hamlet and the Ghost disappear, and the

> Whither wilt thou lead me? Speak, I'll go no farther.

of their reappearance. Hamlet thus still "holds" the scene; until, after an empty moment, responding to the effortless

> Mark me.

he surrenders it and himself, with that simple

> I will.

The disclosure follows. There is remoteness in the level melody of the verse, and something of hypnosis too; but, to balance that, its clear syllabic articulation stimulates attention:

> But that I am forbid
> To tell the secrets of my prison-house,
> I could a tale unfold whose lightest word
> Would harrow up thy soul, freeze thy young blood,
> Make thy two eyes, like stars, start from their spheres,
> Thy knotted and combined locks to part
> And each particular hair to stand on end,
> Like quills upon the fretful porcupine. . . .

—while, punctuating such passages, we have the hammer blows of

> So art thou to revenge, when thou shalt hear. . . .

> Revenge his foul and most unnatural murder. . . .

>   but know, thou noble youth,
> The serpent that did sting thy father's life
> Now wears his crown.

To the rest of the truth the approach is more devious; the tone is more rueful:

> Ay, that incestuous, that adulterate beast,
> With witchcraft of his wit, with traitorous gifts—
> O wicked wit and gifts, that have the power
> So to seduce!—won to his shameful lust
> The will of my most seeming virtuous queen. . . .[16]

---

[16] At which point Devrient the actor used to veil his face in his cloak. It is possible also for a Hamlet, taking his cue from "adulterate," to show that he has half expected and dreaded this, and the shame of it.

The infamy of the adultery is stressed, and the physical foulness of the poison made vivid to us—so elaborately vivid that when, much later, there is talk of poisoning Hamlet himself, and when the Queen is dying from its effects, the picture should come before our eyes again. After which, but for the vehement backwash of that

> O, horrible! O, horrible! most horrible!
> If thou hast nature in thee, bear it not. . . .

which itself subsides into the compassion of

> Taint not thy mind, nor let thy soul contrive
> Against thy mother aught . . . .

the occult passion of the speech fades; till, with the

> Adieu, adieu, adieu! remember me.

the Ghost itself fades from our sight.[17]

Hamlet is left as in some limbo, from which to struggle back to the certitudes of the world. He has not spoken since that

> O my prophetic soul! my uncle!

was wrung out of him; he listened in silence to the tale of his mother's shame. Now, with an

> O all you host of heaven! O earth! What else?
> And shall I couple hell? O, fie! . . .

he emerges; "recovers his senses" we cannot say—for that, it will appear, is just what he does not completely do. From this moment indeed until (after that critical night of the adventure of the play,

---

[17] "Fades" is, I fear, an euphemism if one is thinking of Shakespeare's stage. At the Globe it is probable—though not certain—that the Ghost descended by a trap. But note that it did not so disappear in the first scene, when first it stalked away, or later when it

> started like a guilty thing
> Upon a fearful summons.

and passed swiftly out, while the three men were hesitating whether to strike at it or no.

Shakespeare's object would partly be to provide differently for two superficially similar scenes. In the first the sudden crowing of the cock is the signal for a quick disappearance. Here

> The glow-worm shows the matin to be near,
> And 'gins to pale his uneffectual fire . . . .

And, while there was nothing better to be done than lower the Ghost slowly out of sight, the lines would at least give some sense of a slow fading away.

the killing of Polonius and the grim hide-and-seek through the palace) it begins to seem, as he sets out on his journey in the morning, that the ill is purged, from now till then Hamlet is "mad." How mad, whether by a modern alienist's standard certifiably so—Shakespeare does not think in those terms. He uses the word as unprecisely as we still commonly do. Says Polonius,

> to define true madness,
> What is't but to be nothing else but mad?

Hamlet speaks of himself as mad; half ironically, while he is under the spell; when he is free of it, as having been

> punished
> With sore distraction.

He is not ironical there. But he speaks in riddles. And this we may fairly accept as Shakespeare's conclusion too; that the thing in itself is a riddle. He attempts no answer. Nor need he, since he is writing a play, not a pamphlet. All he has to do is to show us what madness amounts to in this particular case. Hamlet will also pretend to be mad, and the pretense and the reality will not easily be distinguished. That there is reality mixed with the pretense—so much is plain. The reality, and the riddle of it, is Shakespeare's addition to the old story and its pretense, and is the leaven which, lifting the character above the story's needs, gives the play its enduring significance. For while few of us have murdered fathers to avenge, and not so many adulterous mothers to shame us, there will be hardly a man in any audience to whom that word "madness," in some one of its meanings, has not at one time or another come dreadfully home.[18]

The lifting of the supernatural spell releases Hamlet to violent physical excitement. His first clear thought:

> And shall I couple hell? O, fie!

is a remorseful rejection of his doubts of the Ghost. It is "a spirit of health" and not a "goblin damned"; and, as if in atonement, he will, from the table of his memory

> wipe away all trivial fond records,
> All saws of books . . .

[18] Madness, it is just worth remarking, is one of the minor issues in the close-neighboring *Twelfth Night*. And the Clown asks Malvolio:
> But tell me true, are you not mad indeed? or do you but counterfeit?

all student scepticism, in fact, so-called philosophy, and such like "baser matter." He swears it.

It is significant that his next thought is not of Claudius' guilt, but his mother's:

> O most pernicious woman!

For there has been his wound, and it is widened now and deepened. And the more fully, vilely filled-in picture of the pair of them, of her and the "smiling"—the seductively smiling—"damned villain," so convulses and shakes him that he tries the seemingly ridiculous remedy of setting down upon the actual tables taken from his pocket

> That one may smile and smile and be a villain.

But the simple steadying of the hand to write the words does steady his mind.[19]

There are all the signs of incipient madness in his greeting to Horatio and Marcellus; in the inconsequent cunning, the crookedly flashing suspicion even of his friend; the as quick sensitiveness to reproach, the taking refuge in a web of words. Here, half involuntary, is already the "antic disposition," a spontaneous lesson given to the still self-observant Hamlet in its putting-on. The two feed suspicion in him, certainly, by their reluctance—natural though it is—to be sworn to silence under these unhallowed auspices. Then comes the yet more equivocal voice from the cellarage; to which he anticly answers rather as to a "goblin damned" than any "spirit of health," as if in surrender to whatever the power may be, will it but serve him!—at the moment, to scare this oath from them. He secures it, if only in silence, and seals it with the regained reverence of

> Rest, rest, perturbed spirit!

And in the simplicity and courtesy of

> So, gentlemen,
> With all my love I do command me to you:
> And what so poor a man as Hamlet is
> May do, to express his love and friending to you,
> God willing, shall not lack.

---

[19] A corrective very much, one may suppose, within Shakespeare's own experience, the reduction of "wild and whirling" thoughts to words on paper.

the Hamlet they know speaks again; in the gentle appeal, too, of

> Let us go in together,
> And still your fingers on your lips, I pray.

But with the sudden cry:

> The time is out of joint! O cursed spite,
> That ever I was born to set it right!

he faces the dawning day opening its new account for him, in which his own now dedicate spirit will find, he knows, no rest.

Note finally that Shakespeare does not end the scene upon this resonant rhymed couplet, but with a repeated, quiet,

> Nay, come, let's go together.

—upon a Hamlet exhausted, in need almost of physical aid, in need of friendship; and this burden promises but to make him a lonelier man than ever.

Note.—Upon the question of the Ghost and upon the implication of this "cellarage" business, what Professor Dover Wilson has to say should be carefully studied. Briefly it comes to this or something like it: These four men that encounter the Ghost might well—as representative Elizabethans—take very different views of it; and so would men like them in the audience. Marcellus and Bernardo seem simply to assume that it is, without doubt, the spirit of the King back from purgatory. That would be, incidentally, the old Catholic view. To the "scholar" and "philosopher" Horatio, it is—till he has seen it—a "fantasy," and, even after, may still be only an "illusion." But when it would lure Hamlet away, his scepticism is resolved into fear that it may be some demon in the King's guise. And this is the orthodox contemporary Protestant view of the matter. Hamlet is something of a "philosopher" himself and is a student at Protestant Wittenberg. But he is more imaginative than the others, and, under the circumstances, more ready to believe. He does not, for a moment, think the Ghost a mere illusion. But he is torn between the two beliefs. When the Ghost is there he feels sure—despite his questionings—that it is the spirit of his father; when the experience is only a memory he thinks that it may have been a "devil." The point is that to Shakespeare's audience these doubts would seem quite natural. The whole matter would be a living—even a burning—question; and, as Dover Wilson insists, it is, until the play-scene provides proof enough, as much the Ghost that is on trial (for its credibility) as Claudius.

As to the "cellarage" business; profiting by what Dover Wilson says, I yet venture to differ a little from his conclusions. This, roughly, is my reading of what happens. Horatio and Marcellus find Hamlet half off his head. For their desire to know what is between him and the Ghost they must overmaster it as they may; and they are never to make known what they have seen. Has this spirit bewitched him? That would be their first question. The voice from the cellarage would increase their suspicions of this, for it obviously belongs rather to a "goblin damned" than a "spirit of health"; and his own conduct and response to it—the "Art thou there, true-penny?" the *"Hic et ubique?"* the "Well said, old mole!"—is the reverse of reassuring. Hamlet does not, I think (and as I say above), do all this quite deliberately. He is in such a state of nervous excitement that he instinctively plays up—as an actor would put it—to the fresh manifestation, and mischievously gives it an extra diabolic twist; it may scare them into keeping silence! For Horatio and Marcellus are very naturally unwilling to take the oath that he demands of them. Would it not be sacrilegious, even spiritually dangerous, to swear a solemn oath under such circumstances? They give their word they will divulge nothing. He asks them to swear it, and they promise further that "in faith" they will not. Horatio procrastinatingly yields to the extent of a "Propose the oath, my lord." But they never do take the oath in words, though Hamlet may choose to assume—and, his frenzy passing, this may content him— that they do so silently.

But the scene is a picture set before us, not a proposition argued. This is, roughly speaking, I suggest, the effect meant to be made. We are not asked to draw more exact conclusions.

I should perhaps here note my personal preference for two Q2 readings, which editors, for some reason, do not commonly adopt.

> HAMLET. Come hither, gentlemen,
> And lay your hands again upon my sword.
> Swear by my sword
> Never to speak of this that you have heard.
> GHOST. Swear by his sword.

This last—which stands in the place of the Folio's repetition for the third time of the simple "Swear"—clearly will give, and surely is meant to, an increased importance to the mysterious voice.

Q2 also, at the third proposing of the oath, makes the Ghost take the word out of Hamlet's mouth altogether. Here again is a far more arresting effect than lies in the Folio's mere echo by the Ghost of Hamlet's own "Swear."

A Second Movement

Polonius sends Reynaldo to Paris with money for Laertes, and to spy upon his conduct there. Ophelia, much affrighted, relates how Hamlet has suddenly appeared in her closet—"mad for thy love," says Polonius, and goes, taking her with him, to tell the King.

THE slightly relaxed tension of the last scene's ending is at once further and very sensibly relaxed by Polonius' prolix injunctions to Reynaldo, with which this scene begins; by such verbiage as

> Look you, sir,
> Inquire me first what Danskers are in Paris;
> And how, and who, what means, and where they keep,
> What company, at what expense; and finding,
> By this encompassment and drift of question,

> That they do know my son, come you more nearer
> Than your particular demands will touch it:
> Take you, as 'twere, some distant knowledge of him;
> As thus . . .

—and so on, for seventy lines and more.[1] The circumlocution and hairsplitting, and the flaccidity of the verse give us besides—and vividly—Polonius himself, the tedious old wiseacre who meddles his way to his doom, a figure manifestly modified from that of the earlier scene,[2] with its terse dispensing of sound worldly wisdom. And the matter of the talk suggests to us that time must have passed, since Laertes is in Paris and needs money.

But the key of the whole action is to be changed, transposed from the mystery and terror of those haunted battlements, the poignancy of Hamlet's grief and shame, to the rippling movement of a Court life now restored to its normal round. In this deceptive climate the tragedy will be becalmed for a while. It is upon such waters that Polonius confidently steers, with his

> See you now:
> Your bait of falsehood takes this carp of truth;
> And thus do we of wisdom and of reach,
> With windlasses and with assays of bias,
> By indirections find directions out.

Such will shortly be the sense of the King's bidding to Rosencrantz and Guildenstern, and something such the method of Hamlet's counterminings. Duplicity, maneuvering, ambush and trap, no one knowing how much the other knows; that is the new phase. And it appropriately falls to Polonius to initiate it with the sending of his mean little embassy to spy upon his son. For he is to make himself the center of its wiles, and to suffer, a type of its futility, at last.

Note one technical detail. Reynaldo is just off on his journey. These last-minute injunctions, heaped hastily one on another, give the scene an impetus, which will compensate somewhat for its slackness of fiber.

---

[1] Nor, to Elizabethan understanding, would the Danskers be at all surprised to find Polonius' agent spying amongst them. A very close watch was kept upon the doings of students abroad—and is, one may remark, by certain European states, not too happy in their home politics and fearful of conspiracies hatched elsewhere, at this day.

[2] Cf. p. 204.

As Reynaldo departs, Ophelia enters, dumbfounded with alarm.
When she can speak we learn that

> as I was sewing in my closet,
> Lord Hamlet, with his doublet all unbraced,
> No hat upon his head, his stockings fouled,
> Ungartered, and down-gyved to his ancle,
> Pale as his shirt, his knees knocking together,
> And with a look so piteous in purport
> As if he had been loosed out of hell
> To speak of horrors—he comes before me—

Polonius finishes the sentence for her:

> Mad—for thy love!

and she fears it may be so.

Hamlet's conduct, here described, has been subject to various
explanations, and much abstruse argument. But what is the
impression the tale of it makes on us; now as we listen, and by
the aid of what we remember, with a little allowance to be made
also for what is to come, and to be seen or heard by the aid of
what we shall then remember of this? Behind that complex of
impressions we are not called upon to peer. And if by chance there
is fuller explanation, the clue to it lodged and now lost in some
earlier, discarded, version of the play, it has no dramatic validity.
If Shakespeare leaves the listener searching after this, there he
blunders. But I do not think he does.

We shall remember, as we listen, that Hamlet had been court-
ing Ophelia "in honourable fashion," but that Polonius, mistrust-
ing this, bade her avoid him—as it happened, at the moment
when the Ghost's shattering revelation was pending. And our
yet more recent sight of him, after the Ghost's disappearance,
looking then indeed

> As if he had been loosed out of hell
> To speak of horrors . . .

will be vivid.

"Mad—for thy love." We may accept the "mad," but not the
explanation: Polonius is plainly on the wrong track. And even the
"mad" will be qualified by recollection of that pointed

> How strange or odd soe'er I bear myself,

As I perchance hereafter shall think meet
  To put an antic disposition on . . .

But this will be qualified again by the descriptive

Long stayed he so;
At last, a little shaking of mine arm,
And thrice his head thus waving up and down,
He raised a sigh so piteous and profound
That it did seem to shatter all his bulk
And end his being. . . .

—for here is surely something more than "antic"; and, "affrighted"
though the girl has been, she is evidently telling the truth. As to
Hamlet, then, we shall be left puzzled. Is he still as frenzied as
we have ourselves seen him to be, or only pretending to be so, or
partly pretending to be so and partly—? But what Shakespeare
wants is just to this extent to puzzle us, to make us curious to see
Hamlet for ourselves again, and to prepare us to put the same
questions when we do see him; when, however, we shall still be
left almost as puzzled.

He could hardly do better, surely, than use Ophelia for this
purpose. Hearsay is necessary; if we saw the scene for ourselves,
Hamlet's conduct could not be left quite inexplicable. The tragic
distortion of the relation between the two is initiated, their second
meeting (which we shall see) is prepared for. And this interim
sight of him through her loving and troubled eyes keeps our
compassion for him alive. For there is much in madness that is
repellent and grotesque, and that side of Hamlet's is soon to be
apparent. To Ophelia, moreover, he will very markedly reveal it;
and his own undoubted suffering, here pictured to us, is something of a setoff to that, and to his later treatment of her.[8]

*Rosencrantz and Guildenstern are set to work. The Ambassadors
return from Norway. Polonius plans to prove that Hamlet is
mad for the love of Ophelia. The Players arrive. Hamlet
awakes from his lethargy and, for his part, plans to prove the
King's guilt by showing him its reflection in* THE MURDER OF
GONZAGO.

---

[8] The modern playing of Hamlet is, as a rule, and by much, both too sane and
too sentimental; and the indecency of some of his talk to Ophelia is lost on
modern audiences. But I fancy that Burbage shirked neither the grotesque nor
the brutal.

THE scene which follows is the play's longest, and it advances the action not a jot. But its dramatic significance lies just in this; in the casual (or so seeming) encounters and the evasively irrelevant talk, diluted at last into topical gossip of theatrical affairs—the smallest of small beer!—silenced only to hear a strolling actor declaim an old-fashioned speech about the burning of Troy. It is a sustained preparation for that outburst of self-reproach:

> O, what a rogue and peasant slave am I! . . .

which, when it comes, is by how much the more effective for the delay! Not that Shakespeare lets the main threads of the action drop or neglects to weave in circumstance as well as character as he goes. There are no real irrelevances, little that is not somehow allusive, nothing quite empty of dramatic purpose.[4]

Rosencrantz and Guildenstern have been sent for, and in haste:

> The need we have to use you did provoke
> Our hasty sending. Something have you heard
> Of Hamlet's transformation. . . .

That "hasty" suggests that some sudden misgiving had seized the King, it arrests our attention and gives the scene an initial impetus; the second sentence tells us that it must be some little while since the "transformation" began, and reinforces the impression of passing time already made on us in the scene before. For the rest, Claudius is as mellifluously charming as at our first sight of him. The young men are "dear Rosencrantz and Guildenstern"; and though he is in effect charging them to spy on their friend, it is with the best intent. There is a pleasant informality about the business, and he does not make too much of it.[5] On the other hand, if his talk of fatherly affection is to ring true, he must show himself sufficiently anxious—as he does a moment later with Polonius—to arrive at the "head and source" of the trouble. But indeed he is so, if only to make quite sure that it comes nowhere near the one fatal source.

[handwritten margin note: No wonder Ham stays aloof + suspicious he has good reason.]

---

[4] Even the topical talk of the "eyrie of children" is not. There, we are inclined to say, the illusion is broken altogether—though it is doubtful if for an Elizabethan audience the division between real and mimic world was so precisely drawn as that. But its dramatic effect is plain; the lowering of the emotional tension to as near zero point as may be.

[5] The customary presenting of the King and Queen on their thrones with the two kneeling before them is quite out of keeping.

But first the returned Ambassadors must be received. This play of hidden struggle is never left for long without the counterpoise —by reference if no more—of the overt march of events; and against inaction here are set tidings of action elsewhere. This is the third reference made to Fortinbras and his affairs. Next we shall see him, but Hamlet and he will pass each other by. At last they will meet, the one living and the other dead.

This is an item, too, in the scene's cumulative suggestion of delay. And, the Ambassadors dismissed, there is the additional delay of Polonius' chatter, which is stressed for us by the Queen's impatience of it. And it is she—careless of the plotting to "loose" Ophelia to him—who suddenly arrests it by her

> But look, where sadly the poor wretch comes reading.

—for Hamlet has appeared. The madman, whom we last saw wrought to distraction, have heard of but a while since piteously suffering, comes quietly in

reading on a Booke.

A surprising and fittingly enigmatic first sight of the Hamlet whose tragedy has now sunk, we are to find, so deep in him, beyond even his own ken.

Polonius' unceremonious ejection of the King and Queen contrasts pleasantly with the obeisances of the Ambassadors. Then he cooingly encounters the madman:

> How does my good Lord Hamlet?

And Hamlet answers: *Ham does not give anything away.*

> Well, God-a-mercy.

There could not be a more unaffected beginning.

Since drama is the presentation of character in action, the concentrating of a play's interest upon a man's inaction must *suffering* give rise to difficulties. Action of some sort there must be; something must continually be happening, and the chief character must have a chief share in it. It must not be too passive a share, lest we lose interest in him. Then, to be illustrative of him, it must be futile or frustrate action. It must pertain to the play's main theme, lest we lose interest in that. Yet it must not trench on it to the point—in this case—of too plainly endanger-

ing Hamlet's secret. For once that is out he must act, and the
play will either end, or his and its character must be changed.
Why does Hamlet delay? Because if he did not, there would be
no play. It is a true but an empty answer. For it blinds us to the
achievement involved in making the very delay dramatic. To
picture inaction in terms of action, and make it as interesting, asks
skillful stagecraft.

Hamlet is now—so he says of himself later—sunk into apathy.
Shock and strain have dulled his feelings and weakened the will
they prompted; and in the background, excusing the weak will,
is doubt.

> The spirit that I have seen
> May be the devil. . . [6]

But such apathy of will only leaves the mind more active, nakedly
sensitive, preternaturally clear. Moral restraint will be lacking,
since that part of the man is sick. And from the disequilibrium
comes this "madness"; the mind falls sick, too, of a fever. So it is
that, dull and muddy-mettled as he *feels*, Hamlet is startlingly
quick to suspect Polonius and his schemes, his schoolfellows' duplicity, Ophelia's innocent guile; quick, yet uncertain, for the
unbalanced mind takes no bearings. He is as quick to retaliate,
though his weapon is but the will-less man's "Words, words,
words"—which he despises, and himself for using it, and for being
masterly in its use. And so at each encounter, after a little watchful
fence, we find him taking the initiative and turning the talk to
his own account; to some distraction from his misery, screening of
his secret, or whetting of his almost blunted purpose; or he may
let it lead him no matter whither, as long as it be away from this
unmanageable world of facts and consequences. And thus Shakespeare manages to keep him—even upon the defensive—the moving spirit of a scene.

Polonius treats him as a harmless lunatic. He obligingly plays
the part, mischievously salting his jargon with a few nuggets of

---

[6] This comes, we notice, towards the end of the "O, what a rogue and peasant
slave . . ." soliloquy, as a comparatively calm sequel to its passion. The implication
is, I think, that, when he considers the matter coolly, he is genuinely uncertain, but
that this is not the chief trouble. It is will that is lacking; he has lost for a while
the will to believe.

the old wiseacre's own brand of wisdom, riddling sardonic approval of the worldly-wise paternal care which has kept Ophelia safe from his gallantries.

He greets Rosencrantz and Guildenstern as cordially as he greeted Horatio. But on the very instant he is chilled, his

> Good lads, how do ye both?

being answered by the self-conscious artifice of Rosencrantz'

> As the indifferent children of the earth.

by Guildenstern's

> Happy in that we are not over-happy;
> On fortune's cap we are not the very button.

So he responds in kind:

> Nor the soles of her shoe? . . .
> Then you live about her waist, or in the middle of her favours?

—and the three chop logic and wit for a while as clever young men will. But the sensitive mind is quickly at work. Why have they so unexpectedly appeared, these "excellent good friends"?

They walk—they the snarers—into the simple snare which he sets:

> what have you, my good friends, deserved at the hands of fortune that she sends you to prison hither?
> Prison, my lord?
> Denmark's a prison.

Upon his repetition of the word, Rosencrantz casts his own bait:

> Why, then your ambition makes it one . . . .

and Guildenstern harps on that "ambition," and Rosencrantz yet again. Claudius did not need to tell two supple young courtiers whereabouts to seek for the disinherited Hamlet's secret.

He knows well enough now why they are here. Let them but confess it, that will be some mitigation. But they shift and shuffle beneath his gaze; and even his appeal—

> by the rights of our fellowship, by the consonancy of our youth, by the obligation of our ever-preserved love, and by what more dear a better proposer could charge you withal, be even and direct with me, whether you were sent for or no.

—barely wrings it out of them. But his means of defense are clear.

He has only to speak the truth, though not all of it. Denmark is but such a prison as the world is. A minute since Polonius was asking him:

> Will you walk out of the air, my lord?
> Into my grave?

He wishes he could; there is all the liberty he longs for. He has only to paint them the world as he sees it:—

> this goodly frame, the earth . . . a sterile promontory; this most excellent canopy the air, look you, this brave o'erhanging firmament, this majestical roof fretted with golden fire—why, it appears no other thing to me than a foul and pestilent congregation of vapours . . . .

—and man as a worthless quintessence of dust, and they will report him merely mad. For so he must seem to their servile wisdom; and so perhaps he is, to see the world so, this merry, sensual, practical world, in which his uncle-father and aunt-mother carry it so triumphantly. But even in that world he is but mad north-north-west. When the wind is southerly, he knows a hawk from a handsaw—and spies from friends.

Through all he says there is threaded the longing to be free from the corrupt realities of life; and he jumps to the subject of the Players—incarnation of the unreal—with a kind of ironic delight.[7] Gossip about their momentous affairs eases the strain; here, with nothing more disquieting than this between them, are the three boyhood friends again. And in a moment the pedant Polonius presents himself, the perfect butt. The Players follow.

We note not the courtesy only, but the friendly warmth of his greeting:

> You are welcome, masters; welcome, all. I am glad to see thee well. Welcome, good friends. O, my old friend!—why, thy face is valanced since I saw thee last; comest thou to beard me in Denmark? What, my young lady and mistress! . . . Masters, you are all welcome . . . .

—and he loses himself forthwith in their mimic world.

This passage with the Players crowns and completes the main

---

[7] It is worth noting how, in the scene-sequence of Q1, this note of longing to escape is sounded hereabouts far more intensely but also far more obviously by the "To be or not to be" soliloquy. Cf. pp. 162 *et seq.*

dramatic purpose of the scene. An idle prince, indeed, who not only walks reading and musing by the hour together in the lobby, but will sit fastidiously exchanging with a player the recital of Æneas' tale to Dido! And a weakling, who can seek refuge from his own "cue for passion" in facile pity for Hecuba! We shall learn in a moment that, even as he sat there listening, this stultifying self-picture was forming in his own mind. But Shakespeare has first painted it thus elaborately for us, and stressed the febrile talk with his friends, the mocking of Polonius, the keen interest in the petty politics of the theater, the call for "a passionate speech," the contented surrender to its music, so that we may first begin to wonder when, if ever, the revulsion will come. Then, when it comes, we welcome it the more.

There is the seed of remorse in that demand for "a passionate speech." He is asking the actor—how far consciously?—to simulate for his amusement what he is incapable of feeling himself. And the woes of Troy bring reminder of his own. The chord in him is quick to vibrate:

> But who, O, who had seen the mobled queen . . .

Is it only the unusual epithet that makes him exclaim? Does he not see, in his mind's eye, as he repeats it, his mother, muffled in her widow's weeds—yet how unlike Hecuba in her mourning? For the rest of the speech his passive silence should become (so to say) an active one, which will set us asking what fresh train of thought can be firing in his mind. There is a resolved calm, flickering with humor, in his parting with the Players and Polonius; and in the

> Follow him, friends; we'll hear a play to-morrow.

an intent, made more vivid in the oracular sequel:

> Dost thou hear me, old friend? Can you play *The Murder of Gonzago?*

—for we have not heard that fatal word since father and son thrice exchanged it upon the battlements. He continues:

> You could, for a need, study a speech of some dozen or sixteen lines, which I would set down and insert in't . . . .

—and has forgotten Rosencrantz and Guildenstern, whose ears are pricked to hear what is passing apart there with the Player.

He dismisses them impatiently, his mind now pregnant with its purpose. Then comes the

> Now I am alone.

Only a prince, constantly attended, can appreciate to the full the relief in that; Hamlet, moreover, knows that he is attended by spies. But, being alone, instead of pursuing his purpose, he abruptly plunges, we remark, into the self-reproach of

> O, what a rogue and peasant slave am I! . . .

Nor, till he has purged himself of all this disabling poison, can he come back upon his course again, set it with an

> About, my brain! Hum, I have heard
> That guilty creatures, sitting at a play . . .

The soliloquy recharges the action to the full with the emotion which has been so long lacking, and restores to us the Hamlet bent on his revenge. He sums up in it, besides, all the flaws and failings in him that have let him reach this point, time lapsed, and nothing done. It is a most inconclusive summing-up, however; questions asked, and not answered; later to be asked again, and never plainly answered. And even were he heartless and a coward —which he certainly is not—and in yet deeper doubt, the cause of this strange impotence, we feel, would not be there. But what we ourselves have seen and heard of him (since that unexpected

> The time is out of joint! O cursed spite,
> That ever I was born to set it right!

warned us of coming change) leaves us, in sum, with about this impression: of a nature whose spiritual integrity that supernatural mandate—like an electric current splitting a substance into its elements—has for the while quite wrecked, completing thus what misery and disillusion had begun. The faculties are dislocated and at war. Feeling, faith, intellect and will; each one is still alert, and only the more alert unfettered by the others, but too aware of the others for concord, and each is too critical of the others for the lending of mutual aid. Hamlet is now at odds, not merely with the ills of this world, but within himself, and cannot but be impotent so.

Finally, we should remark the means by which, despite the scene's distractions, the main theme of the action has been pursued and our interest in it kept alive. When Claudius confides their delicate mission to Rosencrantz and Guildenstern there begins what one may call the countermovement of the play, the King's against Hamlet; defensive at first, to turn offensive later. Polonius joins in it unbidden; and, from then on, he, or the two young men, or all three of them together are there to keep a keen eye on their quarry, to note every gesture, with a keen ear for every phrase. Even while they listen to the Player it is Hamlet they watch. His movement against the King may be at a standstill, but the King's against him is active if only in the eloquent presence of these three; and thus the necessary dramatic tension is sustained. Then, upon their dismissal, we are given the one arresting hint of ". . . *The Murder of Gonzago* . . . a speech of some dozen or sixteen lines. . . ." That is enough to hold us expectant through the self-reproachings of the soliloquy; until, towards its end, the hint is given substance, the plan revealed, our roused curiosity satisfied, and the offensive against the King is started again.

Rosencrantz and Guildenstern report that Hamlet is about to distract himself—and amuse the Court—with the performance of a play. Ophelia is set in his way while the King and Polonius hide and watch. Hamlet discovers this, and suspects Ophelia of being a willing decoy. The King is satisfied that it is not love which has driven him mad, that indeed he is not mad at all.

THE next scene opens at a sensibly lower pitch. But fresh impetus is given to the King's countermovement by his appearance with the Queen, accompanied by all four instruments of its policy: Rosencrantz and Guildenstern, already apter for their task and talking of "crafty madness"; Polonius, who now yields initiative to the King; and Ophelia, docile, silent. The tension is keyed up a little too; first by the advancing of the prospect of the play to "this night," then by the imminence of Hamlet's approach. But Shakespeare delays this for an instant; to show us Ophelia and the Queen together, and to point the contrast between them, between the sensitive, innocent girl and the pretty, kindly, smirched, bedizened woman; also to let Polonius "sugar o'er" his slight misgiving over this ambush they are setting, and the baiting of

it, with an accustomed platitude (is he a little less ready since that
"Let her not walk i' the sun . . ." to "loose" his daughter to the
madman?), which, in turn, provokes a revealing aside from the
King. From now on, we need have no doubt of his guilt.[8] The
two "bestow" themselves behind the arras. Ophelia obediently
walks apart, and Hamlet appears.

Before his last quiet entrance, reading on a book, we had heard
of him distractedly intruding upon Ophelia. But a few moments
since we have seen him equally torn with emotion; and here he
is, outwardly calm and self-contained as never before. It is a
similar effect of contrast and surprise. But while that

> The play's the thing
> Wherein I'll catch the conscience of the King.

was wrought with passion, it was set in concentrated purpose too;
and this succeeding calm is far from passionless, it is passion at
a still, white heat, fused into thought.

> To be or not to be, that is the question. . . .

These unmodulated changes from storm to calm smack a little
—and are meant to—of "madness." But how the man's moral
quality shows in the fact that he can thus escape from his suffering to this stoically detached contemplation of greater issues!
Only towards the soliloquy's end, with the

> And thus the native hue of resolution
> Is sicklied o'er with the pale cast of thought;
> And enterprises of great pitch and moment
> With this regard their currents turn awry
> And lose the name of action.

does its thought turn a point or so inward—to regain touch with
the main trend of the action. Note besides the technical skill
which, lodging this parenthesis of calm and seeming irrelevance
before the nervous outbreak to come, has first made us conscious
of Ophelia there in the background, thus keeping us expectant,
and the tension sustained.[9]

---

[8] For some discussion of this, see p. 218.

[9] I think it most likely that Ophelia is meant to enter upon the inner stage and
kneel at her faldstool (but she rises again at once at the sound of Hamlet's voice)
at about the cue ". . . lose the name of action." It is just possible that she is kneeling there the whole time. But Polonius' "Walk you here" is against this, and more

The meeting, for its first few moments, passes as any such meeting may between two sensitive creatures sundered by no quarrel of their own; in reserve, in reproachful sorrow that they have let themselves be sundered, and a provoking of more misunderstanding by which to justify reproach. He may choose to think her

> Good my lord,
> How does your honour for this many a day?

a little uncandid, ignoring the fact that if she shut herself away from him it was by her father's orders. She will hear princely irony in his

> I humbly thank you; well, well, well.

She has brought back his gifts, and that will wound him. He roughly denies them; she can then tax him with unkindness. She knows that they are being watched; and though it is all done for his good, she supposes, this will add to her constraint.

In his sardonic

> are you honest? . . . Are you fair?

sounds an unspoken "so my mother seemed"; and at her first close approach to him with the gifts he cannot but have gained—supersensitive as he now is, she unskilled in deceit—a sense of her discomfort. But in a little his abiding sense of his own profounder guilt draws from him the

> I did love you once. . . . You should not have believed me. . . .
> I loved you not.

—that also being a paradox to which the time has given proof. And he passes to the pitiful conclusion:

> Get thee to a nunnery; why wouldst thou be a breeder of sinners? I am myself indifferent honest, but yet I could accuse me of such things that it were better my mother had not borne me. . . . What should such fellows as I do crawling between earth and heaven? We are arrant knaves all; believe none of us. Go thy ways to a nunnery.

—conclusion likewise to the train of thought begun upon "To be or not to be . . ," and answer to that question.

He suddenly becomes aware that they are being watched; and

---

so the fact that her presence, even so aloof, would distract our attention from the soliloquy.

can he resist the conclusion that she is in league with the watchers? It is one more spy and decoy set in his way, that is all. By stage tradition his inconsequent:

> Where's your father?

is prompted by a movement of the arras and an actual glimpse of Polonius, or the King, or both. Something of the sort, no doubt, is intended. But it should not be too obvious, for that will discount the peculiar sensitiveness to things and thoughts hidden around him, the quick, uncertain clairvoyance of the "mad" mind.

Her clumsy, fearful lie:

> At home, my lord.

(but there is danger in his look; what if he did find her father lurking?—the question has its tragic answer later) shatters her credit with him. It is the second such wound. The first ranked his mother an adultress; and the poison of it infected all womanhood for him. But he has let himself still believe in this seeming innocence; and now it proves in its own fashion as false. And just such a brainstorm sweeps him as followed the Ghost's disappearance, and as will sweep him again when the King's guilt is proved; but it is an angrier, and therefore harsher, outbreak than these. The mind's lack of mastery is betrayed in the rash threat to the King:

> those that are married already, all but one, shall live. . . .

And here is the vengeful iconoclast, distorting the image he once worshiped to the shape of his new loathing of it, that he may the better break and forget it:

> I have heard of your paintings too, well enough; God has given you one face, and you make yourselves another; you jig, you amble, and you lisp, and nickname God's creatures, and make your wantonness your ignorance. Go to, I'll no more on't; it hath made me mad. . . .

[margin handwritten note: strange logic which we understand as audience]

That is Ophelia in the guise of his mother the harlot; Ophelia made symbol and scapegoat of her kind.[10]

Her bewildered, heart-broken outcry when he leaves her:

---

[10] Note the significant change from the "thou" and the "get thee to a nunnery" to the "your . . . you . . . yourselves."

> O, what a noble mind is here o'erthrown!
> The courtier's, soldier's, scholar's eye, tongue, sword,
> The expectancy and rose of the fair state . . .

completes by likeness (in the return to verse) and contrast (between his calm thought and her agony) this section of the scene, soliloquy and duologue.[11]

Next the King and Polonius reappear. Their minds are upon Hamlet, and they all but ignore the miserably sobbing girl, now that she has served her turn.[12] The King's disquiet is visibly increased; his misgivings are turning like a compass needle towards the truth:

> There's something in his soul
> O'er which his melancholy sits on brood;
> And I do doubt the hatch and the disclose
> Will be some danger . . .

and the countermovement (and the lagging action of the play) is promptly advanced a step:

> which for to prevent,
> I have in quick determination
> Thus set it down: he shall with speed to England. . . .

Another valuable stroke of contrast; his "quick determination" is set against Hamlet's interminable talk and delay.

Ophelia may well overhear the

> he shall with speed to England,
> For the demand of our neglected tribute . . . .

since, as we are to learn a few scenes later, the matter is not kept secret; also her father's more sinister:

> or confine him where
> Your wisdom best shall think.

---

[11] It is more minutely studied on pp. 213; 241 *et seq.*

[12] They do, that is to say, according to F1, and most editors follow it. Q2 gives her an *exit* at the end of her speech and implies a—quite arbitrary—re-entrance later. From every point of view, I think, F1 does better. The continuity of the action will then not be broken by a cleared stage (and applause for Ophelia); and the oblivious concern of the two men with the growing menace of Hamlet's conduct is emphasized. Shakespeare stresses, what is more, this neglect of Ophelia in the text itself by giving Polonius that offhand

> How now, Ophelia;
> You need not tell us what Lord Hamlet said;
> We heard it all.

She has been caught in the toil of matters too high and too hard for her. She stands apart; shaken, silent, ignored. Then she escapes.[18]

Hamlet prepares the play, and it is acted and answers its purpose. He is excitedly triumphant, for the King's guilt is now manifest. But when he seems to be at last about to "swoop" to his revenge, he is summoned to his mother's closet, and the thought of her guilt takes first place again in his mind.

BUT no sooner has the King departed with his

> Madness in great ones must not unwatched go.

than Hamlet returns. His wild invective is still fresh in our ears; and he is here again, and at his sanest. Nor at his sanest merely, but with his mind wholly occupied by his opinions upon the art of acting.

It is the third use of this trick of surprise and contrast. We heard of him rushing wildly into Ophelia's presence, and next saw him quietly absorbed in a book. He rushed away, excited to full pitch by his plot to trap the King, and returned calmly deliberating upon death—but his own death!—and the hereafter. Now we have just seen him crazed with anger at discovering the trap laid for him, and baited—she consenting—with Ophelia; yet, but a few minutes later[14]:

> Speak the speech, I pray you, as I pronounced it to you, trippingly on the tongue; but if you mouth it, as many of your players do, I had as lief the town-crier spoke my lines. Nor do not saw the air too much with your hand, thus. . . .

and so on for fifty lines more, in an elaborate and delicately ironical conspectus of dramatic criticism!

But it is not a mere dramatic trick, and only the extremes of contrast smack of madness. And these do but exaggerate a normal quality in him, the ability to range swiftly and clearly from one

---

[18] I do not think that this is to impose too much alien imagination upon the text. Ophelia is not dismissed; and, having employed her so far, I do not think they trouble to speak so that she cannot overhear. On the other hand they have done with her—and show it. She would not follow them, then, when they depart, but simply "make herself scarce."

[14] "But a few minutes": this is the actual time involved; and as Shakespeare interposes no other, no *dramatic* time indication, this is the impression sustained.

mood to another. There is a touch of genius in it. We saw it
operate in his first greeting of Horatio, and while he awaited the
Ghost on the platform; we shall see it again when he returns
from his adventurous voyage purged of his madness, and can pass
obliviously from Ophelia's grave and its emotions to the tale of
the plot against him, to amusing himself with Osric, from that
to preparing his mind for death.

Nor, in his seeming absorption here in these superfluously fine
means to his end has he forgotten the end itself. This concern as
to how that fateful speech shall be spoken is both safety valve and
disguise for his secret anxiety. And the clarity and concentration
of his talk (though he lets it run away with him; the unreal world
always more satisfying than the real) are but a measure of the
keen mind alert again and ready to face the imminent issue.[15] We
feel the controlled excitement beneath; and this dramatically
validates the long digression at such a stage of climax.

There follows a notable little piece of Shakespearean stagecraft;
of minor importance, but a good example of what can be done in
the freedom of the platform stage.

> *Exeunt Players. Enter Polonius, Rosencrantz and Guildenstern.*
> HAMLET.   How now, my lord; will the King hear this piece
>   of work?
> POLONIUS.   And the Queen too, and that presently.
> HAMLET.   Bid the players make haste.
> *Exit Polonius.*
>   Will you two help to hasten them?
> Ros.
> GUILD.   } We will, my lord.
> *Exeunt.*
> HAMLET.   What ho, Horatio!
> *Enter Horatio.*
> HORATIO.   Here, sweet lord; at your service.

Those fifty-five lines of digression are offset by this brisk return
to the action and its speeding forward; a moment or so of diversion separating the long speech to the Players and another long
one to Horatio. And see how the slight occasion is enriched. A
messenger to say that the King would hear the play would have

---

[15] Compare this speech to those careless, detached, references to the "eyrie of
children."

sufficed. But Polonius adds the importance of his own self-impor-
tance to the matter, while Hamlet finds mischievous satisfaction
in dispatching him—this high state dignitary and lately detected
eavesdropper—like a lackey, to

> Bid the players make haste.

Here are Rosencrantz and Guildenstern too. Their pretextless
arrival suggests the hovering spies, Hamlet's prompt dismissal of
them his growing distrust; and there is mockery in the very
superfluity of their errand:

> Will you two help to hasten them?

Then, for contrast, the false friends are replaced by the true one;
Hamlet turns contemptuously from them to find him.[16] And
how eloquent is the change:

> Horatio, thou art e'en as just a man
> As e'er my conversation coped withal.

A kaleidoscopic two minutes, barely that; if the actors are alive
to their work, how illuminating! But only against the anonymous
background of the platform stage can the effect be gained so
economically and easily.

The thirty-line speech to Horatio, thus begun, serves a manifold
purpose. It ballasts and steadies the action by providing a space of
controlled quiet, of smooth-flowing and harmonious verse, between Hamlet's glancing cerebrations and the deeper disturbance
which the play-scene begins. And it does this in showing us the
most equably minded Hamlet we have seen yet. While he waited
with Horatio on the platform for the Ghost to appear he spoke of

> particular men,
> That for some vicious mole of nature in them . . .
> Carrying, I say, the stamp of one defect,
> Being nature's livery, or fortune's star . . .
> Shall in the general censure take corruption
> From that particular fault . . . .

and had, surely, his own tendency to "weakness and melancholy"
in mind—which we have since seen so obsessing him. Now he is

---

[16] By the Folio's stage direction he does find him already standing there; by
Q2's he calls him in. The Folio's may well be the better effect, the contrast being
easier to point, if Hamlet has only to turn from false friends to true and exclaim:
"Horatio, *thou* [a very slight stress will serve] are e'en as just a man . . ."

does not reveal suffering

for the first time alone with Horatio, and they are together for the first time since then.[17] And he forgets himself and his troubles, not in such self-delighting talk as he lavished on the Players, but in loving praise of his friend, whose virtues, he knows, are the very ones he himself lacks; and he seeks, upon the verge of this ordeal, to strengthen himself in their strength. And one might suppose, by this measured calm, that the Hamlet who is passion's slave, the victim of that "vicious mole of nature," was now well in hand. He admits that Horatio's original scepticism may be justified after all. For if the King's

> occulted guilt
> Do not itself unkennel in one speech,
> It is a damned ghost that we have seen,
> And my imaginations are as foul
> As Vulcan's stithy. . . .

No more trade, then, with the supernatural; no more imaginings, be they good or ill; but "grounds more relative":

> Give him heedful note;
> For I mine eyes will rivet to his face,
> And after we will both our judgments join
> In censure of his seeming.

The Murder of Gonzago, that is to say, is to be acted peaceably to its end, the two are to compare notes after and determine—or not —upon a sound plan for a righteous vengeance. That is what Horatio would do; and it is what Hamlet, taking color from him, intends himself to do. So the speech and his demeanor here are meant—ironically by the sequel—to tell us.

Now for the second time we see King, Queen and Court in ceremonial state; and to enhance upon the first occasion, the music of the *kettledrums and trumpets*, the *Danish march* and the guard with their torches are added. Before our eyes Hamlet puts on, as he might a mask, his "antic disposition"; it disguises his excitement, is an ambush from which to shoot his mockeries— arrows, plucked from his own flesh, poisoned by his own misery, which is assuaged when he can see them rankling elsewhere.

A tartness in the King's tone, as they passingly encounter,

---

[17] All this in terms of the action. With what may be supposed to go on behind the scenes, unless Shakespeare indicates it, we have of course no concern. It is inexistent.

might warn him that his enemy was on guard. Polonius is a ridiculously easy prey to a jest. But the sight of his mother, gay and bedecked for the occasion, and her prettily affectionate

Come hither, my dear Hamlet, sit by me.

sting him. He does not retaliate upon her; he cannot, of course, sit by her, for then he could not watch the King. So at whom should he strike but Ophelia?[18] The short exchange that follows is covertly poignant. They parted but a while ago; he savagely enraged, yet suffering too; she heartbroken, yet blaming only his madness. The tragic end, it seemed, to a once-beautiful, an always honorable love. Now, before all the Court, he marks her out for his attentions—with an indecent joke. There was freedom of speech enough in Renaissance Courts. But Ophelia is very young and not light-tongued herself, and the thing is an insult. Yet she cannot as publicly resent it, for Hamlet is a prince. Gossip has given him to her as a lover; in what sense a lover, in what esteem he holds her, must not such joking show? Her answers:

No, my lord. . . . Ay, my lord. . . . I think nothing, my lord. . . . You are merry, my lord.

(the last as reproachful as she dare make it) show her miserably shamed, but turning the dignity of a gentle deference to her defense; until, recovering, and remembering his "madness," she rallies to the smile and the response which courtliness demands. But this will be worse torture to her than his rage, by far. He sees her now as the demure decoy, the hypocrite, the wanton at heart; and on her, at least, he can be swiftly and cruelly revenged. It is the first outcropping of his cruelty; that flaw in a nature sensitive even to weakness, ever tempted to shirk its battle against the strong to triumph over one weaker still.

The Murder of Gonzago, compared to *Hamlet* itself, is a slightly old-fashioned affair, with its dumb show and its lengths of sententious verse. But, for a play within a play to be effective, some such difference, some distinction between the immediate

---

[18] Hamlet and the Queen have not met (always in terms of the play's action) since the scene at the Council table, when she entreated him so lovingly and he so coldly responded. The same thing happens here; he even repeats that ironical "Good mother." We must remember, too, the sort of woman that Gertrude is; the aging beauty, attractive still, but having to make the most of what charms are left her, and not above coquetting in public, even playfully with her son.

illusion and the illusion at second hand, must be made. Its verse
is not of the strength or quality of Æneas' tale to Dido. But that
had to stir Hamlet from his lethargy. This is to provide a quiet
and—till the moment of the poisoning—a negative background to
the drama which must command our chief attention, the tense,
silent and complex drama played by Hamlet, Horatio and the
King, another facet of it by Hamlet and Ophelia, yet another by
Hamlet, the Queen and the courtiers around.

One scene, we have just been told, is to "come near the circumstance" of the old King's murder, and we shall more vaguely
remember that Hamlet meant to write "a speech of some dozen
or sixteen lines"—presumably to point the likeness. We are prepared for such a climax to the business. But before the play
proper can begin:

> *Hoboyes play. The dumbe shewe enters.*
> *Enter a King and Queene, very lovingly; the Queene embracing*
> *him. She kneeles, and makes shew of Protestation unto him. He*
> *takes her up, and declines his head upon her neck. Layes him*
> *downe upon a Banke of Flowers. She seeing him a-sleepe, leaves*
> *him. Anon comes in a Fellow, takes off his Crowne, kisses it, and*
> *powres poyson in the King's eares, and Exits. The Queene returnes,*
> *findes the King dead, and makes passionate Action. The Poysoner,*
> *with some two or three Mutes, comes in againe, seeming to lament*
> *with her. The dead body is carried away: The Poysoner Wooes*
> *the Queene with Gifts, she seemes loath and unwilling awhile, but*
> *in the end accepts his love.*
>
> *Exeunt.*[19]

Does not this fatally anticipate the promised critical scene? Will
Claudius not "blench" at so close a picturing—though a picturing
only—of his crime? Let him do so, and is not Hamlet's purpose
at once served, but Shakespeare's (so to say) aborted, the rest of
the scene being then superfluous? Or, if Claudius manages to
control himself, will he not, since "this show imports the argument of the play," stop the proceedings then and there? These
questions have fomented controversy enough about the Dumb
Show. Editors have answered them variously, producers in the
main by omitting it. One editorial answer is that the King is at

---

[19] Thus F1, which does not vary substantially from Q2, though it is worth
noting that "a Fellow" replaces "another man."

the moment talking to the Queen or Polonius, and does not see it. That can hardly be. Shakespeare does not leave such crucial matters in the air. Failing plain indication to the contrary, we must assume, I think, that whatever there is to be seen the King sees. Another answer is that while he sees the Show he does not suppose it to "import the argument," and is content to let it pass for an unlucky coincidence which no one can remark but he; for dumb shows are apt to be, as Hamlet says, "inexplicable," and the likeness may not be striking. This is more tenable; the Folio's labeling of the murderer as *a Fellow* does, in fact, suggest no such figure as the King's. And it is likely, I think, that the method of acting a dumb show differed greatly from that developed by this time for the acting of a play. It must inevitably have had more of the formal mime in it, which we commonly associate with ballet and the *Commedia dell'Arte*.[20] But the right answer will emerge from the text and the situation involved in it; we have only straightforwardly to work this out, instead of dodging or shirking the issue.

When the King sees the Dumb Show he is at once alert. Though here may be a coincidence and no more, whatever Hamlet has a hand in will now be matter for suspicion. But what should he do? If the thing is mere coincidence, nothing. If it is a trap laid, he is not the man to walk straight into it—as he would by stopping the play for no reason he could give before it had well begun. He must wait and be wary. Ophelia (the acting of the Dumb Show has let her recover herself a little) voices the question for him:

> What means this, my lord? . . . Belike this show imports the argument of the play?

And Hamlet's answer:

> Marry, this is miching mallecho; it means mischief.

and his comment on the Prologue:

> the players cannot keep counsel: they'll tell all.

point disquietingly away from coincidence. "Miching mallecho . . . mischief . . . tell all"; Claudius must be wary indeed.

---

[20] In the 1932 revival by the *Comédie Française*, the Dumb Show was acted in this fashion, fantastically and swiftly, and the King's ignoring it did not seem very strange.

Here, then, is the battle joined at once, between the watcher
and the watched. On the defensive is the King, whose best tactics,
without doubt, are to brave the business out, calmly, smilingly,
giving no slightest sign that he sees anything extraordinary in it;
for the attack, Horatio, whose steady eye—he has assured us—
nothing will escape, and Hamlet, a-quiver with suppressed excitement, who after a while will try—still vainly—by mocking look
and word, to pierce that admirable composure. But for a long
first round, from the entry of the player King and Queen, it is a
still and silent battle. Its background is the line after line of their
smoothly flowing verse, which we hear but need not greatly heed.
Our attention is for the three: for Claudius, conscious that he is
being watched, and Hamlet and Horatio, their eyes riveted to his
face.

The Dumb Show falls quite pertinently into Hamlet's—and
Shakespeare's—scheme. The mimic play as a whole is a calculated
insult both to King and Queen. The "one scene" which "comes
near the circumstance" of the old King's death, and into which
Hamlet has inserted his "dozen or sixteen lines," is to be the
finishing stroke merely. Were it a single one, Claudius might
outface it. It is the prolonged preliminary ordeal which is to wear
him down. Upon the point of dramatic technique, too, if the test
of his guilt is to be limited to the one scrambled and excited
moment of the

> Thoughts black, hands apt, drugs fit . . .

—when our eyes and ears are everywhere at once, upon Hamlet,
Lucianus and the King, upon the Queen and the courtiers, too—
the play's most vital crisis must be half lost in confusion. What
Shakespeare means, surely, is to make this simply the culmina-
tion of a long, tense, deliberate struggle to break down the
King's composure, on his part to maintain it. Treat it thus and
the confusion, when at last it comes, makes its true effect. And the
eighty lines of the spineless verse of *The Murder of Gonzago* are
all they should be as a placid accompaniment to a silent and
enthralling struggle. If the struggle is not the salient thing, if the
ambling of the verse is made so instead, it must lower the tension

of the scene disastrously.[21] And we may, I think, acquit Shakespeare of meaning to do that.

But there is a minor theme for them to accompany, besides. After twenty-five lines the intention of the dialogue sharpens—in the Player Queen's

> In second husband let me be accurst!
> None wed the second but who killed the first . . . .
> The instances that second marriage move
> Are base respects of thrift, but none of love;
> A second time I kill my husband dead,
> When second husband kisses me in bed.

—to a glancing attack upon the Queen herself as she sits there. She, unlike Claudius, winces at once; and Hamlet, with his

> That's wormwood, wormwood!

rashly endorsing this petty, superfluous triumph, encourages thereby the King's growing certitude that here *is* a trap laid for him, no mere coincidence.

This baiting of Gertrude will also set the whole Court agog, will, on the other hand, prevent both her and them from remarking the sterner struggle proceeding. She outfaces the mockery as best she may. They glance aside at her from their watching of the play, scandalized, suppressing their smiles. They glance, apprehensively, at the King; what has he to say to the outrage? He is caught between the obligation to resent it and the need to keep calm under the deadlier and secret accusation. To this enrichment of the foreground picture the background of the mimic play will prove none too ample.

Upon the Player Queen's oath:

> Nor earth to me give food, nor Heaven light!
> Sport and repose lock from me day and night! . . .
> Both here and hence pursue me lasting strife,
> If, once a widow, ever I be wife!

Hamlet seals his complicity by the satiric, audibly muttered:

> If she should break it now!

---

[21] As producers of the play discover. They cut the Dumb Show and with it the cue for the silent struggle with the King. Then there is nothing much left to do but listen to those rather dreary lines and wait for Lucianus. Quite justifiably, that being so, as many of the lines as possible are cut. But Shakespeare did not put them in for nothing.

It is like him that he cannot even now, when his purpose is at least well afoot, pursue it single-mindedly, must endanger it by these sinister diversions. For endanger it he plainly does. Horatio we see sticking to the task set him, steadily watching the King. But here is Hamlet, yielded to the old obsession of his mother's guilt, veritably provoking interference—and upon another count— before the critical scene, the finally revealing moment, is reached. To taunt the Queen to her face; and before Claudius, before the Court, to challenge her with that

> Madam, how like you this play?

is to jeopardize his whole plan. The plan does still succeed; but here also is the seed of his own subsequent failure to exploit its success. Did not the Ghost warn him:

> Taint not thy mind, nor let thy soul contrive
> Against thy mother aught . . . .

But this chance of wounding and publicly shaming her he cannot bear to miss. And later, when she sends for him, the thought of scourging her with reproaches will dominate all else; and he will spare the King at his prayers, because of his unlikeness to a lustful, guilty lover; and, lost in the sating of his wrath against her, he will kill Polonius, and so deliver himself into his enemy's hands.

But, for the time, the tide is with him. The Queen does not appeal to Claudius to stop the play; she puts up no better defense than the wryly merry:

> The lady doth protest too much, methinks.

And Claudius dare not stop it, lest that should prove him guilty upon the graver count. He is reduced to demanding, lamely:

> Have you heard the argument? is there no offence in't?

No offense!—when already his Queen and his marriage have been publicly insulted by these hired and abetted players. Hamlet, seeing that the courage is out of him, lashes him, stingingly, pointedly, casting, for the first time, the one fatal word full in his face:

> No, no, they do but jest, *poison* in jest; no offence i' the world!

—mockingly dares him to unmask, knowing he dare not; and, upon the still supiner

> What do you call the play?

himself unmasks, scornfully sure now of victory. His savagely comic impromptu title labels his enemy mere vermin:

> The Mouse-trap. Marry, how? Tropically. This play is the image of a murder done in Vienna: Gonzago is the duke's name; his wife, Baptista. You shall see anon; 'tis a knavish piece of work: but what of that? your majesty, and we that have free souls, it touches us not: let the galled jade wince, our withers are unwrung.
>
> *Enter Lucianus*. . . .

The critical scene has come. Again, how like Hamlet to have forestalled it and discounted its value by giving Claudius such open warning of what was coming! But a sense of triumph possesses him. By the outflung

> This is one Lucianus, nephew to the king.

(to the king, to King Hamlet, not Duke Gonzago) he avows himself master of these puppets. It is with a sort of insolent confidence that he momentarily turns for another bout of bawdry with Ophelia, and then back for his firing of the mine:

> Begin, murderer; pox, leave thy damnable faces, and begin. . . .

He seems indeed to have Claudius beaten. And with the

> He poisons him i' the garden for 's estate. His name's Gonzago; the story is extant, and written in very choice Italian. You shall see anon how the murderer gets the love of Gonzago's wife.

he scourges him from the field.

But it is a barren victory, lacking its conclusive stroke, and to be turned against the victor. Hamlet—all forgetful of the promised joining of judgments with Horatio—was, it would seem, about to bridge fiction to fact, tax Claudius with the murder to his face and before the world, and take his revenge, if it might be, then and there. But, failing to do this, it is a fatal error to unmask. For Claudius, in the safe retreat he gains, will turn that now useless "madness" to his own protection and profit, leaving his enemy meanwhile to vaunt his triumph in sounding words.[22]

---

[22] Since I owe so much to Dr. Dover Wilson's latest editing of the play, it is perhaps only right to record my total disagreement with his interpretation of the play-scene.

He thinks the King does not see the Dumb Show. I have already given my reasons against that. But the Dumb Show is also, he holds, a deliberate betrayal by the Players of Hamlet's plan; the fact that the King does not see it is a

King, Queen, Court, attendants and Players all vanish clamor-
ously. At this point, and with this help, the actor of Hamlet is
accustomed to lift his part in the scene to such a high pitch of
emotion that descent from it is most difficult, and transition into
the key of what follows must seem forced. Hamlet is, of course,
intensely excited; but it is an intellectual excitement and one not
beyond his control. Hence Shakespeare's use of the light and inconsequent lyric:

> Why, let the stricken deer go weep,
>   The hart ungalled play;
> For some must watch, while some must sleep:
>   So runs the world away . . . .

and the ironically fanciful:

> Would not this, sir, and a forest of feathers, if the rest of my
> fortunes turn Turk with me, with two Provincial roses on my
> razed shoes, get me a fellowship in a cry of players, sir?

instead of such verse—into which emotion more naturally flows—
as follows the Ghost's disappearance, or as we shall find in the
scene to come with his mother, or of such hammering phrases as
those he leveled at Ophelia when she denied that her father was
spying on them. And the fantasy and banter serve to relieve the
strain of what has gone before.

---

providential stroke of luck; Hamlet's "miching mallecho" is an expression of
anger at the mishap, his "the players cannot keep counsel . . ." an apprehension
of more trouble to come. The "posy-prologue" is another offense and Lucianus'
"damnable faces" and his speaking of "thoughts black . . ." yet another, a willful
disregard of the advice to speak the speech "trippingly," not to "strut and bellow."
The scene, by this reading of it, faces, so to speak, two ways. There is the effect
of the play upon the King and Queen (duplicate already in itself) and there will
be the effect upon Hamlet of the jeopardy of his plan.
  I might argue that with the material Dr. Dover Wilson selects no actor of
Hamlet could convey to an audience all this extra and very different kind of
anxiety. Nor do I see how the actors of *The Murder of Gonzago* could help him
much. But the proof of that pudding, it might be answered, is in the eating; who
is to decide that the thing cannot be done? I prefer to plead that it is, in itself, a
thing which Shakespeare would never try to do. He would never dissipate the force
of such a scene by so dividing its interest, or handicap Hamlet at this juncture
with a quite extraneous difficulty. Besides, there is literally nothing in the play
which is not, in some way or another, germane to its story or illustrative of
Hamlet's character, or a consequence, direct or indirect, of what he does or
leaves undone. Such an irrelevancy as this betrayal of his plan by the Players,
springing from nothing, leading nowhere, would be a rift in the fabric, and
dramatically meaningless.

Then follows:

> O good Horatio! I'll take the ghost's word for a thousand
> pound. Didst perceive?
> Very well, my lord.
> Upon the talk of the poisoning?
> I did very well note him.

—and we are back into the main current of the action again.
Rosencrantz and Guildenstern return.[23] At a glance he reads
something of their mission in their faces; and, for a mischievous
impediment to it, calls after the Players to bring back their music,[24]
coolly observing, as he waits, and keeps them waiting there,
chafing and ignored:

> For if the king like not the comedy,
> Why, then, belike, he likes it not, perdy.
> Come, some music!

[23] Here, I think, F1's directions are certainly preferable to Q2's, which bring the
two on only after music and the recorders have been called for. F1 makes them
enter upon Horatio's

> I did verie well note him.

and Hamlet to exclaim, surely at the sight of them:

> Oh, ha! Come some Musick. Come ye Recorders. . . .

—makes him, that is to say, since he guesses that they come from the King,
promptly provide himself with a distraction and a screen against their unwelcome
attentions. Even the difference between Q2's "Ah ha!" and F1's "Oh ha!" is an
effective one, as a direction to the actor.

[24] The Dumb Show had been accompanied by music. Q2 merely says, *The
Trumpets sound. Dumbe show followes*; F1 has *Hoboyes play. The dumbe shewe
enters.* Music was customary at private theaters and Court performances before
the play began, and between the acts if the play was so divided. The public
theaters had music when the play needed it, and it would be a great addition to
a dumb show. For *The Murder of Gonzago* played at the Court of Elsinore
Shakespeare's company would make the most appropriate provision they could
afford. The later stage direction in Q2

> *Enter the Players with Recorders.*

may well imply that this had been the accompaniment of the Dumb Show. F1
has only:

> *Enter one with a Recorder.*

and the subsequent text is altered accordingly. But then the Dumb Show here has
been accompanied by "Hoboyes," and a hoboye cannot be used in the business of
the scene. All that matters in a modern production is that there should have been
suitable music, if possible visibly played. What is absurd is for Hamlet to exclaim:

> Come, some music. Come, the recorders . . . .

as if it were an entirely new idea; and, later, for the Player to bring one on, as if
it had been produced from nowhere.

—or, in other words: This entertainment, my good friends, is not over yet.

The severe tone his good friends take with him reflects the temper in which the King has sent them, though they filter this through a sort of sorrowful reproach. Hamlet is a little hard on these young men. They are courtiers, and timeservers, no doubt, and moral nonentities; but their behavior, the circumstances considered, is surely unexceptionable. All ease of comradeship between the three has, however, now vanished. Guildenstern broaches their errand—to Hamlet's still oblivious back, it would seem:

> Good my lord, vouchsafe me a word with you.

He is turned on with a menacingly bland

> Sir, a whole history.

and a veritable duel begins; "Sirs" and "my lord" on one side and the other; Hamlet bitingly ironic, Guildenstern helpless to pass his guard. He does touch him, however, with the unexpected

> The Queen, your mother, in most great affliction of spirit, hath sent me to you.

That canker spot is set throbbing again; and there could be no better way—we may imagine or not the King thinking so—tc distract Hamlet's mind from its deadly purpose. He responds, on the instant, blandly still:

> You are welcome.

But a second, too familiar "your mother . . ." foments such a dangerously teeming

> Sir, I cannot. . . . Make you a wholesome answer; my wit's diseased; but, sir, such answer as I can make, you shall command; or rather, as you say, my mother: therefore no more, but to the matter: my mother, you say,—

that Guildenstern gives way and Rosencrantz comes fresh to the rescue. The Queen also is amazed at his conduct. The infection works on; this "mother . . . mother . . . mother . . ." beating like a pulse:

> O wonderful son, that can so astonish a mother! But is there no sequel at the heels of this mother's admiration? Impart.

He is to speak with her in her closet ere he goes to bed.

We shall obey, were she ten times our mother.

—and obeying, and slaking his stored bitterness upon her, he will avenge, not a father's murder, but a husband's shame, hers too and his own, and gratify and exhaust and betray himself in doing so. While Claudius is assuring his own safety, this will absorb him.

The diplomat Rosencrantz, to his royally harsh

Have you any further trade with us?

offers a pathetic

My lord, you once did love me.

But the frank, confiding Hamlet is no more. He does not trouble to put a term to such friendship, derides it instead:

So I do still, by these pickers and stealers.

And in place of the secret they would pick and steal from him (yet how should they even now imagine what this "grief" is that he denies them?) he pays them once more with the false coin of

Sir, I lack advancement.

and mischievously turns—the dilettante prince again!—to give impressive greeting to the recorders.

He then turns back to the now somewhat sulky Guildenstern; first with a warning question:

why do you go about to recover the wind of me, as if you would drive me into a toil?

and, since that draws a canting answer, to deriding him also, with the

Will you play upon this pipe? . . .

and the rest. And he ends with a sharper warning still:

'Sblood, do you think I am easier to be played on than a pipe? Call me what instrument you will, though you can fret me, you cannot play upon me.

They had better have taken it in time, those two. At which point Polonius appears.

Here is in some sort a repetition of the earlier picture of Hamlet, Polonius, the two friends, and the Players in attendance, when he sat trifling his time away, they smilingly subservient to his mood, and the notion of *The Murder of Gonzago* was about to dawn on him. All four are harshly astrain now, and Polonius is peremptory and—though precariously—much upon his dignity:

> My lord, the Queen would speak with you, and presently.[25]

But an extra and outrageous turn of the antic disposition effectively deflates him:

> Do you see yonder cloud that's almost in shape of a camel?
> By the mass and 'tis like a camel, indeed.
> Methinks it is like a weasel.
> It is backed like a weasel.
> Or like a whale?
> Very like a whale.
> Then will I come to my mother by and by.

(Fool a madman to the top of his bent; if, less mad than you think, he fools you in return, that is but fair.) Then, with a single gesture, and a

> Leave me, friends.

he rids himself of them all.[26]

Does that repeated "by and by," which he opposes to Polonius' sharp "presently," speak of a suddenly stinging thought that he might best go to his mother after—only after!—he had done his deadly business with the King?[27] I think so; and the actor can convey it well enough by look and intonation, and by now letting the swift, irritable sequence ignite and flame out in

> 'Tis now the very witching time of night,
> 'When churchyards yawn and hell itself breathes out

------

[25] The word, so continually used by Shakespeare for "at once," has unluckily lost that meaning to us; though, to Scottish audiences, it has not.

[26] Another instance of the frictionless technique of the Elizabethan stage. Here are five or six characters dismissed from the scene at a word, yet the effect will not be one of rabbits scurrying mutely into their holes, as it would be upon a realistically scenic stage. For when Rosencrantz and Guildenstern appeared, Horatio lapsed into onlooking; so did they when Polonius came; and the Players with the recorders are impersonal figures. Therefore all of them but Polonius, when the moment comes for their dismissal, have, against the negative background, lost individuality a little, have been brought, in comparison with the solid and vital figure of Hamlet, to something the dramatic value of a bas-relief; and they can—this is the point—disappear without distracting our attention from Hamlet, or checking the impetus of the scene. And this is a very important point, since the end of the scene is now so near.

[27] "By and by" can also mean "at once," but I think that in this instance it does not. The O.E.D. gives earlier examples of both senses.

Contagion to this world: now could I drink hot blood,
And do such bitter business as the day
Would quake to look on.

But with that the little blaze of excitement—for it is no more, it
does not resolve into purpose—dies down. The more deeply rankling injury in him stirs again:

Soft! now to my mother. . . .

But he pauses before he goes, in a sort of dread, in something
very like prayer:

O heart! lose not thy nature; let not ever
The soul of Nero enter this firm bosom;
Let me be cruel, not unnatural;
I will speak daggers to her, but use none. . . .

For it comes to him that he has changed and hardened since his
task was laid on him, and he learned with what he had to do;
with treachery, and adultery, and murder at its foulest. And self-
thwarting and self-contempt have helped to make him cruel of
heart. But he needs to be cruel, to be callous and ruthless too. Of
what use are finer qualities, with everything around him—comradeship, love, even his mother's love for him—turned by his
enemy to instruments of evil? He must strike, and spare no one.
Yet along what paths, and towards what spiritual abysses may not
this temper lead him? We have seen him vengefully torturing
Ophelia. His love for his mother lies deeper than that love lay,
its ruin in him may be the more destructive.

*The King, momentarily secure, decides to expedite Hamlet's de-
parture for England. The sight of the mimic murder has
roused his sleeping, stubborn conscience, and, left alone, he
struggles with it. And—Hamlet being by now, he must suppose, safe in his mother's closet—he even kneels and tries to
pray. But Hamlet, as it happens, is still only on his way there;
and passing by, he has the unknowing King at his mercy.
Yet he spares him, lest, killed at prayer, his enemy should
escape everlasting damnation.*

SHAKESPEARE, at this juncture, must make sure that, despite the
excitement, the threads of his story hold taut, and that none of its
various interests is forgotten. So while the King has been out of

our sight his messengers have kept us in mind of him, and the coming scene with the Queen has been prepared. Here is more preparation for it and for what is to happen after it. Hamlet shall be sent "forthwith" to England. Claudius looks ahead; his adversary only tangles himself in each new snare set in his path. Then comes Polonius with the news that Hamlet is on his way to the Queen. The old gentleman moves like a rapidly connecting shuttle between these three scenes—the present, the last and the next, very usefully links them together, they themselves being the link between the crisis of the play-scene and the strenuous closet-scene —and helps speed them along.

But this scene at the outset has been rather oddly held up by Rosencrantz and Guildenstern. The King tells them that such outbreaks of lunacy begin to make him fear for his life—which is both the truth and a politic reason for what he means to do. It behooves them to express their concern; but Guildenstern's

> Most holy and religious fear it is
> To keep those many many bodies safe
> That live and feed upon your majesty.

and Rosencrantz' heavily charged homily which follows, upon the transcendent value of a kingly life, come strangely from these two. The whole passage has an artificial air. "Topical allusion," one exclaims; and the assassination of kings was, indeed, in Shakespeare's day a perennially topical subject. But there is explanation enough within the play's own bounds.

Claudius will not send the heir to the throne overseas without consulting his Council. A scene or so later we have his

> Come, Gertrude, we'll call up our wisest friends
> And let them know both what we mean to do,
> And what's untimely done . . . .

—the case against Hamlet being by then an even better one, since he has killed Polonius. And when, soon after that, he appears to pass judgment on the culprit, he does so attended by his Councilors—though Q2 must put it thriftily: *Enter King and two or three* —his authority sustained by theirs. Shakespeare's first idea, I fancy, was to bring this Council into the present scene; and these speeches, inappropriately given now to Rosencrantz and Guildenstern, are the remnant of it. The change—if there was one—is certainly an improvement. The action flows more swiftly here without the Councilors; and they are more dramatically useful later when they confront, hands on swords, the then convictedly dangerous Hamlet.

Rosencrantz and Guildenstern departed to arm them for their "speedy voyage," Polonius to warn the Queen of Hamlet's coming and "convey" himself behind the arras before he can arrive, Claudius is left alone. It is the first time that we see him so. And the adulterer, the murderer and usurper, so cool and collected till now—but for that one moment during the mimic play[28]—now incontinently bends and writhes under the dreadful burden of his remorse. We have been prepared for some such revulsion by the earlier lines, spoken aside, about the harlot's cheek beautied with plastering art being not more ugly than is his deed to his painted word, and by the "O heavy burden!" with which they end. But I strongly suspect that these were inserted as an afterthought (lest the turn here should prove *too* unexpected to be convincing, or seem a mere superficial consequence of the shock of the play-scene,)[29] and that the original effect was meant to be one of arresting surprise. For here, not in the revelation during the play-scene, is the action's true turning point. That was a flash in the pan. But upon what happens now—or, rather, does *not* happen —the rest of the play depends; from this moment the tragedy and its holocaust are precipitated. Incidentally, it is always referred to as "the prayer-scene." But this is a misnomer more than usually misleading; since the whole point is that though Claudius strives to pray he cannot, that Hamlet spares him because he thinks he is praying, while, if he knew what was in his mind, he would presumably dispatch him then and there, and all, but for Gertrude's grief and the scandal, would be well over. It is upon this

[28] And the breakdown there is commonly much exaggerated by actors. Claudius should, even at that moment, keep some measure of self-control and depart as much apparently in anger as in fear. We hear of him immediately after "in his retirement marvellous distempered . . . with choler"—for which he has the excellent excuse of the insult offered to the Queen, the scandalous tenor of the play from that point of view. It is in this that he would wish the Court to see Hamlet's particular offense, and in his madness generally the danger to be dealt with.

[29] They have just that manufactured air about them. The actor may give to the speaking of them all the conviction he can, they remain "dead." For further discussion of this point, see p. 218.

master stroke of irony that everything turns; upon a Claudius battling within himself for his salvation and losing, and a Hamlet refusing to kill him lest he should *not* be damned.

The technical make-up of the scene; Claudius' soliloquy lapsing into the silence of the attempted prayer, the surprise of Hamlet's appearance (we imagine him, as Claudius must, already with his mother, Polonius having outsped him there), *his* surprise at the chance offered him, his soliloquy imposed, so to speak, upon the other—all that is unique in the play. Nor are we anywhere given harder or closer-knit argument. Each competes with the other in this; and we have a solid intellectual knot tied, a steadying interlude between the excitements of the play-scene and the emotions of the coming encounter with the Queen. Each antagonist is unaware of the other, Claudius of Hamlet's presence, Hamlet of what is in Claudius' mind. Each reaches a characteristic conclusion; Hamlet, with his revenge to his hand, is dissatisfied with its quality and refuses it; Claudius faces the truth about himself as he rises from his knees—

> My words fly up, my thoughts remain below;
> Words without thoughts never to heaven go.

—and, his own life spared, goes, single-minded again, to write the letter which is to compass Hamlet's death. And all Hamlet has gained is a fresh reminder of him

> in the incestuous pleasure of his bed. . .

—more fuel, that is to say, for the already dangerous mood in which he now takes his interrupted way to his mother.

Hamlet comes to reproach his mother for her sin. Discovering that for the second time he is being spied on, he "whips out his rapier" and kills the unseen Polonius. Despite his father's bidding, he is upon the point, in his rage, of telling his mother that her lover and husband was her husband's murderer, when the Ghost's reappearance prevents this. It is a gentler "visitation," and softens him for a while. But he departs savage and embittered still. Claudius comes for news of what has passed, learns of Polonius' death, and sends Rosencrantz and Guildenstern with guards to arrest this now provedly dangerous madman.

THE encounter with the Queen, as acted, too often becomes a moral lecture delivered by a grieved young man to a conscience-stricken matron. It is not meant, of course, to be anything of the sort. For one thing, Shakespeare would never bring this most passionate theme to a sententious crisis. For another, he habitually treats age in his characters as freely as he treats time in a play's action, conventionally, or (within the bounds of likelihood) for dramatic effect alone—and so he does here. Hamlet is "young." It looks as if Shakespeare first thought of him as about twenty, as the student returning to Wittenberg; late in the play he takes the trouble to make him a definite thirty, evidently to justify the developed maturity of his mind. But he remains conventionally "young." Gertrude—if we argue the matter out, but we do not— might then be approaching fifty by the calendar, and in real life have come to look matronly and middle-aged enough. But, played by a boy upon Shakespeare's stage, this is just what she could not plausibly be made to look. There she must be either conventionally "old" or conventionally "young." And since she must be shown sensually in love with Claudius, and seductive enough to make him commit murder for her sake, she clearly— the sole choice lying between the two—must be "young." And the force of Hamlet's reproach that at her age

> The heyday in the blood is tame, it's humble,
> And waits upon the judgment . . . .

is that, while to intolerant youth (never so intolerant as upon this issue) this should be so with her, it all too patently is not. From this, in fact, springs the tragedy; poor Gertrude's blood was not tame. In this the story of the play is rooted, and much of its meaning will be missed if the point is not from first to last kept clear.

The "movement" or "make-up" of this scene is also a little unusual. First come five lines of bustling prelude from Polonius, which link it to the two scenes just past. Then we hear Hamlet coming, vociferating as he comes; once more it is that obsessive

> Mother, mother, mother![80]

---

[80] Only the Folio gives it (though Q1 indicates something of the sort), and it has been held to be an interpolation by Burbage. It has, in any case, dramatic value. It helps bind these scenes together, strengthens a little the fresh resurgence of Hamlet's wrath against the Queen, and warns her to brace herself for his coming.

Begging Gertrude to be "round with him," Polonius slips behind
the arras; and the—somewhat tremulous—bravado of her

>   I'll warrant you,
> Fear me not.

prepares us for the imminent clash.

They are alone together for the first time; and their estrangement till now—her gentle efforts to mend it countered by his
constrained courtesy or insolent sarcasm—has been but a longer
preparation for the moment. She has amply enough now to
incense her in the insult of *The Murder of Gonzago*; and her own
anger, as we noted, will blind her to any further reason for the
King's. Without prelude, then (and with an almost childish lack
of dignity), they join battle:

> Now, mother, what's the matter?
> Hamlet, thou hast thy father much offended.
> Mother, you have my father much offended.
> Come, come, you answer with an idle tongue.
> Go, go, you question with a wicked tongue.
> Why, how now, Hamlet!
>   What's the matter now?
> Have you forgot me?
>   No, by the rood, not so:
> You are the queen, your husband's brother's wife;
> And—would it were not so!—you are my mother.

—to which last savage stroke she has no answer. And upon her
impotent and most imprudent

>   Nay then, I'll set those to you that can speak.

she finds herself in his hard grasp and flung back in her chair
again (where she had enthroned herself to receive him), and next
so menaced by the fierceness of his

>   you shall not budge;
> You go not till I set you up a glass
> Where you may see the inmost part of you.

that she cries aloud for help. It is not that threat which frights
her, but plainer danger. For despite him, and as he feared, the
"soul of Nero" is astir in Hamlet. And did not Polonius from his
hiding echo her cry and draw the frenzied rage upon himself, the

sword thrust that despatches him might truly, in a moment more, have been for her.

For there is a mad, Neronic gaiety in the

> How now, a rat? Dead, for a ducat, dead!

the sanguine

> is it the King?

and the jingle of

> A bloody deed! almost as bad, good mother,
> As kill a king and marry with his brother.

In her bewildered horror she can only echo vaguely

> As kill a king!

and he is himself again in the ominously stern

> Ay, lady, 'twas my word.

They face each other, anger purged by calamity. And she is spared the imminent revelation; for Hamlet turns to the slain:

> Thou wretched, rash, intruding fool, farewell!
> I took thee for thy better; take thy fortune;
> Thou find'st to be too busy is some danger.

But this, in cold blood, from the sensitive and chivalrous Hamlet for elegy upon an old man—Ophelia's father too—whom he has recklessly killed![81] It is proof of the dire change worked in him; and for Gertrude, as he turns back to her, some warning of what —be he mad or sane—she may now expect. The deed itself, too, futile as it proves to be, its mere doing (for him, the *doing* of anything after the long thwarting and inaction), gives him, for the moment, a terrible authority, under which she shrinks cowed.

This unusual initial crisis over—but we may call Polonius' fate the catastrophe of his busybodying through the two preceding

---

[81] Is Hamlet meant to think that the eavesdropper is the King, and the actor to show this? I believe not; for we are aware that he has just come swiftly from the King's closet where he has left him on his knees. And this unlikelihood can be pointed if Polonius hides on the opposite side of the stage. He is not, surely, meant to *think* at all. He reacts, as if by instinct, to the cry from behind the arras; he is so excited as to be "beyond himself." The connection of ideas, if any, will be with the former eavesdropping, and his murderous impulse then. His "Is it the King?" is the unreasoningly hopeful question of the imaginative man, who always expects good luck to do better for him than he can for himself.

scenes, and the uninterrupted action makes this view of it effective—the encounter, as Hamlet has meant it to be, begins; with his

> Peace! sit you down,
> And let me wring your heart. . . .

But he talks a language she does not understand, less of ill deeds themselves than the hidden springs of them, and of the infection their evil may spread till the whole world be "thought-sick" with it.

So he begins again, and speaks as to a child—

> Look here, upon this picture, and on this;
> The counterfeit presentment of two brothers. . . .[32]

—to try to make her understand. But that does not move her either. He reasons, he scolds, he bullies; until, battering her with ever grosser and grosser words, he at last has her morally down, and pitifully crying:

> O Hamlet! speak no more;
> Thou turn'st mine eyes into my very soul. . . .

And then he treads her in the mire:

> Nay, but to live
> In the rank sweat of an enseamed bed,
> Stew'd in corruption, honeying and making love
> Over the nasty sty—

Such sparks of the dreaded "soul of Nero" as there were in him flamed and died with the killing of Polonius. But here is cruelty enough, in the loosing upon the wretched woman of this long-pent store of resentful rage. And so transported is he as to come again to the very point of dealing her the deadlier blow, which will turn these mad hints of murder to plain fact—when, providentially, the Ghost appears.

---

[32] Does Hamlet point to two pictures on the wall, compare two miniatures, the one of his father which he wears, the other of Claudius worn by Gertrude, or see—and try to make her see—the two in his mind's eye? Personally, I pronounce without hesitation for the miniatures. The pictures on the wall seem hardly in place, either in Gertrude's closet or the Globe Theatre. That they appear in an illustration to Rowe's edition is no recommendation at all. And the pictures seen in the mind's eye will not point the dramatic contrast between the tremendous and obscure metaphors in the surrounding speeches and the clear simplicity of this imagery, while the miniatures in the actor's hands help to do so.

A very different "visitation" this from the imposing vision of the battlements; no armed imperious figure, but

> My father, in his habit as he liv'd![83]

—lived even here in unsuspicious happiness with wife and son; no sternly renewed mandate, nor the condemnation Hamlet looks for of his lapse in time and passion. But a gently reproachful

> Do not forget . . . .

—a pale, inverted, echo of that parting, commanding "Remember me," and the pitiful

> But, look! amazement on thy mother sits;
> O, step between her and her fighting soul . . . .

—for he divines a grace in her, as Hamlet does not, as she herself, it may be, does not yet. Then, after a little, a silent stealing-away. It is as if, with the passing of time, the spirit had lost material power, was nearer to its rest, and to oblivion.

These thirty-five lines make a center of calm in storm. It is a strange reunion for the three; and its pathos is epitomized in the question and answer between mother and son:

> To whom do you speak this?
>   Do you see nothing there?
> Nothing at all; yet all that is I see.
> Nor did you nothing hear?
>   No, nothing but ourselves.

"Nothing at all; *yet all that is I see.*" So speak the spiritually blind.

Hamlet rages at her no more. But the compassion stirred in him soon hardens to irony. He has, she tells him, cleft her heart in twain. His

> O, throw away the worser part of it,
> And live the purer with the other half. . . .

only preludes the

> Good-night; but go not to mine uncle's bed;
> Assume a virtue if you have it not . . . .

and praise of "that monster custom." Trust not to change of

---

[83] *Enter the Ghost in his night-gowne* (*i.e.* the long robe which the King would have worn at night in the ease of his private apartments) says the occasionally most useful Q1.

heart. Put on the "frock and livery" of repentance, and you may come to be what you pretend to be. The unheroic way is best. For him, he must be Heaven's "scourge and minister" and "cruel to be kind." Yet these so "stern effects" in him are, it would seem, something of a frock and livery too. For, his passion spent, his cruelty sated, he now himself melts into repentant tears over old Polonius' body. But worse than this ill deed "remains behind"; the work prescribed him is still to do.

At which point, upon the rhymed couplet, it looks as if he had once been meant to depart and the scene between the two to conclude. But there were various technical reasons against that. For one, our interest must be guided out of this seething eddy—as the purposeless, forbidden attack upon Gertrude has been—back to the main stream of action again, the struggle between Hamlet and Claudius. Shakespeare provides a short cut to it by making Hamlet already aware of his so-called mission to England (we may suppose, if we question the matter, that the project had not been kept secret: it was spoken of before Ophelia), and even leaps ahead in allowing him prevision of its treachery—of which we have still to learn. For another reason; the action—Claudius in command—is now sweeping forward to his departure, and such a "full close" would badly check its flow.[84] Nor (upon the point of character) will Hamlet finish with his mother in such a gentle mood. He "must be cruel"; and he turns back to whet his cruelty once more on her. No passionate indignation here, nor compassionate appeal to her to repent; but for answer to her miserable

> What shall I do?

the cold sarcasm of

> Not this, by no means, that I bid you do:
> Let the bloat king tempt you again to bed;
> Pinch wanton on your cheek, call you his mouse . . . .

He even taunts her with being ready, no doubt, to sell her son—at such a price!—to her paramour:

> And let him, for a pair of reechy kisses,
> Or paddling in your neck with his damn'd fingers,

---

[84] Shakespeare, as we have already noted (p. 36), does even more to avoid this by not "ending" the scene at all, but "transposing" it into the next.

> Make you to ravel all this matter out,
> That I essentially am not in madness,
> But mad in craft.[35]

He has recovered his cruelty, too, when he turns once more to the dead Polonius; that

>   For this same lord,
>   I do repent . . . .

giving place to

>   I'll lug the guts into the neighbour room.

~~~~~~~~

[35] The scene has not been swept clear of all tokens of the disclosure of the murder—explicit in Q1. Hamlet has given her no particular evidence—as the text now stands—of being only "mad in craft"; rather the contrary. And her protest that she has "no life to breathe" what he has said to her is not what seems called for merely by his ravings against her union with Claudius, or even by his general reckless abuse of him—in which, certainly, the phrase "a murderer and a villain" did occur, but it was of a piece with the rest.

Dover Wilson has it that an important part of Hamlet's problem must be whether or no to justify his killing of the King by telling the world the truth. Will they believe it if he does? Is he thus to blacken his mother's name? Will she not inevitably be accounted an accomplice in the murder? On the other hand, if he does not, or if he only tells the Queen, will he not be accounted a mere murderer himself, striking to recover the crown? But the problem is surely insoluble; and for that excellent reason Shakespeare does not direct our attention to it. At some stage of the play's development Hamlet did explicitly tell the Queen, of that there can be little doubt. Why the change? Because the Queen could not carry the knowledge through the rest of the play without her relations to Claudius being gravely affected by it, and Shakespeare does not want to add this complication to the story. I am disposed to think that at no time did he let himself in for it, but that the postulated "assembler" of Q1 (in which, as it happens, this scene's text is more than usually corrupt) could not resist the temptation to make the more obvious effect, either upon his own account or by borrowing it from the earlier play; the consequences were of small concern to him.

Whether or no the scene was once meant to end upon the "cruel to be kind" couplet, there is a difference of text between F1 and Q2 in its immediate continuation which involves a slight dramatic difference and is worth noting. In F1, Hamlet is brought back by Gertrude's cry—of a woman left lonely and helpless, she can make it:

>   What shall I do?

This carries the scene smoothly on. In Q2, Hamlet, of his own motion, returns with a

>   One word more, good lady.

That marks his deliberate intention not to leave her in any gentle mood. The change was probably made in order to eliminate the "dead moment" occasioned by Hamlet's "false exit" (to use the technical phrase) and his return, the Queen left at a dramatic loss the while.

And in the final

> Good night, mother!

is summed up all his past play of mockery on the word.

Hamlet gone, Claudius arrives.[36] He has been too apprehensive

---

[36] I have dealt on p. 30 with the question of the false act-division here. There is also that of the difference in the text itself between Q2 and F1. Which version should we follow? Q2 gives us:

> *Exit.*
> *Enter King, and Queene, with Rosencraus and Guyldensterne.*
>
> KING.   There's matter in these sighes, these profound heaves,
> You must translate, tis fit we understand them,
> Where is your sonne?
>
> GER.   Bestow this place on us a little while.
> Ah mine owne Lord, what I have seene to-night?

—which can be made to imply either that Hamlet goes out on the inner stage and that the Queen goes out simultaneously in the opposite direction, to re-enter immediately on the outer stage with the King, Rosencrantz and Guildenstern, or that she emerges from the inner stage to encounter them there, or that the King and the two courtiers enter to her on the inner stage—though "this place" is a likelier reference to the no-man's-land of the outer stage than to the closet—and that she and the King emerge upon the outer stage later, possibly upon the King's:

> O Gertrude! come away. . . .

Upon the outer stage they certainly must be six lines later, for Rosencrantz and Guildenstern are told that

> Hamlet in madness hath Polonius slain,
> And from his mother's closet hath he dragg'd him. . . .

i.e. from some place other than this.

The Folio has:

> *Exit Hamlet tugging in Polonius.*
> *Enter King.*

—and the dialogue follows practically as in Q2, except that, Rosencrantz and Guildenstern being absent, the line dismissing them is naturally omitted. The King can, again, either enter on the outer stage, Gertrude emerging to greet him; or on the inner, and they can both emerge later—between which alternatives there is little dramatically to choose. But the Folio text, in omitting Rosencrantz and Guildenstern's first appearance altogether, and sparing us the slight delay of their dismissal, carries the action forward without check to its impulse; and, as there are other signs that this hereabouts is in general Shakespeare's aim, I think it may well represent his own second thoughts, and I recommend it to producers.

There remains the question of the King's opening lines. They fit—though a little clumsily—an entrance *with* Gertrude, as given in Q2; and they would about fill in the time it must take him to advance with her to the center of the outer stage talking the while. They do not fit the Folio's entrance for him, whether it

to wait for Polonius' promised return with news; and we note that
his first thought when he hears of the "good old man's" slaying—
after a somewhat perfunctory "O heavy deed!"—is that

> It had been so with us had we been there.

For though, as we shall see later when he fronts Laertes, he is no
poltroon, his nerve is shaken now. Yet the supple brain works but
the quicker and better under the pressure of fear; casting about
and ahead, anticipating arguments, devising answers and excuses,
planning new moves, and keenly alert—diplomatist that he is—
to the ever-shifting pattern of events. But he is anxious above all
at the moment to be out of the neighborhood of the lurking Hamlet, surrounded by his guards again, and his "wisest friends." And
the scene's concluding rhymed couplet rings with his anxiety.

*Rosencrantz and Guildenstern, with what help they have mus-
tered, find Hamlet and—speaking fair, as they have been bid-
den to—summon him to go with them to the King. He pre-
tends to comply, but suddenly turns and runs, an obvious
lunatic; and they all have to chase after him.*

It is a macabre business, this torchlight hue and cry through the
darkened castle after a lunatic homicide, and the search for the
body—which he has ignominiously bundled beneath a staircase.

The Folio gives us, for the short scene's opening:

Enter Hamlet.

Ham.   Safely stowed.
Gentlemen within.   *Hamlet,* Lord *Hamlet.*
Ham.   What noise? Who calls on *Hamlet?*
      Oh heere they come.

Enter Ros. and Guildensterne.

Take Q2's more cursory

Enter Hamlet, Rosencraus, and others.

~~~~~~

be directly to her on the inner stage, or on the outer to be joined there by her.
The obvious beginning here is with his

<div align="center">

Where is your son?
</div>

or with her

<div align="center">

Ah! my good lord, what have I seen to-night!
</div>

Does not then "There's matter . . . understand them" remain in the Folio text by
oversight, and will not the producer—if he follows the Folio; and I think he should
—be right to omit it?

into consideration also, and we have Hamlet stealing in, possibly from between the now-closed curtains of the inner stage,[87] the distant voices of men seeking him, his sight of their torches as they come. It proves to be Rosencrantz and Guildenstern, securely joined now "with some further aid"; and, though they "speak fair," turned peremptory too:

> What have you done, my lord, with the dead body?

Twenty-five lines of combative dialogue follow; Hamlet, masterly in madness, hitting hard, Rosencrantz driven back upon futile dignity for self-defense. Before fellow-courtiers and servants, to have his princely companion call him a "sponge"!

> Ay, sir; that soaks up the King's countenance, his rewards, his authorities. But such officers do the King best service in the end: he keeps them, like an ape, in the corner of his jaw; first mouthed, to be last swallowed: when he needs what you have gleaned, it is but squeezing you, and, sponge, you shall be dry again.

—a change, indeed, from that first welcome to "my excellent good friends," and most unpleasantly near the mark. But, homicide and madman though he be, Hamlet is still a prince. He must go with them to the King, but they treat him with consideration still. And despite his wild talk he seems about to go quietly:

> The body is with the King, but the King is not with the body
> The King is a thing. . . . Of nothing: bring me to him.

—when suddenly, with a

> Hide fox, and all after.[88]

he bolts away from them down the dark corridors, madder than ever. And the hue and cry goes on.

The King, having hastily called up his "wisest friends," i.e. gathered a few members of his Council round him (and being certainly now attended by his guards), has Hamlet brought before him, to be dispatched at once to England. Against force and authority there is no appeal, and Hamlet makes none. When he is gone we learn that on reaching England he is to be put to death.

---

[87] They must be closed, if only for the removing of the furniture of the closet-scene.

[88] F1 only; and our only indication of the running-away—which may, therefore, be a late addition. But it is a valuable one.

ANOTHER short scene; and this succession of them, by contrast with the long ones gone before, helps to give us a sense of events now speeding on. /

Q2's economical stage direction

Enter King, and two or three.

we may, I think, legitimately translate into his appearance attended by such of his Council—of his "wisest friends"—as could be hastily "called up" to approve of what he means to do.[39] He has regained some outward equanimity at least:

> How dangerous is it that this man goes loose!
> Yet must not we put the strong law on him:
> He's loved of the distracted multitude,
> Who like not in their judgment, but their eyes;
> And where 'tis so, the offender's scourge is weigh'd,
> But never the offence. To bear all smooth and even,
> This sudden sending him away must seem
> Deliberate pause. . . .

It is the first we hear of the distracted multitude and their love—soon, moreover, to be fastened on Laertes. We may even suspect that the idea has only now struck Claudius—and Shakespeare! It is none the worse a one for that. Did the murder of their colleague not move them, fear of the mob is ever wakeful in the Conciliar mind.

Then, with

Enter Rosencrantz and all the rest.

~~~~~~~~

[39] F1's *Enter King*, which turns the following speech into a soliloquy, is, of course, inadmissible. Claudius' private thoughts and plans we are to know later; these are the reasons of state he gives to his Councilors. Modern editions are apt to have *Enter King, attended*—which is a little too vague. Dover Wilson gives us *The King seated at a table on the dais with "two or three" councillors of state.* If this implies a setting upon the inner stage at the Globe, there would hardly be time (between the closet-scene and now) to arrange it. But a more important objection is that while such "a discovery of the King in Council"—or something very like it—will lend importance to the scene itself, it destroys the fluidity of movement which gives us a Claudius, at this juncture, coming to no halt till he has rid himself of his enemy. There are the checks of the "prayer-" and the "closet-" scenes; but, these apart, and to compensate for them, the action from the crisis of the play-scene to Hamlet's departure is—metaphorically and literally—"on foot." The sense of this will be appreciably lessened by even a short passage for Claudius "seated at a table." The mere physical aspect of a play's action can sometimes be as significant as the dialogue itself.

the King finds himself surrounded and supported by courtiers and guards besides, panoplied in authority and power. And Hamlet has been securely caught this time:

> But where is he?
> Without, my lord; guarded, to know your pleasure.
> Bring him before us.
> Ho, Guildenstern! bring in my lord.

It is the haling of a prisoner before his judge.[40]

From their last encounter, from the sight of the mimic poisoning, it was Claudius who fled, leaving Hamlet ecstatically triumphant. And we have had fine verbal displays from him since; in the rating of Rosencrantz and Guildenstern, the refusal to kill the King at prayer, in his moral victory over his mother. But the quieter "counteraction" has proved by so much the more efficient that here he is, captive and disarmed, the sword suspended such a short while since above his unconscious enemy in Guildenstern's safekeeping, a dozen others ready to be drawn against him, and branded as a dangerous maniac before the world.

We are halfway through the story. And not by words, but in this single picture, the situation and its irony (the harvest to date) is summed up and made eloquent. Here is Claudius, the grieved father and merciful king, sympathy and approval surrounding him, and before him stands the culprit, the homicide, Hamlet. And while we listen, with the Councilors and courtiers, to the King's curt questions and Hamlet's oracular replies (he has his "madness" for defense still; it is gladly allowed him), we know, as

---

[40] Once again, stage directions are in question. Most modern editions follow the Folio with a simple *Enter Rosecnrantz*; some add . . . *and others*, and, of their own accord, commit themselves later to a few nondescript "attendants." But the hint to the producer in Q2's *Enter Rosencraus and all the rest* was to bring on the full strength of the company, surround the King with every safeguard and give to Hamlet's banishment all possible importance. A significant and striking dramatic effect. Dover Wilson gives us

> *Rosencrantz, Guildenstern and others enter.*

and prefers Q2's

> Ho [actually "How"], bring in the Lord.

to F1's

> Hoa, Guildensterne? Bring in my Lord.

This last may not be the logical sequel to *and all the rest* (though even that "all" still excludes Hamlet's guards), but it gives us Guildenstern in personal charge, as he would be, of the distinguished prisoner, and carrying the surrendered sword.

they do not, that all this is beside the point. For Claudius cares no
more about the dead Polonius at this juncture than Hamlet does;
and it is in the latent thoughts of the two as they face each other
that the drama lies. At the crisis of the play-scene it seemed as if
the struggle would surge into the open, but here each is back in
his ambush again. We shall guess at Hamlet's thought, when we
hear that so innocently astonished

> For England?

—since behind it, and the blithely reiterated

> But, come; for England! . . . Come, for England!

with which he beckons after him the schoolfellows turned jailers,
will echo for us his recent grim forebodings of treachery in the
"letters sealed," and the mandate marshaling him to knavery. The
remembrance should sharpen too our questioning of Claudius'
gentle

> Hamlet, this deed, for thine especial safety,
> Which we do tender, as we dearly grieve
> For that which thou hast done, must send thee hence
> With fiery quickness . . . .

and his so suspiciously kindly air.

To Claudius' inmost mind we have till now been sparingly
and, as it were, but grudgingly admitted; fitly so, for he does not
love exploring it himself. Shakespeare has let him keep up appearances. Except for a solitary (and it may be a subsequently added)
aside, not till *The Murder of Gonzago* shook him to the depths
was there any avowal of guilt. This apart, we have seen him as
Gertrude and his Court see him, with Hamlet's jealous hatred to
be discounted, with only the Ghost's word for it that he is other
than he seems. He is, moreover, one of those most clever scoun-
drels; he never lies when he need not and lets the straight road
carry him just as far as it will. This dispatch to England; patently,
for Hamlet's sake, it is the right thing to do. And the game seems
so certainly in his hands that he cannot deny himself a little fun
with his victim:

> For England?
>> Ay, Hamlet.
>>> Good.
> So is it, if thou knew'st our purposes.

Hamlet, as we know, suspects something of them, and is an adept himself at equivoque:

> I see a cherub that sees them.

So, for a moment, the two stand there, as if mutually enjoying some secret joke to the confounding of the lookers-on.

They part. Claudius is left alone; the mask comes off, his mind is revealed; Hamlet's intuition is verified:

> And England, if my love thou hold'st at aught,
>   . . . thou mayst not coldly set
> Our sovereign process, which imports at full,
> By letters conjuring to that effect,
> The present death of Hamlet. Do it, England;
> For like the hectic in my blood he rages,
> And thou must cure me. Till I know 'tis done,
> Howe'er my haps, my joys were ne'er begun.

With which conventional full-close this chapter of the story and the struggle ends; and another is foreshadowed, with the "counter-action" definitely in the ascendant and Hamlet on the defensive.

While this is passing at Elsinore, Fortinbras and his army are traversing Danish territory nearby. On his way to the harbor, Hamlet encounters one of its officers. He reflects upon the contrast between Fortinbras' confident march towards victory and glory, and his own present defeat.

> *Enter Fortinbras and his army over the stage.*

—it is again one of Shakespeare's well-tried effects of contrast. Against the treacherous King and his Court are set the frank young soldier and his "lawless resolutes"; he is on his way with them to prove his "unimproved mettle." We have heard enough of him already for the contrast to make its effect. Incidentally the courtesy of his speech belies his and his army's earlier reputation:

> Go, captain, from me greet the Danish King;
> Tell him that, by his licence, Fortinbras
> Craves the conveyance of a promis'd march
> Over his kingdom. You know the rendezvous.
> If that his majesty would aught with us,
> We shall express our duty in his eye,
> And let him know so.

Here then, we are meant to feel, is a leader who is disciplining both himself and his men.

But the contrast is to be intensified. For hardly has the martial little pageant passed than

> *Enter Hamlet, Rosencraus, etc . . .*

—Hamlet the doomed exile, disarmed and under guard.[41]

By just so much he misses an encounter with his spiritual rival. They are not to meet till Fortinbras, "with conquest come from Poland," will pass this way again to find him a conqueror, too, and dead. He detains instead the returning captain, who does not know this prisoner for what he is—they politely "Sir" each other as equals[42]—and, in answer to his questions, tells him that

> We go to gain a little patch of ground
> That hath in it no profit but the name.
> To pay five ducats, five, I would not farm it;
> Nor will it yield to Norway or the Pole
> A ranker rate, should it be sold in fee.

Yet it appears that two armies are to "debate the question of this straw" to the death. The captain goes his way; and the stage is cleared for Hamlet's commentary:

> How all occasions do inform against me,
> And spur my dull revenge! . . .[43]

~~~~~~~~~

[41] This does not, I think, stretch Q2's summary, etc., too far. He is treated with the respect due to a prince. He is under arrest nevertheless.

[42] The intention is stressed in their farewell

> I humbly thank you, sir.
> God be wi' you, sir.

with Rosencrantz'

> Will 't please you go, my lord?

coming immediately after.

[43] "The stage is cleared"—quite undisguisedly.

> ROSENCRANTZ. Will 't please you go, my lord?
> HAMLET. I'll be with you straight. Go a little before.

—and leave me to soliloquize!

Shakespeare was not interested, it would seem, in nice stagecraft for its own sake. Still, he seldom, in his maturity, takes refuge in such simplicities as this. Its verisimilitude will pass, *just* pass. Is his mind so occupied with the *matter* of the scene, that his sense of the theater is in momentary abeyance?

The Folio omits the soliloquy and the rest of Hamlet's share in the scene. If the play had to be shortened, here, at a stroke, were several minutes saved; and, though the character suffers, the story hardly does.

With scenery's scene-division destroying continuity of action, it soon became

He is to pass out of the action for a while. That would be reason
enough for overlaying our most recent sight of him, masked in his
madness, with a juster one. But we are to be given, besides, a view
of Hamlet which we have hardly had before, a judgment at parting. And in the light of it we shall look on him a little differently
when he returns.

He has intimately revealed himself to us more than once. But
till now he has only once measured himself against any standard
but his own; when, upon the brink of the ordeal of the play-scene,
he made Horatio's calm strength the text of some wistful self-
reproach. That adventure is over. He has thrown away the fruits
of it; and he now stands contemplating Fortinbras of the "strong
hand and terms compulsatory," seeing himself in that light as
nakedly as men do upon the morrow of a failure.

His self-indictment is the bitterer for its cold detachment:

> What is a man,
> If his chief good and market of his time
> Be but to sleep and feed? a beast, no more.
> Sure he that made us with such large discourse,
> Looking before and after, gave us not
> That capability and god-like reason
> To fust in us unus'd. . . .

He has not left it unused. Yet to what use has he put it? To
fostering

> some craven scruple
> Of thinking too precisely on the event;
> A thought which, quartered, hath but one part wisdom
> And ever three parts coward. . . .

customary in the theater to omit Fortinbras and his army too; the entire scene
disappears. But upon Shakespeare's stage this would not do. There some bridge
was wanted, which would both separate and link the two scenes, one dealing with
the death of Polonius and the banishing of Hamlet, the other with Ophelia's madness, Polonius by then in his grave and Hamlet far away. Besides which Shakespeare wants, I think, to keep Hamlet's "madness" and Ophelia's madness apart.
Dover Wilson (in *The Manuscript of Shakespeare's Hamlet*, p. 31), arguing
that the soliloquy cannot be, as some critics have held, a late addition to the play,
says, "The Fortinbras scene was patently written in order to give occasion to the
soliloquy." This, I venture to think, goes too far. Hamlet's appearance can certainly be called the most important thing in the scene. But, apart from the technical need for some bridge scene here, the dramatic effect made by Fortinbras and
his army as a contrast to Claudius and his Court is important in itself.

—but even in the misery of defeat he knows he is no coward. The merciless truth suddenly rings out in the baffled

> I do not know
> Why yet I live to say 'This thing's to do';
> Sith I have cause, and will, and strength, and means
> To do't. . . .

He does not know. And if godlike reason cannot tell him why, yet will not let him act in ignorance, what is it but a mockery and a curse? Therefore:

> from this time forth,
> My thoughts be bloody, or be nothing worth!

Upon which negation of all he has been and believed in until now, not envious any longer of "blood and judgment . . . well commingled," but just of brute capacity for deeds of blood, we part from him. A changed and hardened man; yet not so changed. For even while he thinks that at last he is facing facts he is ignoring them, confident that he has not merely "cause and will" but "strength and means" to act—in this very moment of his helplessness and defeat! The idea and not the thing itself, that is what still counts with him.

A Third Movement

THIS will take us to the end of the play. The King's "counteraction" is the main motive force; Hamlet, till the last scene, an all-but-passive figure.

Three scenes interpose between his departure and return. Before examining them in detail, it may be worth while to note their relation to the action as a whole. Shakespeare, as we have seen, carefully confines this to Elsinore.[1] We do not travel with the

---

[1] See p. 38 *et seq.* One must be wary of imputing dramatic motives to Shakespeare. But I think this "carefully" may be justified. With a continuing need of little "bridge scenes" for the spacing-out of the action, the most convenient, and—for most Elizabethan dramatists, Shakespeare among them—the customary thing would be to transport us to wherever the material for one happened at the moment to be. But several other of the plays of this period—*Twelfth Night, Measure for Measure, Othello*—show a tendency to concentrate the action in some single city or district, at any rate. If the story lends itself to such treatment this does give a certain stability to its framework. And in *Hamlet* this modified "unity of place" is certainly turned to definite dramatic account.

story's travelers; neither to Paris with Laertes nor to Norway with the Ambassadors, nor even towards England now with Hamlet. And it will be to the good to be quit of him and the strain of his troubles for a time—or really we might begin to weary of them. Yet the distraction should not be complete. For he and they are the marrow of the play, and the continuity of our interest in them must not be definitely broken.

In these three scenes the double demand is fulfilled and its conflict reconciled. Ophelia's lyric madness strikes a new note; but we are conscious of Hamlet's hand in it, and of something like pretense with him turned tragic reality for her. Horatio is there to remind us of him. Laertes' frontal attack and his frank cry for vengeance, suddenly detonating, contrast sharply with Hamlet's subtleties; but it is against Hamlet that they are soon deflected. And even while the plot against him is hatching we are warned of his return. So the matter of the scenes is not merely incidental, but rooted in the story, knit together in a certain unity and by a close continuity of action. And it makes firm passage across that always difficult interval between a play's mid-crisis and its final climax and catastrophe.

The death of her father at the hands of her lover unhinges Ophelia's mind. Laertes, returned from France and believing the King to blame, raises a rebellion to avenge Polonius. The King courageously faces it, and calms him and proceeds to tell him where the guilt really lies.

Enter the Queen, Horatio and a Gentleman . . . .

—this scene and the three that follow it run to some length, 760 lines and more between them. Except from the last, Hamlet is absent, and even in that, his cause is not in question. We have, then, a fresh range, an exempted interplay, of character and incident, and the stagecraft of it repays close analysis.

The Queen's opening lines—

I will not speak with her. . . . What would she have?

—are keyed to the last we heard of her; she is still nerve-racked and guilt-ridden, and incapable of facing fresh trouble. Ophelia is not named. We guess at her from that

She speaks much of her father . . . .

But there is a sense of grave and uncanny calamity in this very omission of her name.

The Folio thriftily turns over to Horatio the Gentleman's speech describing her. It asks skillful and discreet speaking, certainly, and a minor actor might well not do it full credit. But this is to rob Horatio of the characteristic quiet in which he listens. His considered comment:

> 'Twere good she were spoken with, for she may strew
> Dangerous conjectures in ill-breeding minds.

and the concluding

> Let her come in.

the Folio also gives to the Queen; and modern editors leave her this last, on the ground, presumably, that she should give the order, not he.[2] But I think the Quarto's intention is clear. The Gentleman stands respectfully aloof. Horatio speaks his two lines of prudent counsel in the Queen's ear. She is still too distressed to make more than a gesture of assent, which he translates for her into words. To give the order he leaves her isolated on the outer stage, and her misery finds vent and relief in the plaintive sing-song of

> To my sick soul, as sin's true nature is,
> Each toy seems prologue to some great amiss:
> So full of artless jealousy is guilt,
> It spills itself in fearing to be spilt.

Then she pulls herself together to receive Ophelia.

But Ophelia is already there—if we follow the Quarto; and again, I think, the dramatic intention is plain. The editors not only follow the Folio in politely postponing her appearance till the Queen has quite finished speaking, but of their own accord they have the Gentleman go out to fetch her and formally usher her in. That is far too proper and sane. The Folio only has

> *Enter Ophelia distracted.*

The original intention is, surely, that she should dart through the door when it is opened and stand for a moment or so gazing at

---

[2] The Folio only gives it her as an integral part of the gift of the lines taken from Horatio in exchange for the Gentleman's speech.

the Queen, whom she does not in her madness recognize.[8] Hence her

> Where is the beauteous majesty of Denmark?

and its pathetic irony. Where, indeed, in this haggard, fearful woman, is the "beauteous majesty" that has been the cause of all this ill?

We may even here take a hint from Q1 and its

> *Enter Ofelia playing on a Lute, and her haire downe singing.*

Having had her way and been admitted to the presence of this disappointingly unknown lady, she becomes absorbed in her lute and her singing.[4] The three[5] stand hopelessly gazing at her, and listening to the "conceit upon her father," with its

> He is dead and gone, lady,
> He is dead and gone;
> At his head a grass-green turf;
> At his heels a stone.

The King comes quietly in. She sings on unheeding:

> White his shroud as the mountain snow . . .
> Larded with sweet flowers;
> Which bewept to the grave did go
> With true-love showers.

And from this her poor mind travels to a perverted mirroring of the tragedy of her love for Hamlet:

> To-morrow is Saint Valentine's day,
> All in the morning betime,
> And I a maid at your window,
> To be your Valentine.

> Then up he rose, and donn'd his clothes,
> And dupp'd the chamber door;
> Let in the maid, that out a maid
> Never departed more.

---

[8] That "she is importunate, indeed distract" is the first thing we have heard of her. Shakespeare and his audience would imagine unseen attendants in some anteroom, barring her way. The King later on implies that his "Switzers" are—or ought to be—there.

[4] The dramatic point of the lute is that you must stand—or, better, sit—still if you are to attempt to play it. Modern Ophelias have an ineffective habit of drifting vaguely about the stage. A lute is at least an admirable anchor.

[5] Or, if the Gentleman has gone, the Queen and Horatio.

Wiseacre warnings against that manner of undoing could not save
her from this one. The merry bit of bawdry which follows:

> By Gis and by Saint Charity,
>   Alack, and fie for shame!
> Young men will do't, if they come to't;
>   By cock, they are to blame.

> Quoth she, Before you tumbled me,
>   You promised me to wed.
> So would I ha' done, by yonder sun,
>   An thou hadst not come to my bed.

may remind her listeners (and us) that it was with such humor
Hamlet so brutally bespattered her as they sat watching the play.
Here is its echo now upon her pitiably innocent lips. Then it is
as if she tried to reassemble scattered fragments of the thoughts
she last controlled:

> I hope all will be well. We must be patient. But I cannot choose
> but weep, to think they should lay him i' the cold ground. My
> brother shall know of it . . . .

For the rest, she addresses phantoms—

> Come, my coach! Good-night, ladies; good-night, sweet ladies;
> good-night, good-night.

—and is gone. The kindly Claudius sends Horatio after:

> Follow her close; give her good watch, I pray you . . . .

and is left alone with the Queen.

Gertrude is silent. She has not spoken since, at his coming, she
appealed to him with a

> Alas! look here, my lord.

—for this guiltless suffering confounds her. Claudius can always
find words.

His twenty-line speech that follows is technically remarkable. It
sets the scene in appropriate time and circumstance. Polonius'
death and Hamlet's departure are definitely relegated to the past;
the recent past, for

> we have done but greenly
> In hugger-mugger to inter him . . . .

(the implication is of haste as well as secrecy), yet not so recent
but that Laertes

> is in secret come from France;
> Feeds on his wonder, keeps himself in clouds,
> And wants not buzzers to infect his ear
> With pestilent speeches of his father's death . . . .

—the "in secret" a subtle stroke of imprecision. It sounds—only
sounds—as if the tragic news had brought him from France; but
Claudius does not know how long he has been here. Now, had
Shakespeare put all this in its more obvious place, linked it directly
to Hamlet's parting soliloquy, made it an explanatory prelude to
Ophelia's appearance, it would only have been of bare practical
use. But by placing it here, the lyric madness is left to be a vibrant
sequel to the hard, intellectual drive, the dry sanity, of the soliloquy. It is, moreover, a thing so moving in itself as to banish other
things from our mind. Therefore, in this anticlimax which follows,
we the more passively accept these incongruous time suggestions.
The speech itself is of the very stuff of anticlimax:

> O Gertrude, Gertrude!
> When sorrows come, they come not single spies,
> But in battalions. . . .

Just such unlooked-for, inscrutable, addition to evil it is that will
set us brooding, as Gertrude silently broods, or, with Claudius,
gloomily summing up errors and chances. And it serves besides
to separate Ophelia's pathos from Laertes' anger; they are to be
thrown, a little later, into sharp contrast.

Now comes

> *A noise within.*

and the Queen's nerves are at once on edge again.[6] But the King
—no coward, it would seem, when his conscience is clear—
listens calmly to the scared "messenger's" tale of a Laertes, not
merely bent upon amends for his father's death, but head of a
rabble that "call him lord" and

---

[6] Here again the Folio knits the action a little closer than does Q2, by giving
her the usefully quick, nervous,

> Alack, what noyse is this?

and eliminating the King's "Attend"—his call to someone in the anteroom.

cry 'Choose we; Laertes shall be king!'
Caps, hands and tongues, applaud it to the clouds,
'Laertes shall be king, Laertes king!'

Not that Laertes proves so very treasonable. Once in the royal presence he seems anxious to be free of his "rabble," who, for their part, too, become biddable enough. The messenger's magniloquent

Save yourself, my lord;
The ocean, overpeering of his list,
Eats not the flats with more impetuous haste
Than young Laertes . . . .

and the crash proclaiming that

The doors are broke.

resolve themselves, in fact, into a hubbub in the anteroom and half a dozen fierce speeches from a passionate young man, with whom Claudius very easily deals. The "giant-like" rebellion is stillborn. It is so for a dramatically good reason. Here as elsewhere Shakespeare stops short of enlarging the play's action beyond the bounds of personal conflict. We heard at the outset the tale of Denmark's dangers from abroad, and have seen the formidable Fortinbras and his army march harmlessly by. And here is rebellion—fruit of the rottenness within the state—brought into the very anteroom. But no further. For if once these wider issues took the stage the more intimate ones would lose, by comparison, their intensity and force. It may be owned, however, that this rebellion—shaken in the wings like a thunder-sheet—is not in itself very convincing.[7]

---

[7] The political part of the play's story is told mainly by implication. Claudius, upon his brother's death, and, it would seem, in Hamlet's absence at Wittenberg, has assumed the crown; and his possession of it has been apparently ratified by the Council, over which we first see him presiding. He has been so far "elected" by them that Hamlet can speak of his having

Popped in between the election and my hopes . . .

And among them he finds the "wisest friends" upon whose support he relies when it comes to sending Hamlet to England.

But Hamlet, we have heard, is

lov'd of the distracted multitude,
Who like not in their judgment, but their eyes. . . .

—and he (and Shakespeare) will have had, I fancy, this love in mind when speaking, a scene later, at the very moment of banishment, of having not only the "will" but the "power" to turn the tables on the King. And now the multitude,

Claudius deals with Laertes very skillfully indeed. The quiet dignity, the cool courage:

> Let him go, Gertrude; do not fear our person:
> There's such divinity doth hedge a king,
> That treason can but peep to what it would . . . .

and the old caressing use of the name, such reproach in its soft cadence now:

> What is the cause, Laertes,
> That thy rebellion looks so giant-like?
> . . . Tell me, Laertes,
> Why thou art thus incens'd?

the "rabble," have suddenly given their hearts to another handsome, gallant, and much-wronged young man. This may seem a mere dramatic convenience, and it is one. But it illustrates also their folly and instability; and, for other strokes to the picture, we have the King's contempt for them, the Queen's

false Danish dogs!

(note the implication that she is, by birth, a foreigner to Denmark; such things slip out at such a moment), Laertes' desire to be quit of their compromising help, and their own facile conversion from wolves to sheep. Finally they fade away, no one even troubling to dismiss them. It is certainly not from among them that Laertes himself is to make choice of the "wisest friends" he will; these, as the very phrase tells us, are meant to be men akin to the King's own councilors.

Such strokes and hints the Elizabethan actors could be trusted to color in and elaborate; their implications would be plain to them. A Claudius would instinctively respond to the outrage of the claim:

Choose we, Laertes shall be king!

and the messenger as inevitably accentuate the "*we*"—though, indeed, the verse does it for him. And a Laertes would know just how coldly to temper his

Sirs, stand you all without. . . . I pray you, give me leave. . . . I thank you; keep the door.

Small matters; but, if they stay unadjusted, picture and characters will lack their exact value.

An Elizabethan audience, moreover, could co-ordinate this and other such fragments; and from their knowledge of kindred actualities fill in the gaps for themselves, and so make a sufficiently definite political background for the play. A king and his Privy Council, a dispossessed heir sent into banishment, an excitable populace, a rebellious young noble; they evaluated and related them each to other without thinking, for it was a familiar scheme of things. To us it is not. The political story of Hamlet is a sentence left with half the words missing. Shakespeare purposely left it so that it might not encumber the more intimate theme. But with no conjecture of the missing words the others must inevitably lack something of their sense. Dover Wilson, both in his edition and his separate study of the play, has dealt very illuminatingly with this aspect of it.

—what better defense against windy, overreaching wrath?[8] What better counter to the fierce

> Where is my father?

than the honest, uncompromising

> Dead.

He encourages the young man, not merely to "demand his fill," but to storm his fill also. And to such stuff as

> To hell, allegiance! vows, to the blackest devil!
> Conscience and grace, to the profoundest pit!
> I dare damnation . . . .
> . . . only I'll be reveng'd
> Most throughly for my father.

responds only with a

> Who shall stay you?

nor even allows the vaunting response:

> My will, not all the world!

to draw from him an ironic smile. And he has reduced his rebel to a readiness, at least, to listen to reason, when the rabble voices are again heard at the door—awed voices now!—and Ophelia reappears.

She stands silent; she does not know him. We shall remember their pretty, familiar parting. This is how they meet again.[9]

There is every difference between this and our recent sight of her, between that phantom of a happy girl singing to her lute and this subdued, silent figure. She has been to the garden to gather herbs and flowers—halfway, so to speak, to the meadow where

---

[8] "The old caressing use of the name": we may not recall it, but the instruction to the actor to repeat the trick of that first

> And now, Laertes, what's the news with you?
> . . . what is't, Laertes?
> . . . What would'st thou beg, Laertes . . . ?

is plain.

[9] "This is how they meet again"—in terms of the play, that is to say; and (once more) these are the only effective terms. Shakespeare does not underline this, for that would only raise the question of its likelihood; and we might then recollect that Laertes had "in secret come from France" and ask: how could he not have seen her and already known of her madness? As it is, the effect is made that he sees her thus for the first time.

she is soon to meet her death. And she now begins a solemn sort of mimicry of the funeral her father was denied. She chants:

> They bore him barefac'd on the bier;
> Hey non nonny, nonny hey, nonny;
> And in his grave rain'd many a tear . . . .

and bends over the bier, which only she can see, with a

> Fare you well, my dove!

She reproaches the rest of them for not singing too:

> You must sing, 'a-down a-down,' An you call him a-down-a.[10]

She ceremoniously scatters her rosemary and rue, and distributes it and the flowers to her fellow-mourners. Then the poor brain loses hold for a moment even of its own fantasy, and she carols out a

> For bonny sweet Robin is all my joy.

but recollects, and chants for a second psalm:

> And will he not come again?
> And will he not come again?
> No, no, he is dead,
> Go to thy death-bed,
> He never will come again.
>
> His beard was as white as snow,
> All flaxen was his poll,
> He is gone, he is gone,
> And we cast away moan,
> God ha' mercy on his soul!

adding reverently

> And of all Christian souls, I pray God.

She cannot quite make out, I think, why they are not ready to follow with her to the grave. But if they will not go, she must. So she bids them a solemn

> God be wi' ye!

and departs, head bowed, hands folded, as quietly as she came;

---

10 Dover Wilson's reading.

and the rough crowd at the door stand silent to let her pass.[11]

To this main melody of the action (so to call it) have been added the grace notes of the imagery of the flowers; rosemary for remembrance, pansies for thoughts, fennel and columbines:

> there's rue for you; and here's some for me; we may call it herb of grace o' Sundays. O! you must wear your rue with a difference. There's a daisy; I would give you some violets, but they withered all when my father died. . . .

And Laertes' part must be noted. His confidence of a moment since turns to bewildered helplessness:

> O rose of May!
> Dear maid, kind sister, sweet Ophelia!

But he can win no answer from her:

> O heavens! is't possible a young maid's wits
> Should be as mortal as an old man's life? . . .

—for indeed he might be speaking to the dead. He has lost her, too, and even more tragically; and, as she goes, he sums all up in the accusing:

> Do you see this, O God?

But his grief has left him malleable, and the King is quick to the advantage. Sympathy itself—

> Go but apart,
> Make choice of whom your wisest friends you will,
> And they shall hear and judge 'twixt you and me:

---

[11] Whatever the origin and value of Q1 as a text, we may take it, I think, that *Enter Ofelia playing on a Lute, and her haire downe singing* is a genuinely Shakespearian stage direction and that the later *Enter Ofelia as before* merely means "still mad." She will not be encumbered now with her lute; and—though it is a small point—the flowers are pretty certainly real, not imaginary.

The mimicking of a funeral ceremony is, I believe, to be justified by the text. At first Ophelia is spoken of as "importunate and distract." The second entry is, to begin with, a silent one. Its songs—in contrast, at least, to "Saint Valentine's day"—are grave and slow; and it is the first line of the first one—

> They bore him barefac'd on the bier . . .

—that gives, as I take it, the cue for the action intended. And the distribution of the herbs and flowers was an ordinary funeral custom. Carew Hazlitt, in *Popular Antiquities of Great Britain* (1870, Vol. 2, p. 175), quotes Misson: ". . . when the Funeral Procession is ready to set out they nail up the coffin and a Servant presents the Company with sprigs of Rosemary; everyone takes a sprig and carries it in his hand, till the Body is put into the Grave, at which time they all throw in their sprigs after it." There is ample authority besides for the use of other flowers.

If by direct or by collateral hand
They find us touch'd, we will our kingdom give,
Our crown, our life and all that we call ours,
To you in satisfaction . . . .

—he leads the young man away, and the rest disperse. The rebellion is forgotten.

Horatio receives news of Hamlet's return.

WHILE the King and Laertes are conferring elsewhere, Horatio hears of seafaring men who have letters for him. These prove to be from

the ambassador that was bound for England . . .

and that is Hamlet, thus anonymously returned. From the reading of one letter, we learn the story—and incidentally that the seafaring men (who may thus look a little apprehensive, perhaps, in these royal and judicatory surroundings) are pirates. They have both attacked and rescued Hamlet:

They have dealt with me like thieves of mercy; but they knew what they did; I am to do a good turn for them. Let the King have the letters I have sent; and repair thou to me with as much haste as thou wouldst fly death. . . . These good fellows will bring thee where I am. Rosencrantz and Guildenstern hold their course for England: of them I have much to tell thee. . . .

It is a scene of thirty-five lines only; its use to prepare Hamlet's return and save cumbersome explanations when he does appear. But there are signs that Shakespeare means to give it a slight dramatic coloring of its own. Q2 begins it with

Enter Horatio and others.

What others? There is only need for an attendant, to be sent to fetch the sailors. The "others" are then, I fancy, meant to be another Rosencrantz and Guildenstern or the like, keeping a polite watch on the King's behalf upon Horatio, upon Hamlet's friend. It is noticeable that, though they know who he is ("but they knew what they did"), the pirates do not name Hamlet. "The ambassador that was bound for England" would be hint enough to the eavesdroppers; but this could be whispered. Horatio, of course, reads the letter to himself, and, departing with the pirates, only says:

> Come, I will give you way for these your letters;
> And do't the speedier that you may direct me
> To him from whom you brought them.

But (as we hear later) they do not—very wisely—go themselves to the King; the letters are given to one Claudio, and by him again to the "messenger" who does deliver them. A phrase in the letter itself ("These good fellows will bring thee where I am") suggests a hiding-place; and, till he was safely back at Court, Hamlet might well want to keep his whereabouts a secret, lest Claudius should have him privily murdered. It will be quite possible—the watchful courtiers at one side of the stage; Horatio and the pirates, conscious of their attention, at the other—to express enough of this in the scene's acting, to extract it from the dialogue, with no more than legitimate byplay added.[12] And whether or no Horatio is being watched, the pirates certainly make their mission as mysterious as possible.

The King has just proved his own innocence of Polonius' death when the news reaches him that Hamlet has returned. Laertes rejoices at the chance of vengeance thus offered him. The King devises a means for it. The Queen comes to tell them that Ophelia, in her madness, has drowned herself.

THE King and Laertes return, still in talk. The suggestion is—it keeps the action going—that there has been no break in their parley. The revelation of Hamlet's guilt we have not heard; Shakespeare does not want to overmultiply occasions for angry outbreaks by Laertes. And as to the "wisest friends" who were to "hear and judge"—that matter has gone the way of the rebellion —technically, rather in the interests of compression; but Claudius

---

[12] F1 begins the scene

Enter Horatio with an attendant.

(and most modern editors substantially follow). This is of a piece with the rest of its economizing of actors; and it may well be that the Quarto reading and its business—if I am right about it—was not thought important enough to preserve. It is not important. But the play is full of such superfluous touches, which yet enrich its dramatic life and, as in this case, rescue a scene from mere utility.

can do his own persuading, and it is clear that his smooth tongue
has already made good play:

> Now must your conscience my acquittance seal,
> And you must put me in your heart for friend,
> Sith you have heard, and with a knowing ear,
> That he which hath your noble father slain
> Pursu'd my life.

Remaining doubts he flatters away. Why was not Hamlet put
on public trial?

> The Queen his mother
> Lives almost by his looks; and for myself—
> My virtue or my plague, be it either which—
> She's so conjunctive to my life and soul,
> That, as the star moves not but in his sphere,
> I could not but by her. . . .

To have your sovereign so confess himself to you bespeaks intimate friendship indeed! An even likelier reason follows, and a
darker confidence is hinted at:

> you must not think
> That we are made of stuff so flat and dull
> That we can let our beard be shook with danger
> And think it pastime. You shortly shall hear more. . . .

Upon which—shortly indeed!—news comes; but not the expected
happy news of Hamlet's death. He is alive and back in Denmark.
  Since we already know it we can the better mark the different
effects of the surprise upon the two of them; the King's perplexity
(and at the queer mockery of the letter, so mysteriously delivered,
the sense of lurking danger stirs in him again); Laertes' joy:

> But let him come;
> It warms the very sickness in my heart
> That I shall live and tell him to his teeth,
> 'Thus didest thou.'

But that prospect does not suit Claudius at all; for what has not
Hamlet to tell in return? We perceive his mind momentarily fum-
bling; it is for the first time:

> If it be so, Laertes,
> As how should it be so? how otherwise? . . .

Then he sees his way clear, and is soon circumspectly leading his tamed young rebel along it.

In the scales against much masterly compression, however, we now find Shakespeare dispensing a hundred lines and more for the winning of Laertes to a murderous plot against Hamlet, and lavishing in the process abundant and very variously relevant talk about Lamord the Norman and his horsemanship, Laertes' own skill in fence and Hamlet's jealousy of it with, besides, some philosophizing by Claudius, which comes, at first blush, a little strangely from him.

Truly the thing could be more thriftily[18] done; but its amplitude can be accounted for. Claudius must advance cautiously, he would feel, towards the very unpleasant proposal he has in mind, and he habitually moves behind a smoke screen of words. Will this exuberant young man consent to forgo an overt, a spectacular revenge? And, say he can be persuaded to agree to the duel in the guise of a fencing match, will he—for he is a gallant fellow—be a party to the "little shuffling" that is to leave him with the "unabated sword," which will be Hamlet's death?

But the management of Laertes here is really masterly; and Claudius, the arch-diplomat, cannot but enjoy—and be ready to linger over—the exercise of his craft. First, we have tonic to vanity in a subtly reinforced dose of praise. The eulogy of the horsemanship of the gentleman of Normandy makes the account of *his* praise of Laertes the swordsman the sweeter hearing:

> He made confession of you,
> And gave you such a masterly report
> For art and exercise in your defence,
> And for your rapier most especially,
> That he cried out, 'twould be a sight indeed
> If one could match you; the scrimers of their nation,
> He swore, had neither motion, guard, nor eye,
> If you oppos'd them. . . .

---

[18] Dover Wilson (agreeing with Verity) scents something like topical allusion in the talk of the horsemanship, an indirect reference to Southampton's prowess in this kind. If this be so—and it has something the air of being so—it is another instance (cf. the talk of the "eyrie of children") of Shakespeare's skill at dragging in such things where they will do his play least harm, though we cannot say they do it none. But the passage survives in the Folio. Did its interest, then, prove more than topical, did it justify itself dramatically? Or, a further possibility (privately suggested to me by Dr. R. B. McKerrow); was it never a part of the acted text?

And talk of Hamlet's envy of such skill is a last drop to the mixture, and the sweetest of all.

Youthful complacency is then ruffled by the suddenly distrustful

> Laertes, was your father dear to you?
> Or are you like the painting of a sorrow,
> A face without a heart?

And a dozen sententious lines follow—wide of the mark for Laertes in their talk of the mortality of love and the need to seize the moment as it passes—which have, indeed, for an immediate dramatic excuse only the stoking of his impatience to come to the point. Shakespeare makes them serve also for a rather vague revelation of a Claudius grown conscious that Gertrude's love is lost to him (he knows not why, but, since the scene in her closet, we know), too vague, one must own, to be very effective. Then a touch sets the fume ablaze:

> But to the quick o' the ulcer:
> Hamlet comes back; what would you undertake
> To show yourself your father's son in deed
> More than in words?
>   To cut his throat i' the church.

That is the ripe mood. And the King's bland and (for us) admirably ambiguous response—

> No place, indeed, should murder sanctuarize;
> Revenge should have no bounds.

—should steady him in it. The young man is well in hand. Success indeed betters expectation; for not merely is the trick of the unbated sword embraced, but, says Laertes,

> for that purpose I'll anoint my sword.
> I bought an unction of a mountebank,
> So mortal that but dip a knife in it,
> Where it draws blood no cataplasm so rare,
> Collected from all simples that have virtue
> Under the moon, can save the thing from death
> That is but scratched withal. . . .

Poison! How will Claudius, of all people, respond to that? Interesting to watch him first play with the notion, a little reluctantly; then, with that feline

> Soft! let me see . . . .

yield—once more!—to its fascination. For even so must he have looked when he pictured to himself his brother sleeping in the orchard; even so, perhaps, he may have turned as—at another rumor in his anteroom—he here turns with a tender

> How now, sweet queen!

She comes with the tale of Ophelia's death, its candid beauty in sharp contrast to the secret wickedness brewing. The "fantastic garlands" themselves:

> Of crow-flowers, nettles, daisies and long purples,
> That liberal shepherds give a grosser name,
> But our cold maids do dead men's fingers call them . .

seem an innocent reproach to the unction which

> no cataplasm so rare,
> Collected from all simples that have virtue
> Under the moon . . .

can counteract.

The speech fulfills divers ends. It gives actuality to Ophelia's unseen death. We have seen her sitting singing to her lute, and back from the garden with flowers in her hands. We now hear how

> There, on the pendant boughs her coronet weeds
> Clambering to hang, an envious sliver broke,
> When down her weedy trophies and herself
> Fell in the weeping brook. Her clothes spread wide,
> And, mermaid-like, awhile they bore her up;
> Which time she chanted snatches of old lauds,
> As one incapable of her own distress,
> Or like a creature native and indu'd
> Unto that element; but long it could not be
> Till that her garments, heavy with their drink,
> Pull'd the poor wretch from her melodious lay
> To muddy death.

—which matches in vividness our last sight of her living. And the beauty and pity of it incidentally help to rescue Gertrude in our eyes from the degradation of Hamlet's painting of her

> In the rank sweat of an enseamed bed,
> Stewed in corruption, honeying and making love
> Over the nasty sty . . .

with the much more to that purpose in the closet-scene. She is to have no further very prominent part in the play. We shall remember her as well as Ophelia by this.

The effect upon Laertes is interesting too. He has just, for vengeance' sake, committed himself to an act of callous treachery. After the first shock he listens quietly, and has no more to say when the story ends than

> Alas, then she is drown'd.

The Queen's speech has been a-brim with tears; and she now—upon that

> Drown'd, drown'd!

—breaks into a passion of weeping. Such grief and the solace of it are not for him. Still,

> It is our trick; nature her custom holds,
> Let shame say what it will . . . .

and in spite of him the tears flow. He is not quite so satanic as he thinks himself.

Hamlet, purged of his "madness," returning with Horatio to Elsinore, pauses by the way to talk to an old man digging a grave. It proves to be Ophelia's, and he hears himself cursed by Laertes as the cause of her death. His love for her surges up again; he cries his grief aloud. At which seeming mockery, Laertes flies at his throat. They are parted. He is evidently as mad as ever. He leaves them to think so; for how can he explain?

To the contrast between the ugliness of the poison-plot and the innocence of Ophelia's death succeeds another, between the sophistications of the Court and the simplicity of

> *Enter two clowns.*

Is she to be buried in Christian burial that wilfully seeks her own salvation?

I tell thee she is; and therefore make her grave straight; the crowner hath sat on her, and finds it Christian burial.[14]

---

[14] Note the slight but sufficient indication of the passing of time, "the crowner hath sat on her": at least a day has passed. And Hamlet, by his letter in the last scene, was to reach the Court "to-morrow."

And, while he gets some refreshing fun out of them, Shakespeare turns these two to more than comic use. They are ignorant hinds, with their "argal" and their "*se offendendo*"; but their perversion of an abstruse legal argument—

> Here lies the water; good: here stands the man; good: if the man go to this water and drown himself, it is, will he, nill he, he goes; mark you that; but if the water come to him, and drown him, he drowns not himself: argal, he that is not guilty of his own death shortens not his own life.

—is little more ridiculous than the argument itself[15]; and they pierce through verbiage and pretense to the heart of the present business with

> Will you ha' the truth on't? If this had not been a gentlewoman, she should have been buried out of Christian burial.
>
> Why, there thou sayest; and the more pity that great folk should have countenance in this world to drown or hang themselves more than their even Christian.

Here, indeed, in this simplicity, is an important element, which has been till now lacking in the play's scheme, and in the various provocations to thought set before Hamlet upon his spiritual journey. But with its addition the gamut will be fairly complete; in its range from the Players and their fiction to these ultimate facts, mirrored in the digging of a grave and in its harvest of Yorick's skull.

While the two bandy their shrewd humor:

> *Enter Hamlet and Horatio afarre off.*

It is the Folio's stage direction, and an unusual one. It brings the two on eight lines before Q2 does and leaves them there, "*afarre off*," listening. I see dramatic intention in this. From the tenor of the letters to Horatio and the King do we not expect a Hamlet returning primed to prompt vengeance—for his own attempted murder also now? It is one more in the series of such surprises that he should quietly glide back into the action, and stand there so indifferent and detached. He is spiritually far off too. For it is Ophelia's grave that is digging, the Clown's song is a counterpart to hers:

---

15 For which see Furness and Dover Wilson.

> In youth, when I did love, did love,
>   Methought it was very sweet,
> To contract, O! the time, for—ah!—my behove,
>   O! methought there was nothing meet.

and the allusive pattern is completed by Hamlet's fastidious comment:

> Has this fellow no feeling of his business, that he sings at grave-making?

Had he no feeling either, who could turn his back obliviously upon the havoc he had made? It is he that is digging his grave.[16]

Even as Gertrude was spared by a hairsbreadth the knowledge —though at last she will learn—that her lover and husband is her husband's murderer, so Hamlet is here brought to the very edge of discovering that this grave over which he so serenely chops logic is Ophelia's. Within a little, we feel, he must learn it.

> Whose grave's this, sirrah? . . . What man dost thou dig it for?
> For no man, sir.
> What woman, then?
> For none, neither.
> Who is to be buried in't?

—to which, surely, the shattering answer must be given. But the Clown is his match at a quibble:

> One that was a woman, sir; but, rest her soul, she's dead.

And Hamlet enjoys the joke, and goes on to sentimentalize over Yorick, twenty years and more in his grave, now ousted from it for this newcomer—whoever she may be!—and to spin fancies round Alexander's dust. But so men who have greatly suffered do turn away to wistful sentiment and idle fancy. Hamlet lingers here because, once back at Elsinore, his duty must be done. And, behind this forgetfulness of Ophelia, there is the wish to forget.[17]

---

[16] Strange in reality that Horatio should not have spoken to Hamlet of Ophelia's madness, but dramatically this passes unnoticed. Of her death, however, Shakespeare takes care to leave him ignorant. He had gone off in haste to meet Hamlet before it occurred.

[17] But we shall not appreciate this irony—of Hamlet's ignorance that it is Ophelia's grave over which he weaves his fancies—unless the Clowns are kept in their place. Even though they speak no more than is set down for them, they can still (and habitually do) set on the more barren spectators to laugh—not at the natural shrewd humor with which Shakespeare has endowed them, but at the mere

A strange little procession now advances; the King and Queen, two or three courtiers, a meager coffin with its bearers, Laertes, a solitary priest.[18] We can interpret its strangeness well enough, and we watch Hamlet as, little by little, the truth dawns on him:

> But soft! but soft! aside: here comes the King,
> The Queen, the courtiers: who is that they follow?
> And with such maimed rites? This doth betoken
> The corse they follow did with desperate hand
> Fordo its own life; 'twas of some estate. . . .

Now, indeed, he cannot but soon guess, as he listens to the recalcitrant priest answering Laertes, who it is that lies here:

> Her obsequies have been as far enlarg'd
> As we have warrantise; her death was doubtful,
> And, but that great command o'ersways the order,
> She should in ground unsanctified have lodg'd
> Till the last trumpet; for charitable prayers,
> Shards, flints and pebbles should be thrown on her;
> Yet here she is allowed her virgin crants,
> Her maiden strewments . . . .

Yet he listens on and makes no sign. For this is the Hamlet who cried "Let me be cruel!"—shards, flints and pebbles themselves no harder than his heart to Ophelia!—and he dreads and resists the breaking of the callous crust that still armors him. Nor does it

clowning they impose on it. The coarseness of this and the guffaws which greet it will fatally break the finer threads of implication and allusion by which the continuity of cause and effect—in this subsidiary story of Hamlet, Ophelia and Laertes—is sustained. Much depends upon continuity of action too; upon the connection—and Shakespeare has woven it all very closely—between his "mad" departure and her madness, the news of his return, the plot against him, her death, the digging of her grave, his arrival; if these things are not kept physically connected, their metaphysical connection will certainly be missed. Here, in a moment, Hamlet is to apostrophize Laertes as "a very noble youth." The irony of that too will be lost, unless Laertes' last appearance, when he was plotting to poison his adversary, is fresh in our memory, its vividness unspoiled by some "act-interval" of distracting talk.

[18] The Folio has *lords attendant*, and there is need of them to pluck Hamlet and Laertes asunder, though at a pinch the bearers of the coffin could do this. But otherwise the rites should be as "maimed" as possible; the text explicitly dictates this; and how the editors, even down to Craig, Dowden and Adams, have allowed a full procession of priests and mourners to intrude it is hard to understand. For a salutary correction read what Dover Wilson has to say on the subject.

break until Laertes—the Church's benison as cruelly denied—claims Nature's kindlier one:

> Lay her i' the earth;
> And from her fair and unpolluted flesh
> May violets spring! I tell thee, churlish priest,
> A ministering angel shall my sister be,
> When thou liest howling.

This touches his heart, as the soft cry tells us:

> What! the fair Ophelia?

but he listens still. Two more blows fall on him; one from the lost past, the Queen's

> Sweets to the sweet: farewell!
> I hop'd thou shouldst have been my Hamlet's wife. . . .

the other from Laertes:

> O! treble woe
> Fall ten times treble on that cursed head
> Whose wicked deed thy most ingenious sense
> Depriv'd thee of. . . .

Then the stillness (Hamlet and Horatio motionless in their hiding-place, the rest held so by the presence of the stiller dead) is suddenly broken by the extravagant emotion of Laertes' leap into the grave and his cry to them to pile the earth upon him too:

> Till of this flat a mountain you have made
> To o'er-top old Pelion or the skyish head
> Of blue Olympus.

and that brings Hamlet forth. For a moment they will hardly know him in his rough "sea-gown" and traveling gear. There is something new to them besides in the measured, potent scorn of

> What is he whose grief
> Bear such an emphasis? whose phrase of sorrow
> Conjures the wandering stars, and makes them stand
> Like wonder-wounded hearers? . . .

and something minatory—to Claudius, at least—in the prerogatively royal ending

> This is I,
> Hamlet the Dane.

It is his first assertion in that kind. Laertes, in a flash, is out of the grave and at his throat.[19]

It is a Hamlet now royally master of himself indeed—the Hamlet once resolute to face his father's ghost and his own fate, the Hamlet Fortinbras will mourn and praise—who can sustain the onslaught with the mettled steadiness of

> Thou pray'st not well.
> I prithee take thy fingers from my throat;
> For, though I am not splenitive and rash,
> Yet have I something in me dangerous,
> Which let thy wisdom fear. Hold off thy hand!

But, the next instant, the spiritual schism in him gapes again:

> Why, I will fight with him upon this theme
> Until my eyelids will no longer wag. . . .

[19] Neither Q2 nor F1 direct Hamlet to leap into the grave beside Laertes. But Q1 (the text itself being very corrupt at this point) does: *Hamlet leapes in after Laertes.* And Rowe, not copying Q1, which he probably never saw (though, as it happens, his earlier *Laertes leaps into the grave* is Q1 word for word and does not follow F1's *leaps in the grave*), says simply: *Hamlet leaps into the grave.* And editors have—unanimously, as far as I know—followed Rowe. We seem, then, to have here a stage practice, dating from Shakespeare's time, and alive at the Restoration. But even this does not prove, I think, that it represents Shakespeare's intention. It is just the sort of thing that an actor of Hamlet, carried away by his own emotion, his mind anticipating the verbal onslaught, might do; it would prove startingly effective (why stop to consider the incongruity of two men struggling together upon the top of a coffin?) and editorial sanction would perpetuate it.

Against that what can be cited? The absence of any such stage direction from the two authoritative texts? There are many similar omissions, when the directions are nevertheless plainly implied. The implications of the text itself, therefore, are more important, if Shakespeare's intentions can be discerned in them. And the text here, I think, furnishes two sound arguments against it having been Shakespeare's intention, when he wrote the lines, that Hamlet should leap into the grave. He can only do so at one point, upon the

> This is I,
> Hamlet the Dane.

and the royal dignity of the phrase must be quite ridiculously compromised by such an action. Secondly, it is plain that Laertes is meant to be the aggressor. But if Hamlet leaps into the grave, it can only look as if it was he that attacked Laertes. Therefore Laertes must leap out of the grave to attack him.

I fancy, then, that we may have here a little history of Shakespeare's betrayal by his actors. We need not suppose that he took it very seriously. But the lapse was never justified in the play's official records, Q2 and F1. It is merely thanks to actors and editors that the scene is played to this day in a muddle of excitement which confuses its dramatic intentions, when these are fairly plainly to be read in the text itself.

> I lov'd Ophelia; forty thousand brothers
> Could not, with all their quantity of love,
> Make up my sum. . . .

—he loved Ophelia, and he has killed her. In that terrible paradox
is the essence of their tragedy, to which this dullard, glutted with
his own grief, is blind. He knows—who better?—the worth of
such grieving; and he mocks at it, yet less in Laertes than in his
one-time self:

> What wilt thou do for her? . . .
>   Dost thou come here to whine,
> To outface me with leaping in her grave?
> Be buried quick with her, and so will I:
> And, if thou prate of mountains, let them throw
> Millions of acres on us, till our ground,
> Singeing his pate against the burning zone,
> Make Ossa like a wart! Nay, an thou'lt mouth,
> I'll rant as well as thou.

Laertes, kept from strangling him, incapable of other answer,
stands silent. Gertrude—the savage irony lost on her—makes the
only excuse she can for him:

> This is mere madness . . . .

Then Hamlet, as if in pity for such blindness:

> Hear you, sir;
> What is the reason that you use me thus?
> I lov'd you ever. . . .

—but at that he breaks off. For how make plain to them—when
even to himself he cannot—the truth of this tragic discord between
will and deed? So he flings them instead, for their satisfaction, a
jingling reassurance of his "madness":

> But it is no matter;
> Let Hercules himself do what he may,
> The cat will mew and dog will have his day.

and departs.

     The King, watchfully silent so far, now takes command. There
is the old kindly care for the afflicted in his

> I pray you, good Horatio, wait upon him.

The balked Laertes he both soothes and spurs:

Strengthen your patience in our last night's speech;
We'll put the matter to the present push.

—the Queen coming within hearing, he frees himself of her with
another kindly

Good Gertrude, set some watch over your son.

—and departs also; his arm, I think, again linking Laertes', for,
clearly, he must keep an eye on him:

This grave shall have a living monument:
An hour of quiet shortly shall we see;
Till then, in patience our proceeding be.

And to end the scene the curtains of the inner stage would close.[20]

*The story of the embassage to England; the challenge to the fenc-
ing match; the end.*

HAMLET appears again, speaking eagerly to Horatio.[21]

So much for this, sir: now shall you see the other. . . .

The exanimate mood of the talk to the Gravedigger was dis-
pelled by the encounter with Laertes, emotion, it may seem,
finally burnt out of him in that blaze of remorse for Ophelia's
death; and he is purged of his madness. But not of the effects of
it. We feel, in the forced march of his speech and the checks and
divagations of his thought, a still refractory mind, a dangerous
temper. They show too in a trifle, his tone to the faithful Horatio,
in the oddly reiterated "Sir . . . sir . . . sir," and the impatient
requests to that best of listeners to listen. For the first time, moreover, comes a hint that the strain is telling on him physically:

Sir, in my heart there was a kind of fighting
That would not let me sleep; methought I lay
Worse than the mutines in the bilboes. . . .

And what contempt for his own subtle brain and once devious
ways in:

---

[20] That the grave-trap may be closed and the royal "state," etc., prepared for
the fencing match. The intervening scene would allow none too much time for
this, and in this need, it may well be, originated the elaboration of Osric and the
entrance of *A lord.*

[21] What he has been talking about is not clear; but the impression we gain is
of eager businesslike conversation, one subject dismissed for another to be broached.
And this is all that matters.

> Rashly—
> And prais'd be rashness for it—let us know,
> Our indiscretion sometimes serves us well,
> When our deep plots do pall; and that should learn us
> There's a divinity that shapes our ends,
> Rough-hew them how we will.

From this he passes to the tale of his stealing and unsealing the "grand commission," by which Rosencrantz and Guildenstern were to conduct him to his death in England, and forging and sealing another, which is even now conducting them to theirs. He elaborates it beyond need in his grim enjoyment of the business, resavors every detail, the "bugs and goblins" of the King's attainder of him, his skill in the forgery, his parody of his uncle's diplomacy in the

> earnest conjuration from the King,
> As England was his faithful tributary,
> As love between them like the palm should flourish,
> As peace should still her wheaten garland wear,
> And stand a comma 'tween their amities,
> And many such-like 'As'es of great charge. . . .

But Shakespeare makes yet more use of the sixty lines. The gap in the history of his absence is filled, and the Hamlet before us linked to the man of the parting promise:

> O, from this time forth,
> My thoughts be bloody, or be nothing worth!

His task's fulfillment is, in fact, at hand; for we surely need fear no more half measures, nor hysterical self-betrayal, from this expert cracksman, who could sit quietly in his cabin, his one-time friends asleep near him, and forge their death warrant in a fine clerkly hand—and enjoy the work too! Nor have we before heard anything from him quite so cold-blooded as his response to Horatio's

> So Guildenstern and Rosencrantz go to't.

the

> Why, man, they did make love to this employment;
> They are not near my conscience; their defeat
> Does by their own insinuation grow.

'Tis dangerous when the baser nature comes
Between the pass and fell incensed points
Of mighty opposites.

since, base though they may be, the King's stolen letter—which
Horatio has here in his hand and turns to again, exclaiming

Why, what a king is this!

—was sealed, and the two would not have known its contents.[22]
And his tone towards the King has changed. Claudius has now
not only

kill'd my king and whored my mother . . .

but

Popped in between the election and my hopes . . .

It is a sequent thought to that imperious "Hamlet the Dane," a
new weight to his cause. And when Horatio warns him that "It
must be shortly known" what passes in England, the stern

It will be short: the interim is mine;
And a man's life's no more than to say 'One.'

promises imminent and open attack. But *we* know, and have
just been quietly reminded, that attack upon him, by a deadlier
trick than the trick of the play-scene, is imminent also. Which of
the two enemies will strike home first?

For a sudden turn of thought shows him, after all, fatally
guileless:

But I am very sorry, good Horatio,
That to Laertes I forgot myself;
For, by the image of my cause, I see
The portraiture of his: I'll court his favours . . . .

The old sweetness and charm are in that, a little saddened; simplicity besides (he really believes that forgiveness for an injury
should be given for the asking); and in his excuse:

But, sure, the bravery of his grief did put me
Into a towering passion.

---

[22] "There's letters seal'd," says Hamlet, and suspects at once that the two are to
"marshal" him "to knavery" of some sort. But the King has not confided in them;
his last words to them are

Away, for everything is sealed and done . . . .

The implication is plain, I think, that they do not know.

the quizzical self-detachment of the imaginative mind. He and
the hot-headed Laertes are not made to understand each other. At
which point Osric appears. And if the King fears that Hamlet
might suspect something sinister in the fencing match, what
better voucher for its mere diversion than this fantastic waterfly?

The verbal fencing match that follows does yet more to dissipate
our remembrance of Ophelia in her grave, and to separate the
sport from the mourning. Its topical flavor is today at a discount,
but the dramatic effect is valid. We know, as we listen, that behind
this ridiculous gabble about the wager, about the

> six French rapiers and poniards, with their assigns, as girdle,
> hangers, and so . . .

the "carriages" that

> are very dear to fancy, very responsive to the hilts, most delicate
> carriages, and of very liberal conceit.

behind the trippingly sportsmanlike

> The King, sir, hath laid, that in a dozen passes between your-
> self and him, he shall not exceed you three hits; he hath laid on
> twelve for nine, and it would come to immediate trial, if your
> lordship would vouchsafe the answer.

there lurks death.

Hamlet yields, as usual, to the distraction of a little intellectual
cat-and-mouse play. And Osric is easy game; as easy as he himself
is more practically proving to Claudius. We may note that even at
this sort of thing he has grown crueller. The mockery is overt and
brutal, with no "madness" for mitigation. We shall note too that,
having amused himself with the creature, Hamlet, upon that
sudden

> How if I answer no?

comes near to spoiling the whole plan. And he only falls in with
it in impatient indifference:

> Sir, I will walk here in the hall; if it please his majesty, 'tis
> the breathing time of day with me; let the foils be brought, the
> gentleman willing, and the King hold his purpose, I will win for
> him if I can; if not, I will gain nothing but my shame and the
> odd hits.

—with which answer Osric departs; to deliver it to the King, however, with so much "flourish," that a soberer, anonymous Lord has

next to be sent to discover what, beyond the fact that he will walk here in the hall, Hamlet did mean.

The Folio omits this Lord. The need for still more matter here while the throne and the furniture for the fencing match were made ready on the inner stage—the origin, possibly, of his existence—may have gone when its text was settled. But Shakespeare, in Q2, had as usual turned the thing forced on him to good dramatic account. Through the mere repetition—

> his majesty . . . sends to know if your pleasure hold to play with Laertes, or that you will take longer time.

—the King's anxiety peeps out. And the impersonal phrases help resolve the scene (to pass from Osric's flummery direct would have been too abrupt a change) into its next and graver key. For there falls about Hamlet now the shadow of death. He is aware of it without knowing it. Through his answer:

> I am constant to my purposes. They follow the King's pleasure. If his fitness speaks, mine is ready, now or whensoever, provided I be so able as now.

sounds a constancy, a fitness, a readiness to meet a weightier challenge than this. And his quiet

> In happy time.

accepts more than the mere fact that

> The King, and Queen, and all are coming down.

It is as if the vanished "madness" had left something like clairvoyance behind.

Horatio warns his friend:

> You will lose this wager, my lord.

—the faithful eye detecting intolerable strain, which Hamlet (after a cool "I do not think so") owns to, with a childlike

> But thou wouldst not think how ill all's here about my heart. . . .

then dismisses:

> It is but foolery; but it is such a kind of gain-giving as would perhaps trouble a woman.

Shakespeare likes to bring his rarer moments home to us by such familiar touches.

But Horatio is just so troubled for him:

> If your mind dislike anything, obey it; I will forestall their
> repair hither, and say you are not fit.

and the intimate simplicity of it all sets off the simple nobility of
the valediction:

> Not a whit; we defy augury; there's a special providence in the
> fall of a sparrow. If it be now, 'tis not to come; if it be not to come,
> it will be now; if it be not now, yet it will come: the readiness is
> all. Since no man has aught of what he leaves, what is't to leave
> betimes? Let be.

It is to no more than this, at the last, that the subtly questing
mind has come.[23]

As the curtains of the inner stage part, the disquieted Horatio
is silenced by a gesture; and there once more—it is much the
same picture as at the play's beginning—is the sinister brilliance
of Claudius and his Court, Hamlet's somber figure outlined
against it as before.[24]

[23] I venture to prefer the Folio reading of the last sentence, which I understand
(though that may not be the best of reasons), to Q2's, which, despite Dover
Wilson's admirable explanation, I do not. But we need not gather from the
Folio that Hamlet is merely thinking—with St. Paul and the Burial Service—of the
worldly goods a man must leave behind. Surely it is his loss of other things that
he has in mind, of things he loved and valued; his father's care, his faith in his
mother, the ideal love for Ophelia, hers for him. He could keep nothing of all
this. And so, with things such as this, it still would be. What is it, then, to leave
betimes, before he has lost more? But let us own that, whatever the meaning
may be, it is more than vaguely conveyed.

The final "Let be" has disappeared from the Folio, and in strictness perhaps
should not be stolen from Q2 for an addition to its text. But if the Q2 text is
corrupt (as, being to me incomprehensible, I cannot but think it) and the Folio's
a correction of it, the two small words might well, I suppose, have dropped out
in the process. Admit them—as editors commonly do—as an isolated phrase, and
their technical dramatic utility is clear. Hamlet's fatidic speech definitely alarms
Horatio, who makes a move as if to stop the match after all—in which he is
checked by that curt, commanding "Let be." This ends the passage between the
two with a sharp touch of suggested action, links it by an arresting moment to
the "discovery" of King, Queen and Court, and will hold our attention while that
larger spectacle makes good its own hold on us. Therefore, if it is allowable, it
will be a strengthening knot here in the dramatic fabric.

[24] The parting of the curtains and the actual discovery behind them of King,
Queen and Court is indicated with some probability, I think, by the nature of the
stage direction in Q2:

The scene of catastrophe which follows is full of complicated matter, close-packed.[25] Shakespeare will have inherited its holocaust—which may suit him well enough, but he has to harmonize it with his own enrichment of the play's theme. The sudden huddle of violent events is in itself effective after the long delays of plot and counterplot, but character must be eloquent in them still. And this network of action is lucid with character.

We are at the crisis of what we have called the counteraction, the King's war against Hamlet. The first attack—the dispatching him to be murdered in England—has failed. We saw nothing of it, and its mere recounting will not have prejudiced the effect of this, which, doubly provided for, by poisoned sword and cup, can (we are to feel) scarcely fail. On Hamlet's part there is no more plotting, only cold resolution to do what he has to do; but that, seemingly, is in abeyance for the while. Such is our approach to the scene.

The apology to Laertes is candid:

> Give me your pardon, sir; I've done you wrong;
> But pardon 't, as you are a gentleman.
> This presence knows,

> *A table prepard, Trumpets, Drums and officers with Cushions, King,*
> *Queene, and all the state, Foiles, daggers, and Laertes.*

(it is stage direction and property list combined, and entirely businesslike) nor is it even contradicted by the conventional

> *Enter King, Queene, Laertes . . . .*

of the Folio, for "enter" often implies discovery. The drawing of the curtains while Hamlet and Horatio stand there is certain. The King, Queen and Court *could* then enter in procession. But this would involve a slight delay; and, after the extended preliminaries, Shakespeare would be concerned, I fancy, to close up the action and move steadily towards his climax. In this the discovery is an appreciable help. A likely addition to the stage management would be the simultaneous entry through the doors on the outer stage of extra courtiers or guards, and the table for the foils may have had to be moved down. Hamlet, so I believe, is no longer in mourning (cf. pp. 232 *et seq.*). But he would be in his traveling clothes; and these, against the Court splendor, would look somber. Laertes, and even the King and Queen, it may be said, would be in some sort of mourning for Ophelia, having but just returned from the funeral. I do not think so (though Laertes need not be gaily dressed, and, at the graveside, the King and Queen might have worn some mourning outer garments). Realistic likelihood will always give way to legitimate dramatic effect.

[25] It runs to some 170 lines. Compare it and its complexities—if we are studying Shakespeare's technical progress as a playwright—with the long-drawn-out last scene of *Romeo and Juliet*, which is but 30 lines less than twice the length.

> And you must needs have heard, how I am punish'd
> With a sore distraction. . . .

and the explanation, even in its riddling logic—

> What I have done,
> That might your nature, honour and exception
> Roughly awake, I here proclaim was madness.
> Was 't Hamlet wrong'd Laertes? Never Hamlet:
> If Hamlet from himself be ta'en away,
> And when he's not himself does wrong Laertes, .
> Then Hamlet does it not; Hamlet denies it.
> Who does it then? His madness. If 't be so,
> Hamlet is of the faction that is wrong'd;
> His madness is poor Hamlet's enemy.

—is meant to be so. Did his aping of madness send him verily mad? In the Player who

> But in a fiction, in a dream of passion,
> Could force his soul so to his own conceit . . .

he had discerned that strange confusion between the imagined and the real (which Shakespeare himself had cause enough to know). He can look back calmly to the delirium of it now. But who else will understand? So he ends with a simpler plea:

> Sir, in this audience,
> Let my disclaiming from a purpos'd evil
> Free me so far in your most generous thoughts,
> That I have shot mine arrow o'er the house,
> And hurt my brother.

—and in the sad cadence of that "brother" is the last echo of Ophelia's story.

Laertes is a still unpracticed scoundrel; and it will not be too easy for him, with the phial of poison for his sword ready in his pocket, to respond to the appeal to his "most generous thoughts." But, with a little quibbling about honor, he manages it. A jury of gentlemen shall judge his cause against Hamlet later—when he has murdered him! He can even brave his conscience with an outspoken

> But till that time
> I do receive your offer'd love like love,
> And will not wrong it.

The two of them thus reconciled, the customary pleasant stir of preparation for such a match begins; the foils are brought, compliments pass and deprecating protests, and Osric adds his expedient touch of frivolity to the affair.

Hamlet is satisfied with the first foil he takes. Laertes demands another, and selects it from among the spare ones on the table. The King is speaking now, with everyone attentive:

> Set me the stoups of wine upon that table.
> If Hamlet give the first or second hit,
> Or quit in answer of the third exchange,
> Let all the battlements their ordnance fire ....

and so the "sword unbated" can be secured unnoticed. This screen of oratory, in fact—

> The King shall drink to Hamlet's better breath;
> And in the cup an union shall he throw,
> Richer than that which four successive kings
> In Denmark's crown have worn. Give me the cups;
> And let the kettle to the trumpet speak,
> The trumpet to the cannoneer without,
> The cannons to the heavens, the heaven to earth,
> 'Now the King drinks to Hamlet!' ...

—permits the "noble youth" privily to "anoint" the sword besides.[26]

[26] These preliminaries to the fight have to be deduced from the text; they should conform to dramatic effect and likelihood combined, but not to one of these at the expense of the other. The King orders Osric to present the foils. If they were modern fencing foils he could carry half a dozen on his arm; of the long Elizabethan sword not more than three or four. But he may well leave two or three upon the table, and it will not do for him to carry them all, or Hamlet (we may think) might select the one that is unbated. This, then, will have been among those left on the table, and Laertes—pretending that his first choice is "too heavy"—can, under cover of the King's speech, secure it later. But does not its merely being left there make Osric an accomplice? If we had time to reason the matter out, there would be grounds for suspicion. But if the foils are discovered on the table when the curtains part, and Osric simply takes the first three or four to his hand, we shall hardly ask ourselves that question. Moreover, when Laertes says "Let me see another" and moves (as I think) towards the table, Osric is answering Hamlet's question:

> These foils have all a length?

and will have his back turned to it. Then, as the King says

> Set me the stoups of wine upon that table.

—*i.e.* upon a table on the opposite side of the stage—we shall see Laertes take the unbated sword, and we shall know by his expression that he has it. It will be even more effective to see him take the phial from his pouch and dip the tip of

The match begun, its conduct becomes for a while the main action of the scene, the dialogue diminishing to an accompaniment. The first bout, indeed, would pass in a tense silence but for the inspiriting

Trumpets the while.[27]

—a silence only broken when Hamlet scores and claims:

One.

the sword in it; and the King's jovial oratory is, I feel sure, intended—both by Shakespeare and the King—to provide occasion for this; all eyes but ours turned upon Claudius. Even Horatio, that faithful watcher of the play-scene, does not observe Laertes.

Dr. Dover Wilson thinks that Osric is necessarily an accomplice; the chief proof of it that it is to him Laertes says later that he is justly killed with his own treachery. I can only answer that Shakespeare "does not do these things"—does not introduce a ridiculous fribble, and by one *ex post facto* hint in the text convert him to a scoundrel; and, moreover, leave it at that. Nor do I see how the actor of Osric could, merely by facial expression, convey his guilt. Laertes begins his confession—

Why, as a woodcock to mine own springe . . .

—to Osric, because it is he who has gone to his aid, asking him how he does. He continues it to Hamlet a moment after with

Hamlet, thou are slain; . . .
The treacherous instrument is in thy hand,
Unbated and envenom'd . . . .

—all the weight of his remorse in that. And in the interval Hamlet's attention and ours has been turned to the dying Queen; too strong a competition by far for an Osric's guilty grimacings. No, I fancy the poor waterfly can be returned "Not guilty," and allowed to announce "young Fortinbras' " arrival from Poland with a clear countenance and conscience.

Both student and producer, however, should take care to master Dover Wilson's explanations of the wager and the fight (in the new Cambridge Shakespeare and in his preface to the Shakespeare Association facsimile of George Silver's *Paradoxes of Defence*).

The wager, indeed, is a minor matter. If we do not grasp its meaning we can still be amused by the jargon; and I expect that not a few among Shakespeare's audience were in that case. But the proper conduct of the fight is important. I owe much to these elucidations of it.

[27] Q2. The omission of the direction in the Folio may well be accidental, for a little lower down the Q's

Drum, trumpets and shot. Florish, a peece goes off.

is abbreviated to

Trumpets sound, and shot goes off.

though not only does its text still demand the "kettle," but, by stage directions elsewhere, drums are in use.

Laertes (touched too in the self-esteem that Claudius took such pains to foster) protests:

> No!

Hamlet curtly appeals:

> Judgment?

and has it from Osric—who is in his element:

> A hit, a very palpable hit.

Laertes, a peg down, takes fresh breath with

> Well, again!

But the King, for an instant, interposes.

We see now why he thought it well to back the poisoned rapier with the poisoned cup. Hamlet is the better fencer; Laertes may not touch him at all. He is running no risks:

> Stay, give me a drink. Hamlet, this pearl is thine;
> Here's to thy health. Give him the cup.

A most gracious ceremonial! He drinks from the cup first, then draws the pearl from his finger and drops it in; and we shall guess, if we cannot see, that he has pressed the spring which releases the poison.[28] Then, as the cup is carried to Hamlet:

> *Drum, trumpets and shot. Florish, a peece goes off.*

In truth a splendid pledge! But Hamlet, when the din is over, says quietly and coldly—for he will not drink amity to his uncle:

> I'll play this bout first; set it by awhile.

The second bout proves strenuous, for the bad blood in Laertes is fermenting. Hamlet wins it, and claims it with a gay

> Another hit; what say you?

And Laertes does not wait for the humiliating judgment this time, but confesses wryly:

> A touch, a touch, I do confess.

Then, while the two recover breath, the King's soft voice is heard:

> Our son shall win.

---

[28] Forewarned as they have been, Shakespeare's audience would be fully alive to what the ring and the gesture must imply. Claudius is an expert poisoner; and such subtle methods as this, and the pouring of the poison in his brother's ear, were a recognized part of the equipment of the "Italianate" villain.

It is spoken smilingly to the Queen. There is a taunt in it for Laertes; let him show his prowess, and quickly, or their enemy may escape them. Its fatherly affection might well anger Hamlet; but, exhilarated with the sport, he does not heed. For the first time (the irony of it!) we see him oblivious to all trouble, as sane in body as in mind, and in the flush of success; the Hamlet of Ophelia's dreams, of the

> unmatched form and feature of blown youth . . .

—a Hamlet that might have been. And his mother is so happy to see the change in him—his madness cured, and with this the bitterness which had parted them ended—that she can even banter him a little:

> He's fat and scant of breath.
> Here, Hamlet, take my napkin, rub thy brows. . . .

She leaves her "state" and trips to where he stands. The page with the King's cup is still waiting near him. In a merry caprice she seizes it, and, mischievously parodying the favorite royal phrase and trumpet-saluted gesture:

> The Queen carouses to thy fortune, Hamlet.

What, upon the instant, is Claudius to do? While Hamlet bows his thanks, he calls out

> Gertrude, do not drink.

But why should she not? Prettily willful, making him, I think, a mock reverence:

> I will, my lord; I pray you, pardon me.

she disobeys him and does drink. She has given him, we note, while she speaks and curtseys, a moment's chance to save her—at the cost of his own safety. The moment passes; he has let it pass:

> It is the poison'd cup! it is too late.

—retribution outwitting even his quick wit! But she finds, for the instant, nothing amiss; and her next gesture is to press, in all innocence and affection, the poisoned cup on her son. If he would not pledge his uncle and make all well between them, surely he will not refuse her. Though he does not positively refuse, his response is cold:

> I dare not drink yet, Madam; by and by.

But she feels so near to winning him again that she bids him, tenderly, as if he were still a child:

> Come, let me wipe thy face.

and, as a child might, he lets her.

While this is passing the thwarted, desperate Laertes is whispering to the King:

> My lord, I'll hit him now.

to get no answer but a grim

> I do not think't.

—for Claudius, his guilty eyes on the doomed Queen, feels himself slipping to confusion and defeat. Is it the sight of mother and son seemingly reunited that prompts Laertes'

> And yet 'tis almost 'gainst my conscience.

Hamlet turns, buoyantly ready for the third bout. This also passes in silence, and is ended by Osric's

> Nothing, neither way.

But is it ended? Hamlet is half off his guard when Laertes gives himself benefit of the doubt, and with a

> Have at you now!

thrusts and scores his first hit. It is all he will need to score, for he has drawn blood!

Stung by the trickery of the attack, the wound, the treachery of the sharpened sword, Hamlet closes with his man and wrests this from him, forcing on him his own in exchange.[29] The King's

---

[29] For what seems to me the simplest and, more importantly, the most dramatic way of effecting the exchange, see Dover Wilson's note in the new Cambridge *Hamlet*. But he does not make it indubitably clear that Hamlet is "enraged," not merely by the smart of the wound, but by the treachery involved. (He guesses half the truth; the rest is to come.) This is needed, however, to account for the fury of his attack on Laertes, an attack so furious that it stretches him on the ground; and it is illustrated by the King's

> Part them! they are incens'd.

The "traditional" stage business—if I remember it rightly—which involved a fight with modern foils only, was that Hamlet should be wounded in the forearm, should note the blood flowing and surmise the unbuttoned foil (I am not sure that Laertes was not supposed to remove the button from his foil upon the "My lord, I'll hit him now"). Then he had to beat Laertes' foil from his hand, put his foot on it, and offer him his own in exchange—which Laertes would shamefacedly take. The idea involved is the same.

Part them! they are incens'd.

passes unheeded; for eyes are now turned on Gertrude, who, the poison at work in her, stands swaying to and fro. Upon Osric's

Look to the Queen there, ho!

attendants go to her aid. The fight suddenly and finally stops; Horatio's steady voice, heard for the first time, interprets to us what has happened:

They bleed on both sides. . . .

So Hamlet has his death wound. We know it, and he does not. Laertes has his, and knows it; and the pluck goes out of him. Hamlet does not answer his friend's

How is it, my lord?

for, free of the fighting, his eyes are on the Queen. But Osric's

How is it, Laertes?

brings the beginning of confession:

Why, as a woodcock to mine own springe, Osric,
I am justly kill'd with mine own treachery.

It is checked for a moment by Hamlet's peremptory

How does the Queen?

which Claudius answers with a desperate

She swounds to see them bleed.

—for his instinct is to save himself; and Laertes (whose own mouth will soon be shut) has accounted for Hamlet, after all, and the poison might be explained away. But retribution outpaces him again. Gertrude speaks:

No, no, the drink, the drink—O my dear Hamlet!
The drink, the drink! I am poison'd.

—and in the "O my dear Hamlet" what agony of remorse! For at last she understands. "As kill a king . . . a second time I kill my husband dead. . . . he poisons him in the garden for his estate . . . !" And she has seen *this* cup sent on its errand.

At the sound of the one fatal, memorable word Hamlet is transformed. The last shreds of self-conscious weakness fall from him; and he stands there, Hamlet the Dane indeed

> O villainy! How? Let the door be lock'd:
> Treachery! seek it out.[80]

His command is obeyed without question. Claudius is trapped.

The answer to that "How?" is to come from Laertes. But he must confess his own guilt to Hamlet first. So the King's doom is suspended for a torturing minute or so; and we are aware of him, the glib diplomatist, jovial drinker and dancer, the "very, very peacock," skulking among his bewildered Court. Hamlet hears from Laertes his own doom; but he pays no heed to that; he waits for the end of the story. When he has it—

> thy mother's poisoned—
> I can no more!—the King—the King's to blame.

—he turns, and, no one staying him, takes vengeance.

At the sword thrust the courtiers raise a perfunctory cry of "Treason!" But, though the wounded man cries pitifully

> O, yet defend me, friends; I am but hurt.

they do nothing. Then Hamlet drops the sword, and takes the cup and drags the creature out, and—as one would medicine a dog—chokes his mouth open and pours the poison down; and he consecrates to the consummate moment his last outburst of mockery:

> Here, thou incestuous, murderous, damned Dane,
> Drink of this potion! Is thy union here?
> Follow my mother!

Into the silence which follows, steals Laertes dying

> He is justly served;
> It is a poison tempered by himself.
> Exchange forgiveness with me, noble Hamlet;
> Mine and my father's death come not upon thee,
> Nor thine on me!

He dies, and Hamlet feels death coming upon him too.

His first thought is for his friend:

> I am dead, Horatio . . . .

[80] This is (spelling excepted) the Folio's reading. Q2's does not differ except in punctuation. Rowe follows the Folio. Theobald would seem to have been the first to turn the "How?" into a "Ho!" and modern editors, even Dover Wilson, have followed him. Why, I cannot imagine. The "How?" is an obvious question, to which Laertes makes answer; and it knits the sense together and sustains the tension of the moment better than a redundant exclamation can.

only his next for his still-agonizing mother, the source of all this ill. Speechless, she can yet have heard all; at the end nothing has been spared her. And from her son comes only a

> Wretched queen, adieu!

He feels men's eyes on him, the assassin of their King:

> You that look pale and tremble at this chance,
> That are but mutes or audience to this act,
> Had I but time—as this fell sergeant, death,
> Is strict in his arrest—O! I could tell you—
> But let it be . . . .

And once more, and for the last time, he seeks help where he has ever found it:

> Horatio, I am dead;
> Thou liv'st; report me and my cause aright
> To the unsatisfied.

One certain sign of the great writer is that his resourcefulness does not fail him as he nears the end of book or play. So here. All, we shall be feeling, is about over; and suddenly the imperturbable Horatio, the man

> that fortune's buffets and rewards
> Hath ta'en with equal thanks . . .

passionately resolves not to survive his friend:

> Never believe it!
> I'm more an antique Roman than a Dane:
> Here's yet some liquor left.

Hamlet's dying strength cannot wrest the cup from him; but he knows a better means:

> O God, Horatio, what a wounded name,
> Things standing thus unknown, shall live behind me!
> If thou didst ever hold me in thy heart,
> Absent thee from felicity awhile
> And in this harsh world draw thy breath in pain,
> To tell my story.

New duty laid on him, this friend will be faithful still. And at once, for reminder of that world without and its claims, we hear

> *A march afarre off.*

an army's drums and fifes, and a shot of salute. It is, says Osric,

> Young Fortinbras, with conquest come from Poland . . .

ambassadors from England too.[31] Hamlet, self-forgetful, calm, orders affairs of state:

> I do prophesy the election lights
> On Fortinbras; he has my dying voice;
> So tell him . . . .

Then, upon

> the rest is silence.

he slips peacefully out of life—to the rhythm of the drumbeats of the triumphant approach of the man whose "divine ambition" put him to such shame.[32] A last quiet stroke of tragic irony.

But the story which Horatio will tell

> to the yet unknowing world . . .

is not that of his weakness and melancholy, his scruples and failings. These are dead with him. Even his blunders, the

> accidental judgments, casual slaughters . . .

will find a less tenebrous place in the picture seen as a whole. For finally he has not failed. The wrong to be righted led him to no such gallant adventure as his father or this hero, whose prowess he

[31] Q2 and F. both mark an *Enter Osric* here, having given him no exit. But it looks as if the giving of the speech itself to him had been a matter of theatrical economy on Shakespeare's part—as if this particular actor had been the most competent person available to speak these three important lines; and that implies a shedding of the waterfly—unless we are to suppose an Osric shocked quite out of his fantastic self by what has happened. But such niceties in a minor character would not come into question at such a moment. The lines belong to a "messenger" and they are spoken by Osric (what, however, has become of the anonymous Lord, who reinforced the invitation to the duel? Surely he could have served this turn). His *exit* is of no importance and need not be editorially provided. If he passes for a second or so into the anteroom or is seen to encounter an attendant in the doorway—anything of that sort will be amply sufficient.

[32] He says here besides

> I cannot live to hear the news from England . . . .

into which might—by the so-minded—be read regret that he will never know for certain whether Rosencrantz and Guildenstern have been satisfactorily "hoist with their own petar." But this is certainly not the intention of the line. The ambassadors from England are heralded to him as to Denmark's rightful ruler at the moment, and, so answering, he says he will not live to receive them; that is all.

so envied, would have confidently taken in hand. It was a cancer-
ous wrong—

> carnal, bloody and unnatural . . .

—eating into the sanctities of life and his faith in them. But at
the cost of his life he has righted it at last; and Fortinbras comes
to a heritage purged of evil.

> O, proud death!
> What feast is toward in thine eternal cell,
> That thou so many princes at a shot
> So bloodily hast struck!

—he may well exclaim it! And the whole stately ending reminds
us that this most introspective of plays has also been a tragedy of
great events, which have added their dignity to its own. The note
was early struck; in talk of war, in the ominous

> Something is rotten in the state of Denmark.

and it has echoed through the play. And we are sent from the
theater now with our minds not simply upon the pity of Hamlet's
death, but stirred to some pride in him.

Fortinbras is the fortunate man, the enemy whom happy chance
turns friend, the welcomed stranger with the easier work to do.
The future is his. He the more owes (as he will know when he
has heard Horatio's tale) a tribute to the life here sacrificed. He
pays it as an honorable soldier should:

> Let four captains
> Bear Hamlet, like a soldier, to the stage:
> For he was likely, had he been put on,
> To have proved most royally; and for his passage,
> The soldiers' music and the rites of war
> Speak loudly for him. . . .

> *Exeunt marching: after the which a peal of ordnance are shot off.*

It is not by mere convention that Shakespeare allots him a hero's
end.

A Note on the First Quarto

THE PIRATE AND HIS METHODS

THE *Hamlet* which Shakespeare left us is in the Second Quarto and the Folio. From the First Quarto the positive harvest is a few interesting stage directions and a way of reducing the action to such a "two hours' traffic" (or less) as would be passable on the Elizabethan stage. And a performance of it—the merely verbal corruptions set straight—would be an instructive experiment. We should see what, to the mind of the pirate-compiler, were the qualities which made the play popular.[1]

The theory most commonly accepted at the moment is, I believe, that Q1 does not represent an earlier version by Shakespeare, nor even an earlier alien play partly amended by him; but that it is a "surreptitious" and "assembled" text, a garbling and debasing of the mature *Hamlet* which we have. From a bibliographical standpoint I am incompetent to argue the matter. But it seemed worth while to consider Q1 simply as a piece of playwriting, and, comparing it with Q2, to ask how far, as such, it can or cannot be accommodated to the theory. In the main, no doubt, it can be; but not, I think, altogether.

We have, to begin with, such truncate and clumsy lines as are the likeliest possible result of an attempt to remember the speeches containing them made by someone who had listened to them fairly often (not too intelligently) but had never learned them:

> To be, or not to be, I there's the point,
> To Die, to sleepe, is that all? I all:
> No, to sleepe, to dreame, I mary there it goes . . . .

—the crude sense of the real thing. As to the unrelated lines mixed in with the garbled text:

> And borne before an everlasting Judge . . .
> The happy smile, and the accursed damn'd . . .
> Scorned by the right rich, the rich curssed of the poore?
> The widow being oppressed, the orphan wrong'd,
> The taste of hunger, or a tirant's raigne
> And thousand more calamities besides . . .

---

[1] William Poel, among his many other useful services to Elizabethan drama, did, I think, do something like this.

—they are the sort of thing which, recollection failing, anybody familiar with the Elizabethan theater could improvise out of the scraps and ends of plays floating in his memory.

On the other hand, there is Voltimand's speech, which seemingly comes direct from the mouth of an actor who had spoken it in a performance of Q2, or some very similar text (and, if it does, here is a sign that the minor actors in a company were expected to be fairly word-perfect), or from the "part" itself from which he had learned it.

Then there are the twenty-eight lines, peculiar to Q1, which Furnivall declares to be Shakespeare's own.[2] That they might well be is undeniable, and this is a point against a simple acceptance of the "pirated Q2" theory. But they might also have been provided by somebody familiar with Shakespeare's style. In one of them—

> As would have moov'd the stoniest breast alive . . .

—there is a faint echo of *Twelfth Night's*

> Lady, you are the cruellest she alive . . .
> Love make his heart of flint that you shall love. . . .

—the more noticeable, perhaps, because Corambis' lines (which Furnivall does not cite):

> such men often prove
> Great in their wordes, but little in their love.

must surely also derive from Viola's

> for still we prove
> Much in our vows but little in our love.

On the other hand, again, a large proportion of the more memorable phrases—popular tags to this day, likeliest to be so then, and easy quarry for a pirate—come through correctly:

> Frailtie, thy name is Woman.

> He was a man, take him for all in all,
> I shall not looke upon his like againe.

> Angels and Ministers of grace defend us . . . .

> There are more things in heaven and earth *Horatio*,
> Then are Dream't of, in your philosophie.

---

[2] See his introduction to the N.S.S. Grigg's facsimile.

Rest, rest, perturbed spirit.

The time is out of joynt. O, cursed spite
That ever I was borne to set it right.

—and this is but a selection from the first two scenes.

Another very famous tag comes through with the actor trick
of repetition attached to it:

O my prophetike soul, my uncle! my uncle!

And Q2's elaborate variations upon

Get thee to a nunnery. . . .

become a mere gabbling, eight times reiterated

to a Nunnery goe.

This is just the sort of thing which an inferior actor, when the
substance of a scene has failed to hold the audience (and the
emotional structure and the sequences of this one are not easily
made clear), is tempted to do; to finish it, that is to say, with a
series of effective flourishes. And something of the same sort is
to be seen in the triple repetition of Yorick's name, which anticipates—and prejudices—Q2's effective repetition of Alexander's,
which is in its turn, when the warrantor of Q1 deals with it, spoiled
by being overdone.

These things all point, in the main, to a piracy and a garbling of
Q2. Besides which, Q1 gives us a play just as elaborate in plan as
the genuine and matured *Hamlet*; as many characters, though they
are less fully characterized; and an abundance of incidental
material. Fortinbras and Denmark's foreign policy are there; so
(his name changed) are Reynaldo and his spying expedition; so,
despite compression, is all that is material of the Players and their
play, with a reference, even, to "private plays" and "the humour
of children"; so are all the circumstances of the journey to England; we have the Gravediggers, we have even an anonymous
Osric—not merely, then, the major but most of the minor fea-
tures of the authentic *Hamlet*. The pirate crams all he can into
the smaller space permitted him. And, if slapdash, he is competent after his kind; for the cardinal point of each scene will
generally be left us.

Something else suggests the pirate: the fact that it is in the last third of the play that the text is most contracted and corrupt and the botching at its worst.[8] The last third of any play will be apt to suffer so at the hands of a man who fancies himself as no poet, of course, or "serious" dramatist, but a practical man of the theater. For there is nothing he so fears as the impatience of his audience once the excitement of a play's mid-crisis is past. After that push on quickly to the end, will be his rule. Now Shakespeare, writing generously throughout, is even more generous in the last third of the play, of incidental matter, and of what a "practical" pirate might well consider "mere talk." Hamlet is absent from the action too; that the audience (and possibly the actor) may not like. And when he does return he has left emotional rhetoric—stuff, says the practical man, much to the taste of the audience—behind him. Ample reasons here, then, for the extra contraction we find.

THE CHANGED SCENE-SEQUENCE

But two things at least (apart from the question of Furnivall's Shakespearean lines) do not fit the theory that Q1 is nothing but a stolen and garbled version of the mature Q2.

Why should a pirate rename Polonius "Corambis," and Reynaldo "Montano"? I know of no convincing answer.

And why should he displace the "To be or not to be . . ." soliloquy and Hamlet's scene with Ophelia? If he had gotten the rest of the action right it would surely be hard to make this mistake. And why intentionally make such a change? But did he? Must there not have been some version of the play with this scene-sequence in it?

There is the trace of one in Q2. In Q1:

> Lets to the King . . . .

says Corambis to Ophelia; and he takes her to the King and Queen, and the rest follows naturally. In Q2:

> goe we to the King . . . .

---

[8] Compare the pagination of the two Quartos. To the end of the closet-scene (the mid-crisis); Q1, roughly, 45 pp.; Q2, 64. But from here to the end; Q2, 35 pp.; Q1, 18 only; hardly more than half. It may be worth while remarking that the more legitimate omissions of the Folio are also mainly to be found in this last third of the play.

says Polonius; and they set off. But Ophelia never arrives. The thing is not explained; but, of course, in the Q2 scene-sequence she is not wanted. Does this show Shakespeare merely changing his plan of action, or revising an earlier play, either his own or another man's, without troubling to alter the telltale phrase? If it shows a mere currently made change of plan, then the pirate took a hint from Shakespeare, but devised Q1's scene-sequence for himself—which is more than unlikely. If he found his scene-sequence somewhere, was it in an earlier play by Shakespeare, or another man's? One can give a guessing answer to both questions at once. It is as unlikely that he would take so much as he almost provably has done in the shape of character and dialogue from Q2, and go back to a very different play, be it Shakespeare's or another's, simply for this scene-sequence and the change of names.[4] Does it not look, therefore, as if there had existed a version of the play, written by Shakespeare, substantially mature, but which yet contained the Q1 scene-sequence, a Corambis and Montano, and, possibly, the Shakespearean lines (or better versions of them) which Furnivall cites?

There is much to be said, from a more narrowly dramatic point of view, for Q1's scene-sequence. The "To be or not to be . . ." soliloquy comes well from a Hamlet last heard lamenting that the time was out of joint, last pictured to us (in Q1) parting from Ophelia,

> Silent, as in the midtime of the night . . .

And from this picturing of the one encounter to their next, which we ourselves are to see, the thread of their story will be sustained without interruption, save for the few lines given to the introducing of Rosencrantz and Guildenstern and the episode of the returned Ambassadors. And his puzzling talk to her about beauty transforming honesty to a bawd will then follow so much more closely than in Q2 upon his angry grief for his mother's frailty, that the connection between the two should be as much more apparent.

In what, then, is the Q2 scene-sequence an improvement?

---

[4] It is worth noting that Montano-Reynaldo appears only at this point, where the structural difference between Q1 and Q2 is rooted. Also I have ventured to diagnose a reconsideration of the character of Corambis-Polonius at this very juncture also. See p. 205.

It enables Shakespeare (as we have seen) to develop in the long discursive scene with Rosencrantz and Guildenstern, Polonius and the Players, the imaginative, speculative, passive and unpractical side of Hamlet, and to develop it in an appropriately uneventful setting. And from this passivity it is Hamlet who rouses himself, to the self-reproach of

O, what a rogue and peasant slave am I! . . .

and to devising the test of the play-scene. That he should do this of his own accord, self-stimulated, and not (as in Q1) after his nerves have been rewrought upon by the meeting with Ophelia, and he has discovered that the King and Polonius-Corambis have baited their trap with her and are spying on him, adds much moral weight to his character. It is dramatically better too that the hero should keep the initiative; should plot, not merely counter-plot.

The postponing of the scene with Ophelia, and of the shock to the King of the overheard

those that are married already, all but one, shall live. . . .

until the very eve of the play-scene, has advantages of its own besides. The King will not be left sitting still under such a threat, or leaving a leisurely elucidation of it to Rosencrantz and Guildenstern. In Q2 he at once projects Hamlet's dispatch to England. This then becomes—as we have already noted[5]—an important turning point in the play's counteraction, the King's against Hamlet. And, with the train of Hamlet's plot now about to be fired, action and counteraction can, after the discursive delays, be pressed forward together, and the story carried unchecked to its exciting mid-crisis and Hamlet's foiling and departure.

Yet there are signs which could be held to show that the pirate *had* two versions of the play to pick and choose between: one yielding him his Q1 scene-sequence: the other, more lately written dialogue.

For instance; though Corambis does bring Ophelia to the King, she stands there completely ignored while he tells the tale of her love affair with Hamlet and of his own part in it. He tells it, in fact, just as it is more naturally told by Polonius in Q2—of an Ophelia who is really absent.

[5] See pp. 41: 76.

Then there is the matter of Hamlet's talk with Corambis-Polonius. In Q1 this follows close upon his discovery that Ophelia has been set in his path as a decoy, and that Corambis and the King have been spying on them. Does not that give much point to the sarcasm of

> y'are a fishmonger.

(a bawd, a pandar), and of

> I would you were so honest a man.

—so much that one is tempted to say: Shakespeare could only have written the lines in this connection?[6] On the other hand, if this beginning best suits Corambis, Hamlet's final and frankly expressive aside, Q1's

> Olde doating foole.

is hardly harsh enough comment upon a so recently detected trap-baiter and spy. And it plainly, one would say, must derive from Q2's

> These tedious old fools!

—which is suitable enough summing-up of the still guiltless Polonius.

What explanation can be offered here? One is, of course, only piling guess upon guess. But is it not possible that the "fish-monger" passage—with, it would be likely, the even more pointed

> if the sun breed maggots in a dead dog. . . Have you a daughter? . . . Let her not walk i' the sun. . . .

which Q1, economizing time, makes no use of—was originally written for the Q1 sequence, to follow close upon the Ophelia-baited trap and Hamlet's discovery of it? But why, then, did Shakespeare not omit the lines when, addressed to a still guiltless Polonius, they had lost their primary point? They are effective lines in themselves; he would be loath to part with them. And he found, besides, I suggest, that the whole passage could as well be interpreted as sardonically oracular praise of the Polonius who has so prudently withdrawn his daughter from the dangers of a corrupt world, in which men—Hamlet not least—are "arrant knaves

---

[6] There is, moreover, the stressed opposition of "honesty" and "bawd" in the scene with Ophelia.

all," and as fishmongerly-minded as he. Moreover, while Corambis, fresh from his spying and trap-setting, could hardly help seeing the point of the sarcasms, with Polonius they will pass, thus
fined down, for madness; and with us, in so far as we miss the
point of them, as being among those many twilight sayings, whose
meaning is rather to be felt than comprehended—a quite legitimate dramatic effect where Hamlet and his "madness" are concerned.[7]

This implies, then, a correction of dialogue just sufficient to
suit the change in the action, and our pirate left, for his chief
resource, with a play pretty well as mature in plan and characteri-
zation as Q2, but still differing in the matter of this scene-sequence.
But it looks also as if he must have had some knowledge of Q2
itself and of the changes in its dialogue which followed upon the
new scene-sequence, though he did not appreciate their significance.

Not that I have the temerity to offer this as a definite solution
of the Q1 problem. There are other difficulties, and other answers,
doubtless, to these; and I have a dozen times repented the putting
my foot into such a critical quagmire. But Q1's scene-sequence,
and "Corambis" and "Montano," are surely not the pirate's invention, and he plainly has a mature play to pilfer from, and Q2's
scene-sequence is the more favorable to the exhibiting of Hamlet's
character. One is tempted, therefore, to see that change as one of
Shakespeare's (probably latest) contributions to the subduing and
adapting of the story and the storytelling to this maturer end, and
what is left cryptic in the scene between Hamlet and Polonius as
an item, then, in the consequent process of subtilizing the character under cover of its madness.[8]

[7] These oracular passages, of course, abound; and the quality of their content
ranges from the tragically bitter implication of the "dear mother" farewell to the
King, through the cold irony of this one, to the sheer nonsense of the "camel . . .
weasel . . . whale" bamboozling of Polonius. It is for the critic and the actor to
master their latent significance, where this exists; the audience stands midway
between Hamlet and his victim, between the puzzler and the puzzled.

[8] And it is thanks—or otherwise—to Dr. Dover Wilson that I found myself
upon the track of this troublesome and, finally, not very important question. He is
himself so puzzled by the apparent inapplicability of the "fishmonger" passage
that he deduces a now vanished stage direction in Q2, by which Hamlet enters
unseen and overhears the plot to "loose" Ophelia to him. It is such a simple solution that one is strongly tempted to accept it. I was tempted, and to the point of

What, finally, of Q1's explicit disclosure of the murder to the Queen and her explicit denial that she was privy to it? Is that the pirate's, or Kyd's; was it ever Shakespeare's? The question is not upon all fours with that of the scene-sequence; for practically only a single line spoken by Gertrude is involved, and this the pirate—who might well prefer his effects cut and dried—could easily have inserted on his own account. But once again, regard for character—this alone—must rule out the disclosure for Shakespeare. Because once the Queen knows of the murder, how is she, throughout the rest of the play, to be shown docile at the King's side, protecting him from Laertes, carelessly gay during the fencing match, and with no more made of the matter? And that she knew and feigned ignorance is not to be supposed; for this would make her a monster.[9]

The Verse and the Prose

VOCABULARY AND IMAGERY

THE Elizabethan dramatist was in thrall to no critical rule. He might do what he would as long as he made what he did effective. He might write as he chose: in prose or verse, and it might be any sort of verse; and he could chop and change from scene to scene, or in the course of a scene, between verse and prose, or one

---

yielding. But my instincts rebelled. I did not like the spoiling of that entrance *reading on a Booke,* nor the commonplace symmetry of letting Hamlet stand there overhearing a plot by which the plotters were to stand there a little later overhearing him. Besides which—and far more important!—Dover Wilson's argument leads him fatally to having Hamlet regard Ophelia as a decoy the minute he (later on) sets eyes on her, and to knowing from the beginning of their scene together that the King and Polonius are listening. None of this can I admit for a moment. For the result will be to rob Hamlet's part in the scene of all the ebb and flow of tenderness and regret, inexplicable suffering and passion, to reduce it to a dead level of resentment, to make him, indeed, something of a self-righteous scold.

But mere objections are not enough. I felt I must propose, if I could, some alternative solution to the difficulty. For difficulty there is, even though it be—as are many dramatic difficulties—more real than apparent, and, therefore, in effect, the less important. This, then, is what I have found; though it surpasses the needs of an answer; and I had, of course, been puzzling over the question of the scene-sequence on its own account.

[9] For a discussion of the effect that Shakespeare does make—once again, a very subtle one—by bringing Gertrude to the very brink of disclosure but no further, see p. 107, note.

sort of verse and another, just as he would. Shakespeare, in this as in other things, claims every freedom. He develops no cut-and-dried method of his own. He tests and discards. His tendency, from the first, is to be rid of artifice and formula, of all forms which do not prove malleable; they break, indeed, under the stress to which he subjects them, of their molding into seemingly spontaneous expression. For that is what he works towards; but to achieve it without sacrificing the force and distinction of essentially poetic speech. Syntax must be as malleable, since it has to shape not thought only, but the unruliest emotions. And his vocabulary and imagery, however fine, must be but an enhancement of familiar parlance if the effect of it is to come directly home to his audience.

Every language accumulates certain devices for emphasis and display, and the dramatist who bases his dialogue on familiar parlance is bound to employ them. The trouble is that a too casual currency will often have effaced their value, and mere exaggeration will not restore it. A cumulation of two or three epithets, for instance, is a common means of emphasis. Shakespeare, fresh to the theater, finds their accumulation into a very catalogue to be a much-practiced dramatic trick, which he practices himself for a time. Amid the many technical confusions of *Romeo and Juliet* comes that

> Accurst, unhappy, wretched, hateful day! . . .
>
> Beguil'd, divorced, wronged, spited, slain! . . .
>
> Despis'd, distressed, hated, martyr'd, killed! . . .

Yet already he may be sensible that he is skirting the edge of the ridiculous, for he thrusts the Nurse's burlesque of the lamentations into the very midst of them; and we know, besides, that Juliet is not really dead. In *Hamlet* he is still using the trick, but he gives it dramatic validity. Hamlet, lashing himself into fury with his

> Bloody, bawdy villain!
> Remorseless, treacherous, lecherous, kindless villain!

is sensible a second later that he is an ass to unpack his heart with words; and the thing is turned to frankly comic account in Polonius'

The best actors in the world, either for tragedy, comedy, history, pastoral, pastoral-comical, historical-pastoral, tragical-historical, tragical-comical-historical-pastoral. . .

while, for a normal use of it, we have that measured and balanced

How weary, stale, flat and unprofitable. . .[1]

A very common English means of emphasis is what may be called "repetition by complement"; but, again, so common is this, its better-known locutions are so hackneyed, that their value is largely lost. "Flesh and blood," "safe and sound," "hue and cry," "kith and kin," "use and wont"—these are worn currency indeed.[2] Shakespeare, in *Hamlet*, shows an extraordinary fondness for this device, and employs it, one would say, as carelessly as constantly. It may at times betoken the teeming mind—his own or his character's—finding two words as easily as one and too eager to be getting on to choose between them. The use of the conjunction makes smooth going for the verse, the familiar form and the bare addition to the meaning easy listening; and even when this last is negligible, as it is—to take four samples out of Hamlet's mouth alone in a single stretch of a single scene—in "book and volume," "grace and mercy," "strange or odd," "love and friending"—the actor's voice can itself color the second word to a richer implication. But the meaning is often definitely amplified or intensified; amplified in "grunt and sweat"; in "slings and arrows" a sense of piercing is added to a mere blow; and the suggestion in "pitch and moment" carries us upward first and then on.[3] The sense is enlarged in "fit and seasoned" and "mortal and unsure"; its force is modified in "scourge and minister."

The concrete imagery of a noun turned adjective can add weight to the weightiest adjective, as with "ponderous and marble jaws"; or the simple image may be elaborated and made beautiful, as in

---

[1] Even as we have had in *Julius Cæsar*, but as speech planned to impress the hearers:

> Brutus is noble, wise, valiant and honest;
> Cæsar was mighty, bold, royal and loving. . . .

[2] For an extended list of them, and an interesting discussion of their use, see Logan Pearsall Smith's *Words and Idioms*.

[3] And that this is a complementary image is alone (I suggest) a reason for preferring Q2's "pitch" to the Folio's "pith."

"the morn and liquid dew of youth." There is, on the other hand, little but redundancy in such a huddled couple of samples as

> That monster, custom . . .
>   . . . is angel yet in this,
> That to the use of actions *fair* and *good*
> He likewise gives a *frock* or *livery*. . . .

This comes, however, from a fatigued Hamlet in the slack-water of a scene. But surely, we feel, Shakespeare is conscious how tiresome the trick can be if it is overemployed when he gives us Rosencrantz' and Guildenstern's

> Most *holy* and *religious* fear it is
> To keep those *many many* bodies safe
> That *live* and *feed* upon your majesty.
> The *single* and *peculiar* life is bound
> With all the *strength* and *armour* of the mind. . . .

and adds, within a few lines, a "*depends* and *rests*" and a "*mortis'd* and *adjoin'd*."

A yet simpler and commoner device—to be found probably in all languages and literatures, since it reflects what must surely be a universal trick of the mind—is the reiterating of a single significant word, its use as a sort of refrain. As an encouraging watchword; in reiteration to persuade oneself or others that this or that is true; in the pulsing obsessions of temptation or remorse; under a dozen different forms the process is familiar.[4] Again, here is a device that the apprentice Shakespeare found turned to an elaborate dramatic artifice; and as such, to begin with, he adopts it. We have it in its crudity in *Romeo and Juliet*; in *Richard II* for the sake of its musical charm; in *Henry V* the speech on ceremony gives it careful employment; and it is appropriate to the oratory in *Julius Cæsar*. In *Hamlet* it is mere artifice no longer, its psychological rights are restored. We have Hamlet's obsessed iteration—when he is summoned to her closet—of "Mother . . . mother . . . mother . . ," his

> O villain, villain, smiling, damned villain!
> My tables—meet it is I set it down,
> That one may smile and smile and be a villain. . . .

---

[4] Dervishes send themselves into a trance by continually repeating the name of Allah. And there is the Bellman's "What I tell you three times is true," which is the psychological basis of advertising.

his "words, words, words," and "Sir . . . sir . . . sir" to Polonius.
And there is the more elaborate flinging-about between Hamlet,
Horatio, Marcellus and the Ghost of the "swear . . . sworn . . .
sword . . . in faith . . . indeed"; and here the mutual ringing of the
changes of emphasis and tone on the reiterated words is like the
weaving of a spell. The effect is now legitimately gained, and by
no sacrifice of spontaneity; it is kept within the bounds of illusion.

The arresting image is not hard to find, nor one which fits
character or occasion. Its employment will be another matter.
However sharply it should arrest, it must not retain our attention
while the action is moving ahead, and other images accumulate.
Its clarity, then, its emotional force, the exact effect of it coming
when and where it does; the dramatist must feel sure of all that.
A painter uses much the same art in placing some object in a
picture. Its independent importance apart, here it will have one
value, there another, here help complete the composition, there
only disintegrate it, or be itself ignored.

Shakespeare's sense of fitness, both to occasion and character, is
very sure. He casts the play's first scene in verse; that lends it
impulse and stimulus, dignifies the story's exposition, helps
heighten the sense of mystery. But it is at the outset forthright
plain stuff; Francisco and Bernardo are just "honest soldiers" both,
and their speech fits them. Marcellus strikes a slightly finer note.
Only Horatio runs to relative clauses, allusion to Rome and "the
mightiest Julius," and, towards the end—as if the supernatural
had worked on his imagination—to imagery. We have the differing mental quality of the three men painted in Bernardo's

> It was about to speak when the cock crew.

Marcellus'

> The bird of dawning singeth all night long. . . .

and Horatio's

> But look, the morn in russet mantle clad,
> Walks o'er the dew of yon high eastern hill. . . .

With the action running smoothly, we may often follow by the
thread of the imagery the very workings of a character's mind. It
is the King's

> How is it that the *clouds* still hang on you?

developed through the Queen's

> Good Hamlet, cast thy *nighted* colour off. . . .

which seems to prompt Hamlet's own

> 'Tis not alone my *inky* cloak, good mother. . . .

And then we see him taking a sour sort of pleasure in elaborating
the idea, which he has, so to speak, snatched from them; first
adding "customary suits" to "solemn black"; next, cutting a layer
inward, so to speak, with his "forc'd breath . . . the fruitful river
in the eye . . . dejected haviour of the visage," as if to warn them
what they may be uncovering; finally, with his "forms, modes,
shows . . . trappings and . . . suits" rounding off the little parable,
his variations upon *their* theme—and they and their courtiers may
make what they will of it!

There are images which recur with the themes that prompted
them. The world, to Hamlet, is

> an unweeded garden,
> That grows to seed; things rank and gross in nature
> Possess it merely.

Hamlet himself would be, the Ghost tells him,

> duller . . . than the fat weed
> That rots itself in ease on Lethe wharf . . .

not to revenge his father's murder and his mother's shame.
Gertrude is to find thorns lodged in her bosom to prick and sting
her. And Hamlet pictures Claudius to her

> like a mildewed ear,
> Blasting his wholesome brother.

and adjures her to keep from him and not to

> spread the compost on the weeds,
> To make them ranker.

But will the ordinarily attentive listener seize on this connection,
spaced out, as it is, across more than half the play's length? That
is the test of its dramatic validity. It is hard to say positively. But
the image is initially very strongly stressed; and no more notable
place could be given it than it has; in Hamlet's first soliloquy
(when we are all curiosity about him), where too it follows im-

mediately upon the initial emotional outburst (when our attention is well held). Probably there will be at least half-conscious recognition, with something the same satisfaction in it as one gains from a half-remembered refrain in music, or the restoring of some half-forgotten phrase to one's memory.

A similar, if not so clearly connected a sequence, images yet more strongly the infectious corruption of Claudius, and Gertrude's sin. The Ghost's "lust" that will "prey on garbage"; Hamlet's "maggots in a dead dog" (Polonius has suspected him, he knows, of lusting after Ophelia); his savage thought of "fatting the region kites with this slave's offal"; his speech to his mother of the "flattering unction" which

> will but skin and film the ulcerous place,
> Whiles rank corruption, mining all within,
> Infects unseen.

his elaborate demonstration to Claudius of how that "convocation of politic worms," to whom Polonius is delivered, will before long be at him, too, "fat" and triumphant though he now is; the talk of "pocky corpses," dust and rottenness and the smell of mortality in the graveyard; Claudius' own

> O, my offence is rank, it smells to heaven . . . .

—the hearer cannot but be affected, consciously or subconsciously, by such an extended recurrence.

And in contrast to the weeds of Gertrude's sin we have flowers for Ophelia. Hamlet's garden grown to seed has set against it in the very next scene Laertes' warning

> The canker galls the infants of the spring
> Too oft before their buttons be disclos'd,
> And in the morn and liquid dew of youth
> Contagious blastments are most imminent . . . .

and her own imaging of such danger is of a "primrose path of dalliance." Hamlet was for her

> The expectancy and rose of the fair state . . .

and she to Laertes is a "rose of May." In her madness she plays with flowers; and, as if to clinch the apposition, the pitiful description of her death, garlanded with flowers, is given—to whom but Gertrude?

The play is, indeed, in one of its aspects a very edifice of related imagery; these three sequences, with their likenesses and contrasts, being but a part, if a salient one, of the whole. It is an edifice no more logically or rigidly constructed than are the schemes of time and place, but as adaptable as these are, a product of the natural economy of the poet's mind, a part of the general lively synthesis of idea which is, for the mature Shakespeare, dramatic form. He submits himself to no other.[5]

The image must never be let pass, leaving us puzzled. A peculiar one in a passage speedy with passion must carry its explanation. To "pigeon-livered" then, is added

> and lack gall
> To make oppression bitter . . .

And if—like the birds in the basket and the famous ape—it needs much explanation, this is perhaps a sign that it had better not have been used.

On the other hand, though exceptionally, a passage crowded with a strange assortment of imagery may make a striking picture of the overwrought mind. But the thing needs to be cunningly done, and the confusion to be more apparent than real. There is Hamlet's speech while he waits for the Ghost to appear, about the "vicious mole of nature" in a man which may corrupt him altogether; with its "pales and forts of reason," "nature's livery," "fortune's star," and "dram of evil."[6] There is the heavily overcharged passage in the scene with Gertrude; when, to his telling her that she is guilty of "such an act" as

> makes marriage vows
> As false as dicers' oaths . . .

he adds:

> O! such a deed
> As from the body of contraction plucks
> The very soul, and sweet religion makes
> A rhapsody of words; heaven's face doth glow,
> Yea, this solidity and compound mass,
> With tristful visage, as against the doom,
> Is thought-sick at the act.

[5] For a thoroughly documented study of Shakespeare's imagery, the student should turn to Dr. Caroline Spurgeon's book on the subject.

[6] For the dramatic purpose and effect of this, see pp. 58 *et seq.*

Spoken as this must be, in all the heat, with all the impulse of passion, the hearer will certainly not grasp its detailed meaning—which leaves, for that matter, editors still disputing. He is not altogether required to. The "body of contraction" is a mere elaboration of the earlier "marriage vows," and "sweet religion" (plainly derivative from "very soul"), with "rhapsody of words," makes a counterpart (therefore easily seized upon) to "false as dicers' oaths"; and all this only leads up to the dominant "heaven's face doth glow. . . ." That having made its clear and vivid effect, the magnificent hyperbole which follows—the "solidity and compound mass . . . tristful visage . . . doom . . . thought-sick . . ."—is meant but to give us a vague sense of the whole world struck pale beneath God's wrath, a thing *not* to be understood but felt, not to be belittled by understanding. This is the *impression* Hamlet means to make on his mother, and Shakespeare on us.

When the elaborating of an image has to be swift and passionate and clear also, cadence and assonance may be put to use:

> Rebellious hell,
> If thou canst mutine in a matron's bones,
> To flaming youth let virtue be as wax,
> And melt in her own fire: proclaim no shame
> When the compulsive ardour gives the charge,
> Since frost itself as actively doth burn,
> And reason panders will.

The sentence is evenly balanced. For a beginning the "Rebellious hell," with its "e's" and doubled "l's," is tellingly arresting. The repeated "m's" ("mutine . . . matron . . . flaming . . . melt") keep the tone of the lines level and clear. "Proclaim no shame" sustains the clarity, while the initial doubled consonants and the half-open vowels (following for contrast upon the "e's" and "i" of "melt in her own fire") add strength and resonance. "Compulsive" gives force to the manifest indignation of the fully open "ardour" and "charge," and the doubled consonants of the final phrase demand and ensure perfect articulation, while its sibilants ("frost itself . . . reason panders") hiss contempt.

THE PROSE

Shakespeare does not try to keep the play at poetic pitch throughout; he has for long seen the dramatic unwisdom of that. But he has also passed beyond any simple mechanical division into poetry and prose; poetry for heroics and sentiment, prose for buffoonery. He has learned how to modulate his verse with ease to the expressing of many moods; his prose too; and to run the gamut, if he will, from the sublime to the commonplace without a break.

Verse prevails, of course. Not only is it by convention the dominant medium for such a play, but he needs, for his subject, its compelling and illusive power. Convention dictates prose for the Gravediggers, and convenience its use for the commentary upon the versified *Murder of Gonzago*. For the rest, Shakespeare will always have, seemingly, a specifically dramatic reason for employing it.

The longest stretch of prose begins when Polonius "boards" Hamlet, continues through the Rosencrantz and Guildenstern examination in lunacy, the reception of the Players (Æneas' tale to Dido relieving it), and is suddenly, violently broken and ended by the outburst of

> O, what a rogue and peasant slave am I! . . .

The reason for its use here is obvious enough. The action is at a standstill; the impulse of verse would be wasted on it. Hamlet himself is adrift upon the slack-water of doubt and impotence, no pulsing emotion left in him, nothing for poetry to express. The detached, sceptical mind—

> What a piece of work is a man! how noble in reason! . . . And yet, to me, what is this quintessence of dust? . . .

—inevitably speaks in prose.

We have prose for the quiet pessimism of the graveyard. What else is possible? How fatally verse would compromise the gentle gravity, the limpid clarity of

> Alas! poor Yorick. I knew him, Horatio; a fellow of infinite jest, of most excellent fancy. . . .

As well try to put the eighteenth chapter of St. Luke into verse! We have prose for the scene with Osric and the anonymous Lord; a dry prelude to the high-colored drama of the final scene. The encounters with Rosencrantz and Guildenstern and with Claudius after the play-scene are all cast in prose; this, I think, is to throw the harsh mask of Hamlet's eccentricities here into contrast with the soliloquies hereabouts and the scene with Gertrude (all cast in verse), in which we see his true visage. And he is made to break suddenly into prose in the scene with Ophelia, to shatter the delicate melody of her tendering back his gifts, her

> Take these again; for to the noble mind
> Rich gifts wax poor when givers prove unkind.

with the strident

> Ha, ha! are you honest? . . . Are you fair? . . . That if you be honest and fair, your honesty should admit no discours~ to your beauty. . . .

—and so, seemingly, to shatter the last of the harmony between them and of the beauty of his love for her. As if for a reversal of the process, the prose of the graveyard-scene shifts, with the arrival of that sorry little procession, to verse, stiff in cadence at first:

> The Queen, the courtiers: who is that they follow?
> And with such maimed rites? This doth betoken
> The corse they follow did with desperate hand
> Fordo its own life. . . .

but kindling to the anguish of

> I lov'd Ophelia; forty thousand brothers
> Could not, with all their quantity of love,
> Make up my sum . . . .

for which prose would never do.

We may say that, in the main, the prose Hamlet is never the innermost man. For the expression of that—of the combination of thought and feeling, instinct and impulse, and of the twilight travail of the spirit which has place there—only poetry will serve.

THE VERSE

Shakespeare's dramatic verse may be said to flow from two fonts: the "lyric" (so to call it) and the rhetorical. His own earliest bent, we are disposed to presume, was towards the delicate discipline of the lyric, and to expanding this, much as Lyly had done, for dramatic use; though—and it at once made a difference—he had men to work for, not children, the virile note must be struck. And if his vein of heroic rhetoric was not quite so happily his own, this

—though only for his theater's and actors' sake—had to be culti-
vated too. He was soon doing masterly work enough of the kind.
In the earlier plays we can sometimes see the currents running
side by side and blending here and there. And he disciplines his
rhetoric by learning to put it to more strictly dramatic use, letting
his captains and kings and orators find him proper occasion for it.
But it is, both for dramatist and actor, a deplorably easy sort of
stuff to "unpack." We have a mischievous fling at its extrava-
gances embodied in Ancient Pistol. And he is taking at the time
ever more extensive refuge in the exactitudes of prose.

There is a sense in which all dramatic speech must have in it
something of the enhancement of poetry. It may be given by
such a convention as in French classic tragedy forbids the very
use of "common" words, by which a spade may be nothing less
"noble" than an agricultural implement. This is not a mere piece
of literary affectation, but a logical development of the convention
employed; nobility of poetic substance being added to the nobility
of poetic form to make, with the other conventions of time and
place, a flawless unity of impression. Or the enhancement may be
cunningly condensed within seemingly commonplace talk. But
there it must be. If speech is to be made to "carry" in the theater
it must have in it some quality equivalent—for a comparison—to
the effective "length" of a well-bowled cricket ball. Nor, in Shakespeare's theater, of all others, can this poetic enhancement be surrendered. For there speech has to fulfill a multiple purpose. Not
only must it be shaped and colored to the exhibiting of character,
but the play's story has to be told far more fully and vividly than
the modern dramatist will tell it, the continuous action continu-
ously explained and its background suggestively filled in too. For
the creating and sustaining on the bare stage of a whole illusionary
world the dramatist has little other resource than picturesque and
persuasive speech.

All poets, presumably, test their lines by ear as they write them,
if not by speech. But with Shakespeare dramatic *writing* was for
convenience of record merely; his verse was not only conceived
as speech, it was to be so born and only so meant to exist. He
provided music for an orchestra of living individual voices that
he knew. As nearly as might be, he spoke through his actors. It is
the mere notation of this once-living music which remains. Pre-

cise notation, moreover, it could not be made. Write for mechanical instruments in a recognized alphabet of crotchets and quavers, tones and semitones, with a metronome marking to rule all, and a large liberty will still be left to the interpreters. And human speech is both more flexible and less biddable than that.[1] Nor does Shakespeare, as he develops dramatically, want to discipline his speakers in measure and cadence. He is not aiming at precision of form, but at an illusion of life. His verse accords even less to measure than to rhythm and stress. Its unity is in an overriding rhythm, its expressiveness in the varying of the stress. Let the actor submit himself to the prevailing rhythm of a passage—he has, presumably, an ear for music and an accordant voice—and he will find that the very cadence of a line gives him its dramatic import, its very melody the due content of emotion. He will note how the shifting of a caesura, the elision or addition of syllables, an assemblage of consonants or profusion of vowels are meant to help produce this or that effect; and he must master the gymnastics of it. But he had then better put such mechanical matters from his mind. For there will be no one correct way of speaking a line or a passage. Within the range of the form Shakespeare invites him to share in the freedom he himself has won—this lifelike freedom. He must first have gained, of course, as intimate a sympathy as may be with Shakespeare's meaning; and the soundness of his sympathy he can test by translating this into his own terms—in just about so much critical detachment from his author may the actor indulge. Then, all study done, let him, as a conscious instrument, simply attune himself to the character he is to play; and he will find it—there is no very rational accounting for the phenomenon—speaking freely through him, and, within the measure of his sympathy, rightly too.

[1] No instrument can be made to compete in variety and significance of expression with the cultured human voice naturally used. Nor, surely, can any system of notation, any conceivable combination of symbols be devised which will represent the scope of its resources. The usual phonetic alphabet very certainly does not. Whatever the uses of this may be (it was a practical means of recording living speech till the gramophone superseded it), a language learned by reliance on it is bound to be inexpressively spoken, if nothing further is done which may set the ear and tongue free from its restraints. A man who has learned a language phonetically speaks it as a deaf man does. A student must hear the music of a language, and the best thing is probably to set him searching for it; for its melodies and cadences in its poetry, and, where English is concerned, in dramatic poetry, since there melody and cadence are at their freest and most characteristic.

There is little pedestrian verse in the play; though Voltimand's account of his mission and a few other such utilitarian passages may be so labeled. But such a one, for instance, as the opening scene's narrative of the Fortinbras quarrel—which might easily be so—is saved by being set in circumstances tensely dramatic in themselves. Horatio, harrowed "with fear and wonder" by one sight of the Ghost, has mind and nerve braced for the next, and puts them to the proof of concentration on his story—whence the close-knit, well-stressed verse, precise in statement, driven rather than flowing along:

> Our last king,
> Whose image even but now appear'd to us,
> Was, as you know, by Fortinbras of Norway,
> Thereto prick'd on by a most emulate pride,
> Dar'd to the combat; in which our valiant Hamlet—
> For so this side of our known world esteem'd him—
> Did slay this Fortinbras, who, by a seal'd compact . . .

—parenthesis preferred to digression, for thus the speech ploughs straight forward; and if this lengthens the line or displaces a caesura, so much the better, for the speaker must then, to keep the rhythm true, speed over the subordinate matter. Melody may be sacrificed to emphasis; ease will not be let prejudice strength.

> Now, sir, young Fortinbras,
> Of unimproved mettle hot and full,
> Hath in the skirts of Norway here and there
> Shark'd up a list of lawless resolutes. . . .

Note in this how the familiar "Now, sir, young Fortinbras . . ." entices our attention for the compressed exactitude of the second line, even as the free flow of the third (its one significant word, "in the *skirts* of . . ." lodged midway; it is not Norway's self that is preparing war) makes easy approach to the richly descriptive

> Shark'd up a list of lawless resolutes . . .

—which asks some assimilation.

It is only after the Ghost has come again and gone and the tension is relaxed that the verse turns melodious and picturesque, with

> The cock, that is the trumpet to the morn,
> Doth with his lofty and shrill-sounding throat
> Awake the god of day; and, at his warning,

> Whether in sea or fire, in earth or air,
> The extravagant and erring spirit hies
> To his confine. . . .

—and so on. Not, that is to say, until Shakespeare has achieved his dramatic purpose does he indulge in a little scene-painting. The lonely dark and cold of the beginning have been somehow blended into the curt exchanges of the two men relieving guard, made part of the action itself.

The verse will always respond better to a dramatic than a prosodic analysis. In Polonius' injunctions to Ophelia to beware of Hamlet's courtship:

> I do know,
> When the blood burns, how prodigal the soul
> Lends the tongue vows: these blazes, daughter,
> Giving more light than heat, extinct in both,
> Even in their promise, as it is a-making,
> You must not take for fire. From this time
> Be somewhat scanter of your maiden presence. . . .

The third line and the sixth are prosodically short. Pope sets things right with a "These blazes, O, my daughter," and various editors follow him. Capell improves it to "gentle daughter," and even Coleridge says "A spondee has, I doubt not, dropped out of the text."[8] The sixth line the Folio itself amends to

> You must not take for fire. From this time, daughter . . .

—and the reading has been authoritatively defended; and, if condemned, partly so on the grounds that the line, as it stands in Q2, can be made regular by treating "fire" as a dissyllable.[9]

But approach the question from the dramatic point of view and there is no difficulty. A midline pause is needed if the sequent "these blazes, daughter . . ." is to be emphatically attacked; and, as Polonius' lines are meant in general to ripple on their way unchecked, a pause of this sort must be specifically indicated. In the

[8] Quoted from Furness: *Apparatus criticus* and footnote.

[9] Dover Wilson says that the second "daughter" here is simply a careless repetition of the first—by, presumably, the transcriber or compositor. I think it as likely and likelier that some actor was the original culprit. He had caught the garrulous flow of the verse, and had ceased to mark the effect Shakespeare makes by these occasional checks to it.

sixth line there is the pause again, put to the same use. And how can any sensitive speaker miss the increased emphasis, the "No nonsense now!" of the three monosyllables, "From this time . . ," with those two firm "m's" comprised in them? As directions to the actor nothing could be plainer; and that is what Shakespeare is putting on paper.[10]

The Polonius tune is unmistakable, and it connotes him to a nicety. The lines, overfull of weak syllables, run rippling along till they seem to be about to run off the rails of the meter altogether, the flow only arrested now and then, while the old gentleman takes breath and collects his thoughts, by a "Mark you," a "See you now" or a "Perpend." Once, indeed, when he loses the thread of his discourse about Laertes, they do run off the rails into two or three lines of prose; and Reynaldo has, so to speak, to help him on again.

There is with Polonius a stiffening of stricter lines; for though wiseacre, he is no mere babbling fool. The famous "precepts" go to a steady measure, to a melody distinguished enough, if dry. But these belong to a conception of the character afterwards somewhat modified.[11] He can drive his royal master and mistress to distraction with

> That he is mad, 'tis true; 'tis true 'tis pity,
> And pity 'tis 'tis true. . . .
> Mad let us grant him, then; and now remains
> That we find out the cause of this effect,
> Or, rather, say, the cause of this defect,
> For this effect defective comes by cause. . . .

—satire as it is besides, upon much such mental and verbal jugglery in contemporary literature and drama; not a little to be found in Shakespeare's own work! But the adroit politician in him can pass, for a peroration, to the plain, practical

---

[10] This trick (so, not depreciatively, to call it) is something of a favorite with Shakespeare. Take, for an instance, in *Julius Cæsar*, Cassius'

> I, as Æneas our great ancestor
> Did from the flames of Troy upon his shoulder
> The old Anchises bear, so, from the waves of Tiber,
> Did I the tired Cæsar. And this man
> Is now become a god.

[11] See p. 204.

> You know, sometimes he walks four hours together
> Here in the lobby. . . .
> At such a time I'll loose my daughter to him. . . .
> Mark the encounter; if he love her not
> And be not from his reason fall'n thereon,
> Let me be no assistant for a state,
> But keep a farm and carters.

with its steadying beat, the tense consonants and broad vowels of its conclusion. For all Polonius in a single line take, however, the parenthetic, casual

> As 'twere a thing a little soil'd i' the working. . .

There, in sense as in sound—Laertes' depravity to be lightly accepted; and in the clipped syllables, the pinched consonants, the thin vowels, the tripping acidity of it—the old worldling is epitomized.

The verse at times may not so much express the speaker's own character as reflect either the occasion or the quality of the person spoken to. But this is dramatically justifiable. People do take the moment's color of some vivid experience, or self-forgetfully suppress themselves in their care for others. And no more assurance is needed of Laertes' love for Ophelia than the limpid simplicity of the verse of his farewell to her, which paints her character, not his own. He will be self-expressive enough when he returns to avenge his father. But, even then, at the sight or thought of her, his verse always yields to the tune of her again. And the Queen, as we have noted, quite forgets herself in her description of the girl's death.[12] It is, indeed, only her father and Hamlet who do not yield in this fashion to Ophelia's defenseless innocence. Even Claudius is pitiful to her.

But it is true also that Laertes is—even as Gertrude is—an unstable character. And this Shakespeare paints for us, before we have other proof of it, in the violence and exaggeration of his phrase, and the quick ranging from one extreme to another; from the

> To hell, allegiance! vows, to the blackest devil!
> Conscience and grace, to the profoundest pit!
> I dare damnation . . . .

[12] Cf. p. 133.

through the strained

> O heat, dry up my brains! tears seven times salt
> Burn out the sense of virtue of mine eye! . . .

to—after the more spontaneous

> O rose of May!
> Dear maid, kind sister, sweet Ophelia! . . .

—the conceit of

> Nature is fine in love, and where 'tis fine
> It sends some precious instance of itself
> After the thing it loves.

That image of "the kind life-rendering pelican" is—for him, and at the moment—rather forced and false; and a little later Ophelia is

> A sister driven into desperate terms,
> Whose worth, if praises may go back again,
> Stood challenger on mount of all the age
> For her perfections.

Continually, amid his naturally plainer speech, there come strokes of this sort; till we reach the leaping in the grave, and the

> Now pile your dust upon the quick and dead,
> Till of this flat a mountain you have made
> To o'ertop old Pelion or the skyish head
> Of blue Olympus.

—and Hamlet gibes at his ranting. This is character painting in a poetic medium; and the technique is legitimate.

Save in his soliloquies, the King's verse can hardly be expressive of him, only of the mask he wears, or the occasion he is improving. But this, to a nicety, it is. And such, besides, are the metaphysical resources of the poetry, its powers of suggestion by tone, cadence and rhythm, that enough of what is behind the mask can be implied. The well-balanced sentences of the address to the Council are proper to the occasion; but are they not a thought too well-balanced? The reproof to Hamlet, with each epithet doubling the weight of its noun ("obsequious sorrow . . . obstinate condolement . . . impious stubbornness") and, after a moment, epithet and noun artfully turned about ("heart unfortified

... mind impatient ... understanding simple and unschooled")
is not this a little too calculated; even as the contrasted silky kind
ness to Laertes a minute since has surely been a thought too
smooth?[18] The silky smoothness is still there in the welcome to
"dear Rosencrantz and Guildenstern," the thanks betimes to
"Rosencrantz and gentle Guildenstern." Even the Ambassadors
earn an elaborately considerate

> It likes us well,
> And at our more consider'd time we'll read,
> Answer, and think upon this business.
> Meantime we thank you for your well-took labour:
> Go to your rest; at night we'll feast together:
> Most welcome home!

The revealing soliloquy after the play-scene moves to a very
different measure:

> O, my offence is rank, it smells to heaven;
> It hath the primal eldest curse upon't,
> A brother's murder! ...

The verse throughout this is dry and unyielding. The sense is
inconsiderate of it. It is hammered out, and the accent never falls
happily upon the illuminating word. It gives us the true temper
of the man; acute, capable, tenacious, but insensible.

With Hamlet a plain danger to him, the smooth mask of
kindliness may be dropped. But through the exhibition of his
judicial severity comes the sound of his fear. We hear it in the
too-sustained stresses of

> How dangerous is it that this man goes loose!
> Yet must not we put the strong law on him:
> He's loved of the distracted multitude. . . .

—the leveled lines and the suppression of the caesura, giving us
the sense of a forced draught of thought; even as in

> To bear all smooth and even,
> This sudden sending him away must seem
> Deliberate pause. Diseases desperate grown
> By desperate appliance are relieved
> Or not at all.

---

[18] One is even tempted to imagine that Shakespeare chose that most unlikely
name because it sounded so smoothly here in the King's mouth.

its displacement and the clumsy midline restarting help to suggest
the speaker checked and harassed by—such secret and unavowable
things as do, nevertheless, find some expression in the mere
dentals and hisses of "This sudden sending . . . deliberate pause
. . . Diseases desperate grown . . . desperate appliance . . ." There
is dread and hate in the very vowels and consonants.

But he shows admirable courage and address in his encounter
with the revolted Laertes; and once again we have the gentle
caressing cadences, in the

> What is the cause, Laertes,
> That thy rebellion looks so giant-like?
> . . . Tell me, Laertes,
> Why thou art thus incensed.

and, later, in that

> Laertes, was your father dear to you?

in the insinuating

> Not that I think you did not love your father. . . .

and the winning simplicity of the repeated

> But that I know . . .
> And that I see . . .

—phrase after phrase flowing so smoothly one into the other.
Here are the "witchcraft of his wit" and the "traitorous gifts" in
full play. To just such a tune, indeed, was Gertrude wooed and
won. Hence the importance of the scene in the upbuilding of the
character.

Hamlet, the student and thinker, is much alive to the import
of words. His very first utterance is a bitter pun.[14] And the speech
that follows, with its ". . . inky cloak . . . windy suspiration of
forc'd breath . . . fruitful river in the eye," shows him nice in his
choice of them, for sound and sense combined. He is speaking in
public, of course; deliberately and for effect.

Yet words come easily to him, and he takes an artistic pleasure
in them. Imagination finds them for him quicker than thought
will; there is delight in that. And, stirred by passion, he will pile

---

[14] A pun with Shakespeare, needless to say, was not necessarily a comic thing
at all.

them up, phrase upon phrase, until he seems possessed by words
—and he despises the futile satisfaction of it. For words themselves he distrusts; they also are things which "seem," "the trappings and the suits" of reality, tricking the speaker as often as the
hearer; and they are a weak man's weapon. Hamlet, in fact,
despises in himself one of his chief abilities, and this is a part of
the discord which disables him.

There is other witness to this than the notable

> This is most brave,
> That I, the son of a dear father murder'd,
> Prompted to my revenge by heaven and hell,
> Must, like a whore, unpack my heart with words. . . .

The

> Words, words, words!

thrown at the wordy old Polonius is a lightly ironic echo from the
same source. The phrase used to the Queen:

> and sweet religion makes
> A rhapsody of words . . .

cuts deeper, and deeper still the outmatching of the rhetoric of
Laertes' grief, and the bitter comment:

> Nay, an thou'lt mouth,
> I'll rant as well as thou.

But not all the rational means of expression of which he is
master will suffice him for self-explanation. Very naturally they
will not. How should a mode of speech framed for the conveying
of ordered thought, and common to all the world, be adequate
to the elucidating of the mysterious conflict within him—of this
madness, as it seems to all the world: and he himself has no better
name for it? He needs must express himself in poetry, the language of metaphysical things, in which words can be given almost
as mysterious a potency. But even in this he has to search for
strange images, and break all bounds in his effort to bring to
terms those

> thoughts beyond the reaches of our souls . . .

It is by no convention that Shakespeare casts Hamlet into terms
of poetry—and the prose is as poetic as the verse. He could be

expressed by no other means. For he also is essentially and perforce a poet.

Again, the dramatic value of the verse lies, not in its sense only, but in its melody and rhythm. The first soliloquy:

> O, that this too too solid flesh would melt . . .

is an emotional piece of music. The second:

> O, what a rogue and peasant slave am I! . . .

is a passionate one. Its gestating thought is compressed into the next seven lines, poured out without pause. But the culminating

> For Hecuba!

is given a line's length to itself. Then comes a section of eight lines:

> What's Hecuba to him or he to Hecuba,
> That he should weep for her? What would he do
> Had he the motive and the cue for passion
> That I have? He would drown the stage with tears
> And cleave the general ear with horrid speech,
> Make mad the guilty and appal the free,
> Confound the ignorant, and amaze indeed
> The very faculties of eyes and ears. . . .

Here we have a line and a half, the halfline stayed by a query at the normal point of the caesura. Next comes a sentence accounting for the rest of the line; a full line; and a line hardly begun before it is broken—by a query again, but this time more abruptly. The rest is another unchecked rush—and speech and ear alike deal easily with the simply articulated sentence and the consecutive thought—its ending, however, suspended in midair. Again a culminating, significant two words are given a line's length's value:

> Yet I,

And a four-and-a-half line section follows; the first two—to compensate for the preceding hysteria—ballasted and retarded by the speaker's need to fabricate "dull and muddy-mettled. . . peak like John-a-dreams, unpregnant . . ."[15]

---

[15] The repeated queries, with their effect of indrawn breath, help to suggest hysteria. And such a line as

> What's Hecuba to him or he to Hecuba. . . ?

can, by reversing the natural process of the aspirates, actually be spoken so, no

Thereafter the more regular lines, coming two or three together, serve to send the speech forward on an even keel; while a crowded one intervening, a

> Tweaks me by the nose? gives me the lie i' the throat . . .

or a

> Remorseless, treacherous, lecherous, kindless villain!

bespeak the choking passion; and a line's length allowed (yet again) to no more than a "Ha!" or an "O, vengeance!" tell now of strength unequal to the strain.[16] Q2 even eloquently prints the petering-out of the storm as

> And fall a-cursing, like a very drab; a stallyon, fie upon't! foh!

Then follows thought:

> About, my brain! Hum, I have heard
> That guilty creatures, sitting at a play,
> Have, by the very cunning of the scene,
> Been struck so to the soul that presently
> They have proclaim'd their malefactions. . . .

Metrically, the first line here is two beats short. Dramatically it is, of course, nothing of the kind, for the actor will speak it more or less thus:

> About, my brain! Hum-m-m. I've heard . . .

This, with the four following regular, smoothly running lines (exceptionally regular; "presently" and "malefactions" given their fullest syllabic value), and the succeeding similar five, give us the brain as smoothly at work. Only one of the nine lines is irregular, the center one of these three:

> For murder, though it have no tongue, will speak
> With most miraculous organ. I'll have these players
> Play something like the murder of my father . . . .

---

vocal tone being required. That will have been supplied in the immediately preceding "Hecuba."

[16] "O, vengeance!" is, however, the Folio's only; and personally I suspect it to be an actor's interpolation. The next line in the Folio is deplorably weakened by the insertion of an "I sure," which everyone agrees to reject. In Q2 the thought travels from the abuse of Claudius directly to the "Why, what an Asse am I." The Folio's "O, vengeance!" only prejudices by anticipation the entry of the idea upon

> Prompted to my revenge by heaven and hell. . .

But it is the decisive line. Also its caesura coincides with the end of a sentence. This involves a pause; the effect of that being to shorten the final word to "org'n"—as if it died on the speaker's lips as the capital "I'll have these players" came into his mind. The breath taken between the sentences involves also the shortening of the line's last word to "play'rs"; but that, again, prevents it from prejudicing the more important initial "Play . . ." of the next line.

This ten-and-a-half line section of the evolving of his plan, which has followed the exhausting emotional outbreak, ends halfway through a line upon the

> I know my course.

And, again, the caesura becomes also an interval between sentences, and the line's completing must be contracted more or less to

> The sp'rit that I've seen . . .

—not so ugly a contraction in the speaking as in the writing. Except for the one main division between the speech's passion and its thought, every "section" in it does end in midline, but that minimizes the slight pause involved and helps to keep the speech a single whole. The very first line, in fact, to end with a definite full stop is the last; and that has its rhyme—the first and only one —to stress this:

> The play's the thing
> Wherein I'll catch the conscience of the King.

It is a musical full close.

The "To be or not to be . . ." soliloquy is just such dramatic music also. The sentences, each drawn out over four or five lines, the even cadences, suggest the sustained tension of thought; and the iterated

> To die; to sleep!
> No more; and by a sleep . . .
> To die, to sleep!
> To sleep . . .

the pendulum swing of insoluble doubt.

The scansion test for a line—of Hamlet's or any other—will always be the dramatic one. Take such a passage as

> Touching this vision here,
> It is an honest ghost, that let me tell you:
> For your desire to know what is between us,
> O'ermaster't as you may. And now, good friends,
> As you are friends, scholars and soldiers,
> Give me one poor request.

Hamlet is, for the moment, tartly on the defensive against any prying into his secret. Note the admonitory whiplash in the elided end of each line; in the "vis'n here . . . tell y' . . . between 's." And the "o'ermaster 't"—Q2 actually spells it "Oremastret"—is yet more peremptory. But, to mark his quick apologetic revulsion to friendliness, practically no pause is allowed between this and the

> And now, good friends . . .

The four simple but progressively weighty monosyllables are in themselves an appeal, and they prelude the more persuasive

> As you are friends, scholars and soldiers . . .

But if this is to be syllabically scanned:

> As/ you/ are/ friends/ scho/ lars/ and/ sol/ di/ ers/

it will not be persuasive at all. Hamlet is standing with Horatio and Marcellus, the scholar and the soldier, at either side of him, and appealing to them together and individually. And what he says is

> As y' are friends// schol'rs// and soldy'rs//

—as far as such symbols can make it clear. The effect lies in the weight and significance given to the three capital words by the slight pause allowed for after each; pauses which, by a skilled speaker, can be made to count in the rhythm without imperiling it in the least.

Lastly, for an example of cadence, color and rhythm turned to dramatic account, dictating the reading, defining the meaning of the lines, take the passage in which Horatio and his two companions reveal to Hamlet that his father's spirit is in arms. For malleable ease and nervous vitality combined there is, moreover, probably no piece of verse-dialogue in all Shakespeare to touch it.

HORATIO.   Hail to your lordship!
                      I'm glad to see you well:
HAMLET.   Horatio,—or I do forget myself.

HORATIO.	The same, my lord, and your poor servant ever.
HAMLET.	Sir, my good friend; I'll change that name with you.
	And what make you from Wittenberg, Horatio?
	Marcellus!
MARCELLUS.	My good lord.
HAMLET.	I'm very glad to see you. (*To Bernardo*) Good e'en, sir. . . .

The main rhythm gives us speed without haste, and prevails over the minor lapses from it. Note the elided endings of "lordship" and "Horatio." The first is customary. The second has dramatic point; glad surprise rings out upon the resonant "a," and the practical suppression of the two last vowels allows for the slightest of pauses in which the gladness can be felt. There is the short line for the more perfunctory greeting of Marcellus, and a return to meter for the amending courtesy—which still takes Bernardo in its stride, for Hamlet's thoughts are on Horatio—of

> I'm very glad to see you. Good e'en, sir.

Then, drawing him apart, he can devote himself to his friend:

	But what, in faith, make you from Wittenberg?
HORATIO.	A truant disposition, good my lord.
HAMLET.	I would not hear your enemy say so;
	Nor shall you do mine ear that violence,
	To make it truster of your own report
	Against yourself; I know you are no truant.
	But what is your affair in Elsinore?
	We'll teach you to drink deep ere you depart.
HORATIO.	My lord, I came to see your father's funeral.
HAMLET.	I pri'thee, do not mock me, fellow-student;
	I think it was to see my mother's wedding.
HORATIO.	Indeed, my lord, it followed hard upon.
HAMLET.	Thrift, thrift, Horatio! the funeral baked meats
	Did coldly furnish forth the marriage tables.
	Would I had met my dearest foe in heaven
	Or ever I had seen that day, Horatio!
	My father! Methinks I see my father!
HORATIO.	O, where, my lord?
HAMLET.	In my mind's eye, Horatio.
HORATIO.	I saw him once; he was a goodly king.

HAMLET. He was a man, take him for all in all,
I shall not look upon his like again.

The rhythm flows easily and evenly; with Horatio, and only with him, is Hamlet continuingly at ease.

Note the effect made by the double echo of the unusual cadence of Horatio's

My lord, I came to see your father's funeral.

There is irony in the very refrain:

I pri'thee, do not mock me, fellow-student;
I think it was to see my mother's wedding.

And, while the words themselves say little, the strict scansion, that firm, five times repeated "d," and the bitten final "n" of

Indeed, my lord, it followed hard upon.

bespeak a Horatio sternly if discreetly of Hamlet's mind about it.

The short space allowed in the line to "Thrift, thrift . . ." tells a Hamlet that, despite their ten consonants to two vowels, he is to speak the words lightly. There is distaste in the very "b . . . k . . . d . . . m . . . ts" of the "funeral baked meats," with which it more levelly ends, and contempt in the repeated "f's" of the "furnish forth." The last line of the speech must be scanned dramatically:

My fath'r!// Methinks I see/ my fath'r!//

—more or less. Allot it its ten written syllables, it will prove practically unspeakable.

Note Hamlet's frequent repetition hereabouts of his friend's name. The word is gentle in itself, and he is always at his gentlest with Horatio; nor ever, till he is dying, gentler than at this moment, for he is no longer lonely in his grief, and the deadlier blow has not yet befallen him.

This section of the scene ends with three simple lines; their rhythm exact; their words—three excepted—of one syllable, fit frame for their simplicity of content. The first line is Horatio's

I saw him once; he was a goodly king.

and, once more, two succeeding lines from Hamlet repeat the cadence; but accordantly, not ironically, this time:

He was a man, take him for all in all,
I shall not look upon his like again.

The three curt final "king . . . all . . . again" give a certain sense
of finality too. But we know, with Horatio, that here is rather a
beginning than an end.[17] And this repetition with a difference of
the three-line duet, the closer drawn accord between the two, the
touch of a finality which we know is none, make quietly arresting
preparation for the revealing:

> My lord, I think I saw him yesternight.

This fires the train; and from this point the excitement mounts
step by step to the scene's crisis, Hamlet's

> I will watch to-night. . . .

The text embodies clear directions to the actors. Hamlet's

> Saw! Who?

is allowed the length of a line. His share of the next line, the
echoed

> The King my father!

must—the verse demanding an elided "fath'r"—fade away into
breathless wonder. Horatio, with his

> Upon the witness of these gentlemen . . .

brings Marcellus and Bernardo into focus; and the action is at
once broadened and strengthened; for, the tale told, Hamlet will
have the three to attend to and question. The subsequent dialogue
between the four of them falls at first into the regular rhythm of
the verse, though the lines are broken:

HORATIO.	I knew your father;
	These hands are not more like.
HAMLET.	But where was this?
MARCELLUS.	My lord, upon the platform where we watched.
HAMLET.	Did you not speak to it?
HORATIO.	My lord, I did;
	But answer made it none. . . .
HAMLET.	Indeed, indeed, sirs, but this troubles me.
	Hold you the watch to-night?

[17] Incidentally, this echoed cadence, as a test, condemns the reading, once
beloved of actors:

> He was a *man*. Take him for all in all . . .

by which Hamlet was oddly made to imply that kings as kings were not of much
account.

MARCELLUS.	}	We do, my lord.
BERNARDO.		
HAMLET.	Armed, say you?	
MARCELLUS.	}	Armed, my lord.
BERNARDO.		
HAMLET.	From top to toe?	
MARCELLUS.	} My lord, from head to foot.	
BERNARDO.		
HAMLET.	Then saw you not his face? . . .	

from which point—the rushed "saw'y'not" initiating it—the beat
degenerates into a scurry, with the stiffening here and there of a
more regular line to prevent the rhythm from disintegrating altogether. The quick unhesitating give-and-take *within* the continuous rhythm gives us Hamlet's mind keen to absorb all that the
three can tell him as fast as they can tell it; the *breaking* of the
rhythm marks the breaking of this close contact of attention; and
his lapse to such *detachment* from it as

> Very like, very like! Stayed it long?

shows us his thought questing beyond their ken.

His mind made up, the verse returns to the consistent strength of

> If it assume my noble father's person,
> I'll speak to it, though hell itself should gape
> And bid me hold my peace. I pray you all,
> If you have hitherto concealed this sight,
> Let it be tenable in your silence still . . . .

which is maintained to the scene's end.[18]

~~~~~~~~~

[18] Neither Q2 nor Folio displays this dialogue as verse, nor, it may well be, did
Shakespeare in his manuscript. The construction would be clear in his mind, and
he could tell the actors at rehearsal how to piece their bits together. This could
not be done for them in their "parts," which would contain their own lines and
cues only. And if he wrote these passages (and the many similar ones) as Q2
vertically displays them, that was probably for the convenience of the prompter,
who had not then to cast his eye clear across the line from *Hamlet* to "From top
to toe?" or from *Horatio* to "In faith," at a continual risk of error during rehearsals,
when prompting is often continuous; and the man who had to copy out the parts
would be liable to make similar mistakes. Were Shakespeare not at rehearsals, the
prompter and the actors might here and there be hard put to it to reconstruct the
verse—even as the editors have sometimes been since. Yet the actors would have
highly trained ears; and the rhythm, if they yielded to it, would assert itself. But
compare this with the careful setting out of (say) certain scenes in Jonson's *Sejanus*.

The Characters

FRANCISCO AND A FEW FUNCTIONARIES

THE minor characters in Hamlet are not highly developed, nor—
but for two or three—very sharply individualized. There is more
than one reason for this. They may be figures from the old play,
whom Shakespeare has not been at the pains to transform. But
even if he has, or let the character be originally his own, should
it move in Hamlet's orbit—and what in the play does not?—it
will tend to turn satellite, moon to his sun. Opposition of character to character is the very life of drama. Yet even of the King
and Queen, of Polonius, Laertes and Ophelia, it may be said that,
in contact with Hamlet, they put up little more than is needed to
keep them their place. We learn most about them when they are
free of him; yet of some consciousness of him they are never free.

But Shakespeare can by now, if he will, give his actor matter
enough for a vivid sketch of character in fifty words. Francisco,
at the play's opening, speaks just fifty-five. He is on guard. Bernardo approaches; so nervous—we learn why in a moment—that
he does not, as he should, wait to be challenged, but lets out a

> Who's there?
> Nay, answer me; stand, and unfold yourself.
> Long live the King!
> Bernardo?
> He.
> You come most carefully upon your hour.
> 'Tis now struck twelve; get thee to bed, Francisco.
> For this relief much thanks; 'tis bitter cold,
> And I am sick at heart.
> Have you had quiet guard?
>   Not a mouse stirring.

In that short swift exchange between the two, place, time and
season are given us, Bernardo's strung-up nerves, his arrival so
carefully upon his hour lest the Ghost appear to Francisco, who
evidently knows nothing and had better be kept ignorant; and
we have the sharply bitten-in sketch of the "honest soldier," too,
brusque of manner, terse of speech, not insensitive to the haunted
atmosphere, but choosing to account for feeling "sick at heart" by
the plain fact that " 'tis bitter cold."

Nor is this too curious an analysis to be valid. If the ordinary reader does not find it all in the eleven lines—but he can if he will look—well, they were not written for reading. If it be said that the spectator, in the few minutes of their speaking and acting, cannot take in so much, this is not quite the question either. We are not asked to think the matter out, nor given the time to. What we have here, packed into the dialogue, are stage directions to the actors; it is material for the effect they are to make on us, and this effect will be, in the strict meaning of the word, sensational; and if we did, at the moment, analyze the sensation and realize how it was made, the effect of it would be largely lost.[1]

We see no more of Francisco; and such vivid minor characters are apt to disappear from a play when they have served their sensational turn. Barnardine in *Measure for Measure*, sent to his death to remind us of the sinister realities of that so-called comedy; Cinna the poet and the jigging rhymester in Brutus' tent, dashing revolution and war with ridicule of the worth of poetry in such times—to elaborate these lively sketches would give them a distracting importance, to prolong their existence merely would commensurately diminish their value.

To another category of minor parts belong the Ambassadors and the Players. They are units in the machinery of the action, functionaries, little more. Characterless characters of the kind are to be found in every play. The individualities of the actors lend them individuality enough. They furnish something of that indifferent background which life itself provides to all poignant spectacles. Voltimand and Cornelius are appropriately colorless. The message from Norway is a formal one; they are the mere instruments of its delivery. Upon the Players Shakespeare does throw enough reflected life—reflected in Hamlet's kindly greeting to them, in his

> Dost thou hear me, old friend? . . .

and his care for their good treatment—to remind us that players are human beings too.

---

[1] Though it is, of course, possible, without wholly sacrificing the sensation, to gain a consciously critical pleasure in the art of the business too.

HORATIO

Horatio dwells in Hamlet's shadow, yet he is very much himself; and (again) few things are more difficult in drama than to give a character standing of its own, except by setting it in opposition to others, and enkindling it, so to speak, by friction.

But he is established in our knowledge before ever Hamlet appears. He dominates the first scene. Not by any insistence upon himself; that would belie him. It is in his talk of the chances of war with Norway, in his attitude towards the Ghost, that he incidentally discloses himself as a conservatively patriotic and educated gentleman. He takes pride in the dead king's fame and disparages the lawless young Fortinbras; and besides Marcellus' word for it that he is a scholar, we have him citing his Plutarch. He is level-headed and open-minded. The Ghost, when he heard of it, was a "fantasy"; but seeing is believing. Yet he has neither fear of it, for he stays it and speaks to it; nor any superstitious respect for it, since he encourages the frightened Marcellus to strike at it with his partisan. For him it will be what it is proved to be. Yet he is sensitive too. He steadies his nerves for the second sight of it; but he trembled and turned pale when it first appeared. And in his final

> But look, the morn, in russet mantle clad,
> Walks o'er the dew of yon high eastern hill . . . .

a gentle spirit speaks.

MARCELLUS; BERNARDO

Marcellus and Bernardo can best be dealt with in a parenthesis here, for they are what they are as a part of the scheme of this first scene. They strike each his complementary and contrasting note in it. Of the three men Bernardo (though nervous enough at the outset) is the stolidest. Horatio looks to him for some mitigating of Marcellus' fantastic tale. He observes the "thing" when it appears more exactly than do the others, and, a moment later, is bantering the converted sceptic:

> How now, Horatio! you tremble and look pale.
> Is not this something more than fantasy?

For the rest, he says what he has to say as plainly and shortly as possible.

Marcellus is of finer temper, and the whole mysterious business has him the more sharply on edge. What does it portend? He has not dared speak to the Ghost himself. When Horatio, armored in scholarship, does, and it will not answer, he fears it is offended. As timorously as desperately he makes to strike at it with his partisan, and at once repents:

> We do it wrong, being so majestical,
> To offer it the show of violence. . .

The supernatural is very real to him:

> Some say that ever 'gainst that season comes
> Wherein our Saviour's birth is celebrated,
> The bird of dawning singeth all night long;
> And then, they say, no spirit dare stir abroad;
> The nights are wholesome; then no planets strike,
> No fairy takes, nor witch hath power to charm,
> So hallowed and so gracious is the time.

—to which Horatio answers:

> So I have heard, and do in part believe it.

saving himself, even at this eerie moment, by the "in part" from too much credulity. Marcellus, we notice also, is anxious for Hamlet to be told; it is he who—to turn their minds from the Ghost— sets Horatio recounting the reasons for the "strict and most observant watch" and all the "post-haste and rummage in the land"; he who, in the later scene, at its most poignant moment, breaks out with

> Something is rotten in the state of Denmark.

As we watch the scene, intent on the story it tells, we may not notice—may not positively remark—such points and aspects of character. But (once again) these things are stage directions to the actors, material by which the scene can be convincingly built up. The matter-of-fact Bernardo, who has seen what he has seen; Marcellus, alive to the mystery beyond; Horatio, won from doubt to belief—within that likely combination we find our own transient belief in what we see.

All good dramatic writing has this double content; the overt, with which the immediate effect is made; the covert, in which the actor finds guidance for the modeling of the figure by which that effect is to be made. And the less prominent the character, the less imposing its immediate effects, the greater the need for this modeling to be complete.

HORATIO, *resumed*

Hamlet's affectionate welcome of him adds to Horatio's status; and he adds to it himself by the quiet good sense with which he responds to Hamlet's hysterical treatment of him after the Ghost's vanishing.

Thereafter he disappears from the play for the best part of an hour; until Hamlet—and Shakespeare—need him again, and he is conjured, as if from nowhere, by a simple

What ho, Horatio!

—and the very simplicity of the business somehow suggests that he has been within call all the time. Shakespeare restores him to importance by the as simple means of giving Hamlet, then and there, twenty lines to speak in his praise. The method is nakedly simple but, as it is employed here, dramatically sound. For we have Hamlet's relief and gratitude, as he turns from false friends to this true one,[2] finding spontaneous utterance. And we learn of Horatio what we could hardly—since he has no direct part in the action—learn from him: that he is poor and what the world calls a failure, yet that good and ill fortune alike leave him unmoved (this praise also, save for one gentle protest; he is as little self-regardful as that). For all of which Hamlet loves him and trusts both his judgment and faith. His task now is to stand, silent and apart, keeping, through the acting of *The Murder of Gonzago*, a steadier watch upon the King than Hamlet's can be; and this (seemingly irrelevant) expansion of his character will lend to the still figure, as we watch it, a fresh quality and strength.

But, for self-expression, Shakespeare gives him thrifty measure indeed. Forty-eight words for moral support of Hamlet in this crisis (that is the exact allowance for the play-scene and its sequel); after which he disappears again, to reappear only when Hamlet has gone to England. And though, watching Ophelia and the first to hear of his friend's return, he is then quite an important figure, he speaks, except for the reading of a letter, exactly

2 Cf. p. 83.

twelve lines. Were there no more to say about it, his presenting is a masterpiece of dramatic economy.

From the instant of Hamlet's return, Horatio never leaves his side again, and the faithful watchful presence now becomes as eloquent as any speech. Two perceptive sentences stand out from his encouragement of the anodyne talk with the Clown, and when he has heard of the events on the ship he warns Hamlet that the King must soon learn of them too. He is glad to have him distracted by the ridiculous Osric. He sees how the long strain is telling on him, counsels him to forgo the fencing match; since he will not, can only stand apart again in watchful silence—to exclaim once when the first blood flows. He helps bar the King's escape. Then, death nearing, Hamlet calls to him.

Till now he has responded to princely professions of affection with a "your poor servant" or a "good my lord." Now he asserts himself and his love by a fierce eloquence of deed, in which a man that even Hamlet has not known—and by no means the equable philosopher—stands suddenly revealed.[8] But, the moment past, he lets the poisoned cup be wrested from him, and vows himself, silently and for the last time, to his friend's service. We hear that service begun. And the Horatio who will speak

> to the yet unknowing world
> How these things came about . . .

is a man who has grown in stature under our eyes.

ROSENCRANTZ AND GUILDENSTERN

Rosencrantz and Guildenstern are set and sustained in sharp contrast to Horatio; false friends against true. The difference extends to all they are, the three of them. Horatio; poor and unself-seeking, the student, the philosopher, with his loyal respect for the old king:

> our valiant Hamlet—
> For so this side of our known world esteem'd him . . .

—he had just once seen him living; he journeyed from Wittenberg to stand, a simple looker-on, at his funeral; and after, it was not for him to intrude upon the son's, upon the Prince's, grief. And

---

[8] Though there was a passing hint of him in the Horatio who reproved his Prince for these "wild and whirling words."

Hamlet's greeting to him as "good friend" and "fellow-student" shows him a chosen friend, and of recent days.[4] It is during his absence from the action that "dear Rosencrantz and Guildenstern" come to pervade it. They have been sent for by the King. They, then, are approved of by the new regime; and

> being of so young days brought up with him,
> And since so neighboured to his youth and humour . . .

being, besides (with their supple "gentry") fitter companions for a prince, will they not be taken even nearer to Hamlet's heart?[5] He greets them, with much the same impulsive affection, as "my excellent good friends." But how different—even before suspicion has kindled in him—the smart chop-logic of the talk from the confident refuge he took in Horatio's understanding! The false relation hardens as he screens himself from their prying by oracular evasions and trivial gossip about the Players. He cannot flatly and finally dismiss them; it is a princely penalty to be so "waited upon," and to have to repay treachery with courtesy. But their second intrusion on him provokes, as we noted, his summons to that other friend, and the fervent

> Horatio, thou art e'en as just a man
> As e'er my conversation cop'd withal.

And the contrast here will be heightened by the very look of the three; the smiling, point-device courtiers making their congee on the one side, the grave, sober-suited, simple-mannered student appearing on the other.

From their summoning of Hamlet to the Queen to the departure with him—their own fatal departure—for England, Shakespeare endows the couple with more and with a somewhat more sinister importance. Pretense to good comradeship is over. There is a touch of regret for it in Hamlet's

> why do you go about to recover the wind of me, as if you would
> drive me into a toil?

but little more than cant, one fears, in Rosencrantz' plaintive

> My lord, you once did love me.

---

[4] Shakespeare, in this part of the play, is still thinking of Hamlet as of student's age.

[5] He speaks of them later on as "schoolfellows," boyhood friends, therefore; and this Horatio specifically is not.

The sprightly schoolfellows, who were "to draw him on to pleasures," are now plainly his enemy's instruments; and he soon finds himself no better than a captive in their hands. Then their tone, quite appropriately, changes:

> What have you done, my lord, with the dead body? . . . Tell us where 'tis, that we may take it thence, and bear it to the chapel. . . . My lord, you must tell us where the body is, and go with us to the King.

That he goes into exile practically their prisoner is clear from the fact that—and for the best of reasons!—it is they who carry, not he, the King's sealed commission; he has to burgle their cabin to secure it. But there is no hint that they knew of its contents.

Horatio (as if to complete the pattern of their relation to him) is allowed a grim comment on their fate:

> So Guildenstern and Rosencrantz go to't.

And Hamlet, hardened to his task by now, callously caps it:

> Why, man, they did make love to this employment;
> They are not near my conscience; their defeat
> Does by their own insinuation grow.
> 'Tis dangerous when the baser nature comes
> Between the pass and fell incensed points
> Of mighty opposites.

Fit epitaph for them, doubtless; and the fate of the nonentity who yields himself in complacent ignorance to evil employment has its due place in tragedy. And if we feel that they might as well have been let lapse, harmless and unharmed, from the story, it will not be so much in compunction for them as because, dramatically, they seem hardly worth the killing.

As parts to be played, unhappy actors cast for them will protest that they are among the very worst in all Shakespeare. They must not, of course, be judged by what a producer's blue pencil may leave of them; though, as it happens, they are too closely knit into the action for this to be very trenchantly wielded. But do all that legitimately may be done with them, they will yet remain, one fears, superior puppets; for Shakespeare himself has not given them life. That he could have by a touch or so, and without making too much of them, the comparison with Horatio shows. The deficiency is explicable. He did not, I fancy, to begin with, mean them to be more in themselves than supple, superficial nonentities. They are less even than that; a single nonentity split into two. Again we see why. One false friend to balance the one true friend, and to make but one more in the series of decoys, Polonius, Ophelia, Gertrude—the mere pattern would be monotonous. An occasional trio is a welcome relief from successive duets and solos. Nor could Hamlet come off from a single inquisitor of the sort as he does from the pair, lightly playing one against the other, using them as springboard for his antic disposition. So far they suffice. But the stress of the action sequent to the play-scene is too hard on them dramatically. They are not quite of the right stuff for the treacherous embassy to England, for Hamlet's escort to his death. Shakespeare may be feeling so when he imposes on them those two surprisingly solid speeches—which do not fit them, which only leave them, therefore, looking more puppetlike than before.[6] But at that crisis of the play, with everything in rapid movement, he can spare them no more consideration. They remain, then, two rather lifeless strands in its lively fabric.

POLONIUS

As if, again, for contrast, two family groups are presented to us: Claudius, Hamlet, Gertrude, united and divided by evil; Polonius, Laertes, Ophelia, happy together in their ignorance that this same evil is already working to destroy them. The play exists within a framework of these contrasts of character and situation, as must every play more or less, for it is the stress of them which gives it stability. Here is the second dimension—so to call it— which the dramatic form needs and pure narrative does not. Its scheme need not be made very patent. We should probably be left about as conscious of it as we are of the comparable means by which some fine building is kept erect; we feel secure when we stand in it, but do not forget its beauty because of that. But without these means to stability, building or play, for all their beauty, will alike collapse.

We can, I think, see Shakespeare changing his mind a little about Polonius. In his first scene (not to count the single speech at the Council) he is far from being a "tedious old fool." His

------

[6] The point is further discussed on p. 98.

injunctions to Laertes and Ophelia are clear and terse, and contain sound worldly wisdom. The change comes with the charge to Reynaldo; and hence, perhaps, the seemingly undue length allowed to that minor matter; our first impressions of the character must be corrected. After the resolution into the more comic key we have him spontaneously and abundantly himself; though the mere abundance is gradually pruned, for once the garrulity has been demonstrated, the effect of it can be gained without much indulgence in the thing itself.

His adjusted place in the play's character-scheme soon becomes plain. Hamlet doubts and delays, questions and suffers. Claudius, all outward candor, keeps his secret close and moves surely to his ends. Polonius is the complacent wiseacre, infatuate in opinion, precipitate in action—and usually wrong. He is not wholly or obviously a fool, nor externally ridiculous at all. He can occupy his high place with dignity enough—only now and then calling pomposity to his aid—so long as everybody else will keep theirs. He is for order and degree, whether he must be telling his own daughter that

> Lord Hamlet is a prince, out of thy star;
> This must not be. . . .

or simply in using the Players

> according to their desert.

He is loyal to the powers that be:

> Assure you, my good liege,
> I hold my duty as I hold my soul,
> Both to my God and to my gracious king. . . .

—as he will, with like fervency, once have assured him whom Claudius has doubly succeeded (for clearly he has held his old place); nor is he the man to have been pained by his "dear majesty" the Queen's "o'er-hasty marriage."

He is kindly; his manner to his retainer "good Reynaldo" is most affable. As a man of the world he will not idealize his fellow-creatures; and at Ophelia's defense of Hamlet—

> My lord, he hath importuned me with love
> In honourable fashion.

—he scoffs. Yet he is tolerant, as a man of the world must be; and when it appears that he was wrong—and he ungrudgingly admits it—his only comment is a perfunctory

> I feared he did but trifle,
> And meant to wreck thee. . . .

Nor do we gather that he will be gravely displeased if Reynaldo does discover Laertes to have been

> drinking, fencing, swearing, quarrelling,
> Drabbing . . .

as long as no great scandal results. For his last sly injunction—something of a comedown from the earlier, sententious "to thine own self be true"—is a

> And let him ply his music.[7]

Of the same pattern as this spying upon Laertes is his "loosing" of Ophelia, decoylike, to Hamlet, Claudius and he to be the "lawful espials" here. His intentions are excellent. To cure this madness one must first know its cause, and he suspects nothing sinister in that. He does not stop to consider that it may be somewhat ignoble, a little cruel, to put his daughter to such a use. It is as like him that, having baited the trap with her and placed a prayer book in her hands, the sight of her, docile in guile, should prompt the incongruous platitude:

> We are oft to blame in this—
> 'Tis too much proved!—that with devotion's visage
> And pious action we do sugar o'er
> The devil himself.

and as like him that, when he and Claudius emerge disappointed from their hiding-place, he ignores her distress.

He is old, of course; and in such shallow natures feelings desiccate with age. He looks back whimsically to when

> in my youth I suffered much extremity for love. . . .[8]

He does not—if the very slightest of touches is there to tell us so

---

[7] Which I can hardly believe is meant to disclose a last moment's interest in this aspect of Laertes' education. It is the equivalent, surely, of "Let him go his own way and enjoy himself." We have a similar, better known saying in "face the music."

[8] He is definitely one of Shakespeare's "old" men, no account being taken of his likelier age as the father of Laertes and, as it concerns the women characters, Ophelia. See p. 226, note, where the question of this convention is discussed.

—find even the sight of mimic suffering to his taste; for, when the Player pauses in the tale of Hecuba, comes his:

> Look, whether he has not turned his colour and has tears in 's eyes. Prithee, no more.

and whenever he can so turn his busy mind from statecraft:

> he's for a jig or a tale of bawdry, or he sleeps.

Poor Polonius! Were this no other than the world he has so successfully learned to live in, where words are potent and ambassadors correctly come and go, where one so pleasantly "hunts . . . the trail of policy," or may with a "bait of falsehood" take a "carp of truth," and

> of wisdom and of reach,
> With windlasses and with assays of bias,
> By indirections find directions out . . .

where human nature must perforce become

> As 'twere a thing a little soiled i' the working . . .

but to no worse effect than that a prince may seduce your daughter and your son be debauched in Paris—were life, in sum, simply the sort of clever game he thinks it, he then would be the man he so complacently feels himself to be, the tried and wise "assistant for a state," who has never

> positively said ' 'tis so,'
> When it proved otherwise . . .

whose never-lacking advice has only to be followed for all to be well! But Shakespeare shows us, by a harsher light, a very different picture; of a silly old gentleman pettily maneuvering among passions and forces that are dark to him. No one wishes him ill. But he will meddle. And at last a sword thrust, meant for his master, incontinently ends him. For an elegy:

> Thou find'st to be too busy is some danger.

And as if to mark his pitiful futility his corpse is let lie there, eavesdropping still, while the revealing quarrel rages between mother and son. Then it is lugged away, like so much carrion.

It is a nicely mischievous touch that at the University he "did enact"—of all possible parts!—Julius Cæsar.

LAERTES

In the two earlier scenes before he leaves for Paris, Laertes is a more or less conventional figure. But even here—in his elder-brother moralizing, and the import of Ophelia's demure

> But, good my brother,
> Do not, as some ungracious pastors do,
> Show me the steep and thorny way to heaven,
> Whilst, like a puff'd and reckless libertine,
> Himself the primrose path of dalliance treads,
> And recks not his own rede.

and in Polonius' hints to Reynaldo of how he is likely to be found passing his time, and that suggestion of

> The flash and outbreak of a fiery mind,
> A savageness in unreclaimed blood. . .

—there is preparation for the contrast to be established later between him and Hamlet, between the pensive idealist and full-blooded confident youth.

When he returns Hamlet, the irresolute bungler, has gone—presumably to his death—leaving disaster behind him; Polonius slain, Ophelia "driven into desperate terms." In his place uprises this gallant fellow, carried into the palace upon a wave of rebellion, but, disdainful of such aid, facing the King alone:

> To hell, allegiance! vows, to the blackest devil!
> Conscience and grace, to the profoundest pit!
> I dare damnation. To this point I stand,
> That both the worlds I give to negligence,
> Let come what comes; only I'll be revenged
> Most throughly for my father.

What—after so much trimming and veering, mining and counter-mining—could be finer? What more tender too than his grief?

> O rose of May!
> Dear maid, kind sister, sweet Ophelia!

And when—the true culprit known and reported to be again within his reach—he is ready straightway.

> To cut his throat i' the church.

even that makes pleasant contrast with Hamlet's late refusal to kill the praying Claudius lest he should spare him hell-fire. Yet the next moment this "very noble youth" is bettering an already scoundrelly plan to assure him his revenge with a secretly sharpened sword by proposing to poison it too. Conventional virtue strangely belied; our edifying young counselor of the earlier scene with his sister turned the wrong side out indeed!

Shakespeare may not have had the anomaly in mind from the beginning; it suffices him to have a character here in hand that is capable of it. His purpose, at its crudest, is to swing our sympathy back to Hamlet, Laertes losing on the balance; but he will enrich his character-scheme in doing so.[9] It looks very much as if—lest, misled by his self-depreciation, we misinterpret Hamlet's failings—he now wished to show us what moral instability may really be, and to what sort of nature it properly belongs. *Morally* unstable Hamlet is not. His

> thinking too precisely on the event. . .

may sap his resolution, but it sharpens, not blunts, his sense of right and wrong. Laertes—swayed by every passion and rash in action; suspicious, as all unreasoning people are, but the more blind to flattery—proves wax in the clever fingers of the King. He is too ignorant of himself to be, by that banal precept, true to himself, and he can be cajoled and provoked into the ignoblest crime.

The man of action, with his

> O, thou vile king,
> Give me my father! . . .
> How came he dead? I'll not be juggled with. . . .

is soon maneuvered to an intellectual standstill; and, when grief for his sister has also worked on him, he becomes the easiest of dupes. Claudius, finding use for him, first flatters him with confidences and—deadlier than plain praise—by reporting others' praise of him; then so stings him with doubts of the worth of his passion and grief that the moment-old honest welcome of the news of Hamlet's return—

---

[9] In Q1 it is Claudius who proposes to poison the sword; Laertes merely acquiesces. Whether this shows us Shakespeare's first intention or is (as current theory about Q1 requires, if it is to be consistently applied; but need it be?) a part of the pirate's bungling, the improvement in the true text is plain.

> But let him come;
> It warms the very sickness in my heart
> That I shall live and tell him to his teeth,
> 'Thus didest thou.'

—is replaced, not simply by consent to an underhand trick, which would itself normally be abhorrent to him, but—for defiant answer to these taunting doubts—by that

> I will do 't:
> And for that purpose I'll anoint my sword. . . .
> I'll touch my point
> With this contagion, that, if I gall him slightly,
> It may be death.[10]

Lured into one infamy, from pure bravado he must outpass it with another.

Committed to such partnership, he is in a trap, from which, till it is too late, he will not have the moral courage to escape. Yet he is no murderer at heart; and, when he follows Ophelia to her grave, while Hamlet's

> That is Laertes, a very noble youth. . . .

may echo a little ironically in our ears, since we know what is brewing, the one-time truth of it is mirrored, and is meant to be, in his anguish, in the tender

> Lay her i' the earth,
> And from her fair and unpolluted flesh
> May violets spring!

—even in his flashing attack, with a

> The devil take thy soul!

upon his outrageous rival in mourning, whose "wicked deed" it truly is that has wrought the ill.

He and his enemy pulled apart, he has to stand and listen to strange things; to that

---

[10] Claudius, it is worth noting, has no great confidence either in the young man's self-control—how should he have!—or powers of deception. Laertes is to keep close within his chamber until the moment of the fencing match. And he is warned:

> If this should fail,
> And that our drift look through our bad performance,
> 'Twere better not assayed. . . .

> I lov'd Ophelia; forty thousand brothers
> Could not, with all their quantity of love,
> Make up my sum. . . .

—no vulgar seducer's cry; to the still stranger

> Hear you, sir;
> What is the reason that you use me thus?
> I lov'd you ever. . . .

And he is not the man to unriddle them. But when he is reminded of what his very effective answer is to be by the King's privy

> Strengthen your patience in our last night's speech. . . .

he does not respond to that either; he goes glumly away.

It is again hard listening for him when, all being ready for the treacherous match, Hamlet, before King and Court, craves his pardon for the wrong done:

> Give me your pardon, sir; I've done you wrong;
> But pardon 't, as you are a gentleman. . . .
> Sir, in this audience,
> Let my disclaiming from a purpos'd evil
> Free me so far in your most generous thoughts,
> That I have shot mine arrow o'er the house,
> And hurt my brother.

—and to this he must reply. A glance exchanged with the King will tell us by whose help he has concocted the quibbling

> I am satisfied in nature,
> Whose motive, in this case, should stir me most
> To my revenge: but in my terms of honour. . .

(honor!) which hardens, as before, to the bravado of

> But till that time
> I do receive your offer'd love like love,
> And will not wrong it.

We need not be surprised that he fences ill. He is at odds with himself even as Hamlet was. And since he cannot fairly come near his man with the poisoned blade, his stroke itself must be treacherous—which featherweight addition to his guilt goes, he finds, "almost" against his conscience; a flashlight upon his moral disorder. But, indeed, into such a tangle of wickedness has he got himself that, when the tables are suddenly turned on him, what we hear in his

> Why, as a woodcock to mine own springe, Osric,
> I am justly kill'd with mine own treachery.

is something like thankfulness. He pays his penalty. He sees to it that Claudius does not escape. Hamlet forgives him, and we are meant to, also.

OPHELIA

But while Laertes deserves his fate, and Polonius invites his by his meddling, of what is Ophelia guilty? At worst, of a single lie told to a madman for his good. We may call her docility a fault, when, as she is bid, she shuts herself away from Hamlet; but how not trust to her brother's care for her and her father's wisdom? How even question the part she is made to play later when not her father only but the King and Queen themselves prepare her for it?

She is no fool. Shakespeare shows us that to begin with by the touch of mischievous humor with which she counters Laertes' homily. And beneath the dutifully diffident

> I do not know, my lord, what I should think.

her feeling is clear that Hamlet's love for her is wholly honorable. As to which she is right. But she must obey her father.

"Many a day"—whatever that may mean in the calendar of frustrate love—passes before the two meet again. She has been sending back his letters and refusing to see him; till, one day as she sits sewing in her closet, he suddenly breaks in upon her, dumbly distraught, suffering, mad.

> Mad—for thy love!
>   My lord, I do not know;
> But truly I do fear it.

By parting her from him, then, they have brought this guilt upon her. And next they must needs thrust her in his path again, so that, since her "good beauties" did the harm, her virtues—the kindly Queen hopes—may somehow

> bring him to his wonted way again . . .

When Hamlet discovers and speaks to her she naturally says nothing of their last strange meeting. One does not remind a madman of his madness; though, indeed, he seems sane enough now. She offers—as any girl would—to set the seal on their parting by giving him back the presents he gave her, the verses he wrote her; "ill at these numbers" though he said he was, they were music to her. If he will not take them back things may then begin to mend between them. So simple are her tactics. He does refuse them; but it is with a harsh, unexpected

> No, not I;
> I never gave you aught.

which is like a blow in the face to her, an unkindness far outpassing her obedient repelling of his letters since, and refusals to see him. For it is a denial that he ever did love her—the estranged lover's cruelest revenge.

Why does she not tell him that she only obeyed her father in shutting herself away from him? At the mere thought that he never loved her she would have no heart to. She puts the little packet of his gifts down somewhere; let happen to it what will. He rouses her pride, too, by his sudden sardonic

> Ha, ha! are you honest? . . . Are you fair?

And if there is a certain self-consciousness in the dignity of her

> What means your lordship?

are not those eavesdroppers chiefly to blame? Once more, and perforce, she is obeying her father; but—though surely they all only mean him well—it is to more questionable purpose now.

Hamlet has his secret from her too. Stung by her seeming fickleness he may have been, but that was not the death of his love for her. He cannot tell her of his mother's guilt; nor is there any but this riddling way of telling her what it has meant to him, of his lost faith not simply in womanhood, but in himself where womanhood is concerned:

> I did love you once. . . . You should not have believed me; for virtue cannot so inoculate our old stock but we shall relish of it; I loved you not.

So her father was right when he scoffed at her tale of her wooing "in honorable fashion." She accepts disillusionment with a miserable

> I was the more deceived.

What with this and with what follows, his bitter

> Get thee to a nunnery; why wouldst thou be a breeder of sin-
> ners? . . .

she might well by now be forgetting the eavesdroppers and her
task here. She is sharply reminded of them by the abrupt, inconsequent, fiercely suspicious

> Where's your father?

What on the instant should she answer? He is "mad," and there
is danger in his looks. She tells her loyally defensive lie:

> At home, my lord.

He knows, as he puts the question, that Polonius is hiding there;
he does not positively know that she knows it and is lying to him,
nor greatly care to know. It is enough that she is a part of the
conspiracy of evil around him, and, in her very womanhood, of
the "wantonness and ignorance," the lusts of the flesh, in which
the evil first took root:

> Go to, I'll no more on 't; it hath made me mad. . . .

For her, the well-meant appeasing lie has merely set a match to
his madness, which now rages over her meaninglessly. Does *she*
paint, jig, amble, lisp? She prays aloud for him. And her thought,
when he has left her, is of the "noble mind . . . o'erthrown," only
later of her "deject and wretched" self. She stays silent and scarce-
regarded while the King and her father, emerging from their
hiding and having had their use of her, discuss weightier matters.
But behind that strained mask of grief her own sanity is already
wavering. When they have gone she goes quietly away.[11]

---

[11] For a discussion of the contradictory stage directions, see p. 80, note.

One can detect in Hamlet here a slight psychological incongruity, for which the
old story or the old play may be responsible, the episode in it which gives us the
"fair woman" sent to seduce him and his secret from him. There is nothing in
the least wanton about Ophelia; yet (well before, in his mad rage, his obsession
about his mother's wantonness shows) his talk to her of beauty transforming
honesty to a bawd sounds a little as if he suspected her of such designs on him.
There is effective irony, of course, in his speaking thus to an innocent girl, who
has been "loosed" to him with a prayer book in her hand; and the subtler thought

Nor will the strain be less when, but a few minutes later, we see her coming with the rest to the performance of the promised play. She has been trained to Court life, and to be merry when merriment is in demand. And here is Hamlet, gaiety itself, no trace of his lunatic passion left on him, joking with the King and her father. And they, seemingly, are as gay as he, and might quite have forgotten their late resolve to send him to banishment or prison. But at least he will have no more to say to her. Far from it; he turns upon her again. She suffers ignorantly, and there is no more pitiful suffering. She is sensible of obscure forces at work around her. She knows now that it is no wrecked love for her insignificant self which has sent him mad. The thing has other roots, and promises—what dreadful harvest? Yet she had to be given by the father she trusts to be scourged by the man she loves; and now she has smilingly to face more unmeet cruelty still. His raging still in her ears, she finds him nearing her again; and, for a sequel to it—sequel besides to that now recanted wooing "in honourable fashion," those "holy vows"!—he sets himself to

—that it is even viler to turn innocence and piety to such uses—is already implicit in Polonius' preparatory

> We are oft to blame in this . . .
>   . . . that with devotion's visage
> And pious action we do sugar o'er
> The devil himself.

Yet it looks as if the genesis of Hamlet's attitude lay in a recollection of the cruder theme. This would fit in, what is more, with the surprisingly indecent treatment of her in the play-scene—since nothing she has said or done gives excuse for that. But again, there is more refined cruelty and more disequilibrium of mind in saying such things to an innocent girl. Have we here then, perhaps, a visible part of the process of Shakespeare's transference of the story from the physical to the psychological plane?

To the generally gentler view of Hamlet—a little out of fashion now—belongs the penetrating remark by Lamb in his essay *On the Tragedies of Shakespeare*: ". . . in all such deep affections as had subsisted between Hamlet and Ophelia there is a stock *supererogatory love* (if I may venture to use the expression) which in any great grief of heart, especially where that which preys upon the mind cannot be communicated, confers a kind of indulgence upon the grieved party to express itself, even to its heart's dearest object, in the language of a temporary alienation. . . ." Lamb was in justified reaction against the ranting bullying Hamlets he too often saw. He touches, needless to say, the heart of the matter, and he must himself have brooded often upon its yet more tragic aspects. But "language of a temporary alienation" is a fairly mild term for what Hamlet does say.

cheapen her before all the Court by squatting familiarly at her feet and launching smutty jokes at her.[12]

She defends herself as best she may, tagging to her distressed interjections a formal "my lord" for some denial of the lewd intimacy—its implications so plain to the smirking courtiers!—thus thrust on her. Later she musters courage to make a little casual conversation herself, even to respond to her Prince, as a Court lady should, with a pretense at his own merry mood. But we shall not have forgotten our recent sight of her desperately praying for him, convulsively weeping for her loss of him; and, for all that she keeps up appearances so bravely, we may wonder, as we look at her now, if the gentle, fragile nature could sustain many more such wrenchings at the root.

She vanishes with the rest when the crisis comes, and we do not see her again. For the mindless wraith that we see is no longer Ophelia. The father she loved and trusted killed by the man she loved; it is the final and fatal wrench. Her madness tragically outmatches his whose work it is.

CLAUDIUS

We have in Claudius the makings of the central figure of a tragedy. Something of him will be found very highly developed in Macbeth. There again is the man who does murder for his crown, cannot repent, and is drawn ever further into ill.[13] But here Hamlet himself is allowed so to sway the action of the play that no other character can be very freely treated if the framework of the accepted story is to be maintained. Claudius in particular, the "incestuous ... adulterate beast" of its beginning, must remain

---

[12] It is not that a little loose talk at a Renaissance Court would be anything very out of the way. But this particular passage of equivoque is, to begin with, exceedingly gross; and, as inflicted by Hamlet, the bookish, fine-minded student, upon the strictly schooled, well-guarded, mere girl that Ophelia is, the effect is exceptionally shocking.

[13] And is there not in

> If 'twere done when 'tis done then 'twere well
> It were done quickly. . . .

a distinct echo of Claudius' lines to Laertes:

> That we would do
> We should do when we would; for this 'would' changes,
> And hath abatements and delays as many
> As there are tongues, are hands, are accidents. . . .

the "incestuous, murderous, damned Dane" at the end, whatever may be done with him in between.

It is long before Shakespeare lets us see him as he is. We encounter him first, before the Ghost has spoken, presiding at his Council, the Queen at his side, speaking of his brother's death with dignified sorrow; discreetly implying as to his marriage—in the

> our sometime sister, now our queen,
> The imperial jointress of this warlike state . . .

—that it is chiefly a dynastic business; benevolent to Laertes; gentle but firm with the recalcitrant Hamlet. His kindliness is a little too feline, perhaps, his discourse somewhat overelaborate, his courtesy too uniform to be quite unfeigned; and his protests of fatherly love for the young man, whose succession—with whatever legal warrant—he has forestalled, may slightly smack of hypocrisy. But these are harsh criticisms. He is new to his throne, and naturally anxious, under the particular circumstances, to stand well with everyone around him. And even Hamlet, left alone, his mind only on the marriage, does not hold Claudius so heavily to blame for it. The shame is his mother's.

So far, then, there does not seem to be much against him; and superficially—seeing him with his courtiers' eyes—there is much in his favor. And when, the Ghost's tale told, we see him again, we look in vain for confirmation of it. Everything he does and says is far more consistent with innocence than guilt. The very point, in fact, of that

> O villain, villain, smiling, damned villain!
> My tables—meet it is I set it down,
> That one may smile and smile and be a villain. . . .

has been that, to look at Claudius, the thing *is* incredible. Picture him thus, an urbane, considerate and convivial gentleman, going quietly and confidently about the business of his Court and State, and we understand why Hamlet, in a calmer moment, may feel that it is perhaps "a damned ghost" that he has seen, and that his

> imaginations are as foul
> As Vulcan's stithy.

Claudius is, then, a consummate hypocrite. But everything till now has gone so smoothly for him that he may well think himself secure. Shakespeare, as it happens, has small choice, in the early part of the play, but to present him to us thus, the mask fitting marvelously, unless he is to be given some counterpart to Horatio for a confidant, or indulged, he also, in soliloquy. The technical constraint is turned to advantage. To have a Hamlet and a Claudius matched in method would be to the prejudice of each. Instead—since we for long never see Claudius alone, nor except among those whom it is his business to deceive—there can be most effectively set against Hamlet's hesitancies, doubts and nervous introspection, this easy, equable assurance. We do see him gradually drawn into ever graver consideration of Hamlet's case, to the point of resolving to dispatch him to England. But even this is no certain evidence of his guilt. While it may at one time be wise to keep a disinherited heir at your Court and under your eye, it may become wiser to send him packing upon some mission abroad. He goes to the entertainment Hamlet has provided apparently in the gayest of moods; and if he lapses into silence—why, even as things are on the surface, he has enough to trouble him. His incontinent flight from its cardinal provocation finally convinces Hamlet of his guilt. But not till even later, till, for the very first time in the play, he is left alone, does he himself definitely confirm it to us, with the

> O, my offence is rank, it smells to heaven;
> It hath the primal eldest curse upon't,
> A brother's murder!

That at least, I am persuaded, is how Shakespeare planned the matter, and I venture to wish he had left it at that. The earlier revealing aside, spoken while Polonius, with his talk of pious action sugaring o'er the devil himself, arms Ophelia with her prayer book for the ambush—that

> Oh, 'tis too true!
> How smart a lash that speech doth give my conscience!
> The harlot's cheek, beautied with plastering art,
> Is not more ugly to the thing that helps it
> Than is my deed to my most painted word.
> O heavy burden!

—has all the look of a subsequently applied patch. It is somewhat flat in itself, and so awkwardly placed, that it can be given no great dramatic force.[14] It is a feeble anticipation of the very effective, long pent outbreak of the soliloquy. What justifies it?

Does Shakespeare want to show us Claudius' conscience at work before risk of discovery rouses it? That may be. Is it that he will not keep us waiting longer for a definite admission of guilt? The dramatic effect so far has not lain, of course, in our doubts of this. We shall have taken the Ghost's word without question. It is Hamlet's own doubting which has been so effectively excused by the sustained appearance of innocence. An audience nowadays not only knows the story of the play, but is insensitive to some of its original significance; and actors have come to suit their reading of the parts to this. The Elizabethan Hamlet had, with his audience, reason enough for doubting whether it was, after all, "an honest ghost" he had seen.[15] His modern successors mostly seem to hold the Ghost's word for gospel and reproach themselves for even momentary disbelief in it. And a modern Claudius, his reputation for all but villainy long lost, plays the villain from the start. If this anticipatory aside is a patch, it may well have been put on to save the Elizabethan Claudius from appearing, on the contrary, too persistently innocent, and for fear the audience should rather come to share Hamlet's doubts than, as they were meant to, detachedly observe them. It must now be accepted, of course, as an integral part of the text; it should equally be a direction to the actor to make—except for this single moment—the "plastering art" of his "most painted word" as convincing as possible.

The "prayer-scene"—but, try as he will, the guilty wretch cannot pray—is a turning point in the presenting of Claudius, as in the action of the whole play. Till now the smiling mask, the mellifluously conventional speech, clouded and frayed but a little even by this alarming business of the play; here, in sharp contrast, the seething mind laid bare. And though the mask goes on again, it will hereafter be transparent to us.

This hard argument about the efficacy of prayer must have been the matter of more than one sermon heard both by Shakespeare

---

[14] Not because it is an aside. Claudius could, indeed, so far isolate himself upon the outer stage as to give it the effect of a soliloquy. But it is irrelevant to the rest of the scene; nothing legitimately leads up to it or away from it.

[15] Cf. (once more) Dover Wilson's convincing argument.

and his audience in those compulsorily theological days—by
Claudius from his Court chaplain too. We have, therefore, no
simple sinner, with confessor at hand to direct him, if he would,
towards penance and absolution, but a man dosed with contro-
versial doctrine, who must struggle with its dilemmas as best he
can. From his guilty heart he cannot pray. Yet God's mercy is for
the guilty, too, and his fault is past. But its fruits are his still, and

> May one be pardoned and retain the offence?

In this world perhaps; yet

> 'tis not so above . . .
> What then? what rests?
> Try what repentance can: what can it not?
> Yet what can it when one can not repent?

After which, and with some more beating of the breast, argument
collapses into

> Help, angels! make assay!
> Bow, stubborn knees, and, heart with strings of steel,
> Be soft as sinews of the new-born babe! . . .

and a weary

> All may be well.

While he is trying what the older submissive routine will do
for him Hamlet passes and pauses; and we are shown to what
twists of savage theology a finer spirit in its perplexity may be
wrought. His sword is out, his enemy helpless. But will it be
revenge enough

> To take him in the purging of his soul,
> When he is fit and seasoned for his passage?
> No. . . .

—not death only but damnation must be assured. So Hamlet
passes on. And by this perverted scruple he opens the way to all
the ills to come; quickly beginning with Polonius' death, Ophelia's
to follow, the Queen's, Laertes', and his own little delayed. Had
he known the truth—which we learn on his departure, from
Claudius' defeated

> My words fly up, my thoughts remain below;
> Words without thoughts never to heaven go.

—that this enemy was *not* purging his soul, but (so we shall gather later on) planning how to save his skin by ridding himself of son as well as father, he might have done straightforward human justice on him. Instead, the adversaries issue from the frustrate encounter—Claudius unaware of Hamlet's presence, Hamlet as blind to what that bowed head hides—these strangely warped religious exercises, the one to worse frustration, the other to dispute for his soul's salvation no more.

This revelation of an inward Claudius does more than rescue the character from conventional villany. Here is a man who can face the truth, not only about his deed and its deserts, but about himself too. His own chaplain could not argue the question better, nor—one may add—to a more orthodox conclusion. But he rises from his knees knowing himself to be as hardened in sin as ever, and so proceeds, with only the more clarity of mind, to give effect to those thoughts which have obstinately remained below. He is in danger, he must act; and it is small wonder that such a weather-cock as Hamlet, veering in spiritual storm, should have, for the time, no chance against him.

Quite naturally, while he is the motive power of the action (as he is from now to near the end of the play), he is more vividly revealed; though the fact may be that only from about now did Shakespeare start developing the borrowed character. But graft and stock are, as usual, made to agree. If the formal, calculated speech belonged to theatrical convention, it also fitted dramatically both the King discoursing and the man of guilty conscience, fearful lest an unguarded word betray him (and the more fearful that, no one suspecting him, he is the likelier to relax his guard). But things, though worse, are now better for him. If Hamlet, by some queer clairvoyance, has happened, as it seems, upon his secret, he has also given him good excuse—and is to make it better by killing Polonius—to deal drastically with such madness. It is the true part of a grieved stepfather and prudent statesman, for the sake of his country's peace, for the culprit's own sake, to get him quickly and quietly out of the way. He subscribes to the madness; for who will believe what a madman may say? Yet once in England the dispossessed heir might turn menacingly sane. There is safety only in his death; so that is duly planned.

And as he cannot—let it cost him his soul—repent the one murder he is the readier to profit by another.[16]

But once that reproachful figure no longer paces his lobbies, he can—being the clear-thinking, practical man he is—banish both the old crime and the new from his mind. And here is the key to the Claudius that we see for a short while, grieving genuinely enough for Polonius' death, over Ophelia's suffering, and facing Laertes with unforced dignity and calm. No merely well-masked villain; but the man that he would be, could his crimes but be left out of account; the man that he likes to be able to feel that he is. And of such is the real and dangerous wickedness of the world! It is this interim picture of him, with its touches of inconsistency, which does most to make Claudius a figure of flesh and blood.

He never relapses after to theatrical convention. And note how by this the writing of the part has changed. For the formal line and sentence we have sensitive, pregnant phrases, which seem to shape themselves spontaneously into verse. We can see his mind at work; and with what agility when, his security shattered by the sudden tidings of the failure of his plot against Hamlet, the awakened devil in him turns on the instant to make Laertes his accomplice in another!

It is masterly diplomacy by which he converts the young man's demand for open justice on his father's murderer into consent to the seemingly friendly fencing match. But if the task were a simple one neither of the two would appear to be such dangerous adversaries to Hamlet as, for this last round of the fight, they must. The biter is bit, however. The fascination of poison—when Laertes so unexpectedly proposes to "anoint" the unbuttoned sword—once more proves too much for him. And he also will be "hoist with his own petar."

Shakespeare finds no occasion to develop him further; he lets him slip back, rather, into the mere machinery of the story. But just so men do, after a period of amnesty, relapse to a routine of guilt. We note his callous silence upon the news of Ophelia's death; his chief care now is to keep Laertes under his eye, under

---

16 Though how it is ever to be explained away, Claudius seemingly does not stop to think. But Shakespeare knows that this chicken will not come home to roost.

his spell. In the last scene the old smiling mask is on again, the
speech is as mellifluous as before. But this is dramatically right;
Hamlet has returned, and there is fresh guilt to hide. A last blot
is added to his swiftly closing account, when he lets the instant
pass in which Gertrude could be saved. And, dosed with his own
poison, he meets a fittingly ignominious end.

Claudius does not come quite unquestionably to life. The material for the character is there, old and new, and it is all consistent
enough. But Shakespeare has left some of it incompletely developed, some indeed to implication only, and the actor must use
judgment in assembling it. And though Claudius is the villain of
the piece, his guilt undoubted and of the blackest, the evidence
for the prosecution must be weighed. But an actor will instinctively make himself Counsel for the Defense of the part he plays,
when he can.

There is the question of his love for Gertrude, and hers for
him. They never themselves refer to its illicitly passionate days.
There are, indeed, no love passages between them. They are only
twice, and for the space of a few lines, left alone together, and
then trouble is heavy on them. It has, at this time, even begun to
separate them; for Gertrude tells him no more than she need of
what has passed with Hamlet in her closet. But throughout the
play, alone with her, or before the Court, Claudius shows her very
much that loving respect which Hamlet says his father showed
her. The relation, as it now is, seems not to lack dignity; and the
actor may justifiably somewhat discount the "Hyperion to a
satyr," and, still more, "the bloat king," and the paddock, bat and
gib of the closet-scene as the language of angry grief, the pent-up
poison of a sick mind. Even the Ghost qualifies his

> that incestuous, that adulterate beast . . .

and the "shameful lust" by

> With witchcraft of his wit, with traitorous gifts—
> O wicked wit and gifts, that have the power
> So to seduce! . .

—which suggests, surely, good gifts turned to ill account, and a

Gertrude fascinated by them, yet not too easily won.[17] We certainly are not meant to see her enamored of an obvious monster.

How far was it love for her which tempted him to crime? To this we have his own clear-headed answer when he is wrestling with himself alone and speaks of

> those effects for which I did the murder,
> My crown, my own ambition and my queen.

She takes neither pride of place in it, nor comes as an afterthought. But it is in his converse with Laertes (when, as we have noted, Shakespeare brings him most spontaneously to life) that his feelings for her show. Is it odd that he should so confess himself to the young man?

> for myself—
> My virtue or my plague, be it either which—
> She's so conjunctive to my life and soul,
> That, as the star moves not but in his sphere,
> I could not but by her. . . .

It sounds, does it not, as if wrung from him? Later comes the rueful (and equally odd, as part of the provocation to the murdering of Hamlet):

> Not that I think you did not love your father;
> But that I know love is begun by time,
> And that I see, in passages of proof,
> Time qualifies the spark and fire of it.
> There lives within the very flame of love
> A kind of wick or snuff that will abate it . . . .

Of what does that covertly speak—those "passages of proof"—but of Gertrude's mute obedience to Hamlet's behest to deny herself to his bed? He does not know the reason; she could not tell him. To him it only seems the inevitable sad satiety of a passion such as theirs, grown "to a plurisy," dead "in his own too much."[18]

---

[17] It is true that a line or so later, the Ghost refers to him as

> a wretch, whose natural gifts were poor
> To those of mine . . .

and even talks of the difference between a "radiant angel" and "garbage." But of all the evidence for the prosecution this is the most—and the most excusably—biased.

[18] In letting any matter of this kind pass unemphasized into the play, Shakespeare would be unconcerned with what we may call its likelihood in time; he

Not that this can be very clearly brought home to the audience. Had Shakespeare given himself a freer hand with Claudius and Gertrude, nor let the play be so overwhelmingly dominated by Hamlet, he would, we may well suppose, have clinched this and other questions about them more effectively. As it is, the chief dramatic value of the passages is (yet once more) as a direction to the actors. If Gertrude, from the closet-scene onwards, does a little self-consciously hold aloof from him (except when, for a moment, he is in danger from Laertes), and if he shows himself somberly aware of it, the lines, when they come to be spoken, will take color from this. And such an attitude one to the other will in itself be eloquent; especially by contrast to the earlier happiness, shown plainly to the world when at last it may be. But it is a pity that these ends of character are left loose.

Is Claudius a drunkard? We have the promise of the "jocund healths" he means to drink, and Hamlet's scornful

> The king doth wake to-night, and takes his rouse,
> Keeps wassail, and the swaggering upspring reels . . . .

with its sequent

> This heavy-headed revel east and west
> Makes us traduced and taxed of other nations;
> They clepe us drunkards. . . .

But we hear no more of this, except when Hamlet would rather kill his enemy "drunk asleep" than at his prayers—which is still only evidence for the prosecution—and we see nothing of it at all. So Shakespeare does not want to stress it. But it helps picture a Court in which the student-philosopher Hamlet would, at best, feel very out of place; and it gives a significant touch to the picture of the King, no more a drunkard than his neighbor, or than a clever man can afford to be, but the consummate sensualist in this too. And he would find, it might well be, comforting forgetfulness in the nightly wassail, and courage in the "swaggering upspring" and the bravado of those trumpets and drums.[19]

---

would not, that is to say—indeed, he does not otherwise—stop to consider whether the closet-scene had taken place a day or so or a week or so earlier.

[19] But I saw once an Italian actor who had evidently been greatly struck by this aspect of the character, for his nose was reddened and he played the part bibulously throughout. This lightened the play very much. And here, my dear Dover Wilson, is another possible answer to the burning question: Did Claudius see the Dumb

GERTRUDE

However else Shakespeare may have envisaged Gertrude upon his stage, it could not have been as the mature matron, the realistic mother of a man of thirty, to which a later-born tradition has unluckily accustomed us. His boys could play the young Ophelia and the fourteen-year-old Juliet and scarcely call convention into question; and one sees them bringing a certain advantageously sexless distinction to the withered Queen Margaret or the stern Volumnia.[20] But the presenting of ripe womanhood and its charm would obviously be beyond them. As far, then, as appearance went (and setting aside the simply comic) he had to choose between spontaneous youth and conventional "age." Juliet is young. It is against all likelihood that Lady Capulet should be old; but she is made so, for here is an effective contrast which nothing in the story forbids. Ophelia is young; and if likelihood were all, Gertrude, who will certainly never see forty-five again, might better be "old." But that would make her relations with Claudius —and *their* likelihood is vital to the play—quite incredible. There-

Show? My Italian, at that juncture, was far too muzzy and hilarious to have seen any offense—or, indeed, any meaning at all in it.

[20] As to the comic old women, it is likely that they were played by men. Dr. W. J. Lawrence thinks so (and allows me to quote him), pointing out that when, with the Restoration, actresses inherited the Juliets and Rosalinds—though even this change was not suddenly complete—such parts as the Nurse in Otway's *Caius Marius* (his adaptation of *Romeo and Juliet*) were till the end of the century, or near it, acted by men. And this, as he justly says, looks very like a survival of Elizabethan practice.

But that, with Shakespeare at any rate, the men did not trespass into this territory beyond the Mistress Overdones and Dame Quicklys and Angelicas is suggested, I think, by the severe limitation of the number of the women's parts. In no play do we find more than five. And this looks like consideration for the likely number of trained apprentices available, a number limited both by law and custom. In *Richard III*, it is true, there are, besides the women's parts, the young King, the Duke of York and Clarence's son to be cast. But for two of these not much skill is needed, and something may be done by doubling. The doubling would be without regard to sex; in *Romeo and Juliet* Lady Montague's death implies the need for a Balthasar or a page for Paris. Such plays as *A Midsummer Night's Dream* and *The Merry Wives of Windsor* ask, of course, for a number of children. But they were originally intended, it is presumed, for private performance, and any public theater would need outside help for their production. Shakespeare, from first to last, is as sparing as possible of women characters, and particularly of the elderly or middle-aged. A heroine he must have, and she perhaps a companion or an attendant or two. For the rest; while fathers and uncles abound, mothers are fairly scarce. And is there an aunt in the canon?

fore she must still be young, only as much older than Ophelia as dress and conduct can suggest. But Shakespeare, by an adroit twist, converts necessity here to profit. He gives us in Gertrude the woman who does not mature, who clings to her youth and all that belongs to it, whose charm will not change but at last fade and wither; a pretty creature, as we see her, desperately refusing to grow old. And it is actually in this pathetic incongruity that the whole tragedy has struck root.

She is drawn for us with unemphatic strokes, and she has but a passive part in the play's action. She moves throughout in Claudius' shadow; he holds her as he has won her, by the witch-craft of his wit. We first see her sitting in Council at his side, formally presented, too, as "the imperial jointress" of his power. But it is plain that she does little except echo his wishes; some-times—as in the welcome to Rosencrantz and Guildenstern—she repeats his very words, inverting, as with a slight effort, their order. We practically never see her apart from him, except when, at his and Polonius' urging, she has sent for Hamlet to her closet; and then he follows to bid her "translate" what has passed. She does not tell him everything. Polonius' death is news enough; the rest, after all, was madness. But here, we may gather, starts a rift between them; from now on they stay conjugally apart, and he feels he has lost her. Later, during the fencing match, when she has momentarily at least recovered her good spirits, in pretty defi-ance she disobeys him and drinks from the cup he has prepared for her son. That trifling disobedience is her death.

She seems to be fond of Hamlet; though whether she really so much wishes him to stay at Court we can hardly tell, for it is under Claudius' eye and influence that she makes the plea. She is gracious to Ophelia; and if the girl's "good beauties" do turn out to be the "happy cause" of her son's "wildness"—why, their marriage would be just what she feels a marriage should be.

For long she does not admit that Hamlet is positively mad; she never uses the word about him until, in her closet, he sees the thing she cannot see. She knows him well enough to know that her own "o'er-hasty marriage" is at the root of his trouble, but her trivial

> Did you assay him
> To any pastime?

—when Rosencrantz and Guildenstern bring their first report of him—shows her quite insensible to the depth of it.

Yet, watching her, *we* know that this shallow, amiable, lymphatic creature was an adulteress, cunning enough to deceive her husband. Hamlet says that

> she would hang on him,
> As if increase of appetite had grown
> By what it fed on. . . .

It was the obvious way of deceiving him. She wept bitterly when he died. We need not, however, see hypocrisy there. She may well have wept the more bitterly because she had been false to him. And husbands, whose love is of too complacent and Hyperion-like a "dignity," are temptingly easy to deceive. Within a month she has married her lover, and she is still the Queen. She owns that—in the eyes of the world—it was overhasty of them. But of any remorse for the past there is no hint at all. Surely everything —if her morose son would but come to his senses and take a more cheerful view of life—has at last turned out very well.

It is upon such a nature, then, that the cathartic storm of Hamlet's stored resentment—the occasion given him—is to break. He has been expressly warned to

> leave her to heaven,
> And to those thorns that in her bosom lodge
> To prick and sting her.

But her seeming bland immunity from anything of the sort so pricks and stings his own incorrigible moral sense that at last he can restrain himself no more; he must set her up a glass wherein she may see, not the still pretty sight she is used to finding there, the mask of virtue she presents to the world, but the "inmost part" of her, the terrible truth.

He is coming to her, so she supposes, to be rated for his "pranks," which have indeed become "too broad to bear with," when he can, under cover of his play, insult before the whole Court both her and his sovereign and stepfather by gibing at their marriage. And she has primed herself—clearly she does not relish the task; the subject is a ticklish one; it is Claudius, she announces, who is offended—to be "round with him." But his lunatic violence terrifies her, his killing of Polonius breaks her nerve. Within a little he has her cowed. The tables are turned, and he is rating her, scourging her towards repentance for deadly sin.

We have had Claudius a few moments since, facing the evil in him honestly enough; but for a while it seems as if she really did not know what Hamlet meant. Still, bewildered though she may be by the rhetoric and moral fervor, his

> makes marriage vows
> As false as dicers' oaths. . .

(for answer to the bravado of her "What have I done. . . ?") tells her plainly that he knows of her adultery. But it is past and respectably atoned for; and there is genuine perplexity in her

> Ay me! what act,
> That roars so loud and thunders in the index?

What *can* she have done to warrant such tremendous execration?

He sets to work, with a kind of painstaking wrath, to demonstrate to her, as to a reprobate child, her moral obliquity. And now it is, her silence tells us, that she will not understand. Very naturally—this from her own son!—she will not. So he coarsens and coarsens his attack, till finding it intolerable, she pleads guilty. And then he will not spare her. If the carnal sin is all she can recognize, she shall have that painted in its true colors too:

> Nay, but to live
> In the rank sweat of an enseamed bed. . .

She has ample excuse at last for her pitifully reiterated

> O! speak to me no more . . . .
> No more, sweet Hamlet!

When the Ghost appears—and she is spared the yet deadlier blow of a revelation of the murder—she is blind to its presence, deaf to the voice:

> Do you see nothing there?
> Nothing at all; yet all that is I see.
> Nor did you nothing hear?
> No, nothing but ourselves.

and it implies, we feel, a blindness of soul in her besides, a sanity which Hamlet's "madness" puts to shame. He has battered her into admission of her fleshly sin; but spiritual perception—what can give her that? The division between mother and son is here at its deepest, in this picture of mother, father and son, united but divided, together, but in understanding curelessly apart. And here is intrinsic tragedy, the tragedy of what human beings are; and the action is stayed while we absorb the sense of it. Yet in kindliness the two are never nearer to each other. The ghostly presence—itself so softened—is a reproach to his anger, and her very incomprehension makes her tenderer to him.

The mystic moment past, his compassion, truly, is as bitter as his wrath. To him bitterer; for he has no faith, he finds, in her repentance. Let her assume the virtue she has not. Having stripped one mask from her he bids her wear another; the pretense may become reality in time. He turns bitterer still. She will betray her son to her paramour. What else should she do? He ranks her with his traitor schoolfellows, whom he will trust as he would "adders fanged."

But in all this he is wrong. She is repentant and she does not betray him. He is no more just to her than we need expect the one-time chastely romantic adorer of Ophelia, turned misogynist, to be. For truer insight there is the Ghost's

> O, step between her and her fighting soul. . . .

—knowledge, befitting the dead, that even unawares something within her is struggling for salvation. But, with Gertrude as with Claudius, Shakespeare leaves these last threads of their story loose-ended. And Hamlet so dominates the play that we are too apt to see things through his eyes.

A few strokes, however, have still to be added to the character, and in its acting they can be given some significance. The morrow of this ordeal finds her so sick of soul and conscious of guilt, so broken in nerve, that only her ingrain royal sense of duty forces her to receive the "distract" Ophelia. But (in quick and effective contrast) she can gallantly throw herself between the enraged Laertes and her husband. And she can momentarily forget her own trouble in grief for the girl's death; the detached beauty of her tale of it tells us so. Hamlet, when she sees him again at the graveside, is still, it seems, in the grip of his madness, and she pleads for indulgence for him. She is the happier when, at the fencing match, he quietly speaks of it as a thing conquered and left behind; and for a little while—because he is so happily restored to her—her natural gaiety has play again. It is for a very little while. And the terrible knowledge that Hamlet was commanded to spare her, Shakespeare more ruthlessly will not.

The poison does not kill her so quickly but that she must suffer this agony besides. Laertes' last words; the back-rushing memory of much not understood till now, of the mimic murder in the garden, Hamlet's mysterious ". . . as kill a king"; the sight of Claudius here in his grip—she dies companioned by the meaning of all this, conscious even, it may be, of her dying son's implacable farewell. It is the very death her cheated husband died.[21]

HAMLET

As with the play, so—but for one vital difference—with the character. Shakespeare has to reconcile the creature of his imagination with the figure of the borrowed story; the Hamlet we have is the tragic product of his very failure to do so.

The unfitness of the man for his task is at once plain. But Hamlet's continuing effort to be at the same time—so to put it—Kyd's hero and Shakespeare's reveals deeper incongruities. It involves him in a rupture of the entire spiritual treaty between

---

[21] And we have had the effects of such a poison most vigorously painted for us by the Ghost:

> The leperous distilment, whose effect
> Holds such an enmity with blood of man,
> That swift as quicksilver it courses through
> The natural gates and alleys of the body;
> And with a sudden vigour it doth posset
> And curd, like eager droppings into milk,
> The thin and wholesome blood; so did it mine;
> And a most instant tetter barked about,
> Most lazar-like, with vile and loathsome crust,
> All my smooth body. . . .

Shakespeare could have done that at half or a quarter the length (and the modern producer—of opinion, no doubt, that he should have—usually omits the last six lines); but he clearly wants the physical effects of the poison to make a deep impression on us. I do not say that we shall remember the actual lines for so long. But when we see the Queen stricken, the impression made by them should be spontaneously, if only vaguely, renewed. There is nothing in the text to mark the moment of her death; but since she speaks after she has collapsed into the arms of her attendants there is no reason she should not live on, long enough, at least to learn the truth. The King dies swiftly; but by sword as well as poison.

himself and the world in which he must live, and in a conflict between two selves within him, the one that could agree with this world, the other that cannot. There is the fundamental tragedy, exhibited by setting him in contact with a variety of his world's inhabitants; his mother, the girl he has loved, a true friend and two false ones, his secret enemy, the man he unwittingly wrongs, an old Court wiseacre, a shrewd old peasant, those shadows of reality, the Players, and that other shadow, his father's ghost. Each contact has its discord, and sets him playing false to what common sense would expect of him, and to what he once might have expected of himself.

Before the play begins this schism has begun; his mother's remarriage its immediate cause. It is suddenly intensified by the supernatural discovery of his father's murder, shamefully linked to this; so intensified that a salutary intermittent fever of the brain is seemingly all that enables him to discharge its poisons and survive. This fever—called, for want of a better name, his madness—fracturing the surface of his mind, adds yet more facets to our view of him. It adds, too, a fascinating iridescence to the cruder colors of the story, and it gives a fluctuating pulse to the action. Shakespeare found it—this madness—a mechanical trick. He makes it a dramatic symbol of the true tragedy of his Hamlet, which is the tragedy of a spiritual revolution.

HIS LOOKS AND CONDUCT

The exigencies of the action will not let us see a happy Hamlet —if ever there was one. But we have Ophelia's reference to him as he seemed to her to be:

> The expectancy and rose of the fair state,
> The glass of fashion and the mould of form,
> The observed of all observers. . .

And in the forgetful pleasure he finds in the mimic world of the Players is the reflection of a happier man.

We see him directly in three quite distinct guises. There is the black-suited Hamlet, rebelliously singular amid the peacock brilliancy of the Council. Then, in drastic contrast, there will be the Hamlet of the "antic disposition," who must not merely answer, in some degree, to Ophelia's account of him—

> with his doublet all unbraced,
> No hat upon his head, his stockings fouled,
> Ungartered, and down-gyved to his ancle . . .

—but who will (is it not likely?) have "cast his nighted colour off" also. Would he, after promising "in all his best" to obey his mother, have disregarded this command, persisted in his public reproach to her? Would he not, moreover, wish to give Claudius every reason to think that he was no longer brooding on his loss? Tradition is against it; but all Shakespearean tradition is, strictly speaking, truncated at 1660. Most Hamlets, at any rate, in this middle section of the play make too much of their grief (they duplicate, that is to say, the effect of the earlier scenes) and too little of their madness. Except in the scene with Gertrude, the one outspoken reference to the past is not sorrowful at all; it is the bitterly mocking:

> look you, how cheerfully my mother looks, and my father died
> within 's two hours.

When he is alone we have the truth of him, but it is his madness which is on public exhibition. And a very "antic disposition" he will at times display—for he must, if he is to claim the madman's privilege and security—till at last "his pranks" become "too broad to bear with."[22] The description of him and those phrases are specific directions to the actor.

All this will again be changed when he emerges safe from the ambush of his voyage. He should probably appear at the grave-side with his "sea-gown scarfed about" him. By the wistfully humorous detachment of his mood we are to know that the fever in his brain is now burned out. That his one passionately remorse-ful outburst when he learns of Ophelia's death should be greeted as madness is only a last ironic instance of his spiritual schism with his surroundings. This behind him, what could be more ruth-lessly sane than his talk of those exterminated vermin, Rosen-crantz and Guildenstern, or shrewder than his sense of his polit-ical position? And he takes his intellectual ease with Osric. We see that his strength is worn. He has forebodings of death. Then, to the wronged Laertes, and before King, Queen and Court, he

[22] Cf. what Dover Wilson says about the accepted appearance of the stage madman.

makes his apology, purges his offenses, and seemingly would be reconciled to the estranged world. It is a deceptive sunset gleam. The threat of the poisoned sword apart, his heritage of ill and his failure so far to cope with it are taking their own revenge on him. But it is thus that, before the terrible end, Shakespeare shows us the Hamlet that might have been, something the nobler for his ordeal than the romantic figure of Ophelia's adoration, the Hamlet, rather, of whom Fortinbras is to say

> For he was likely, had he been put on,
> To have proved most royally. . . .

HAMLET AND GERTRUDE

The turning point of the play, as we have seen, is when Hamlet postpones his vengeance on the King because it would not be cruel enough to kill him at his prayers, and passes on to wreak as cruel a vengeance as he can upon his mother, hoping only that he may be able to stop short of killing her. For vengeance in large part this is. And while that which is to be fulfilled at last upon the King is a duty laid on him (he has welcomed it truly, and his will and conscience are engaged in it; but the keeping them so is a hard task, and a harder the turning purpose into action), to this impeachment of his mother, which has been expressly forbidden him, he goes with a dreadful zest. Nor does the offense against his father account for the ferocity of his attack. Her sin against herself moves him more. But the springs of his wrath are bared in the climax to the scene's beginning, when she asks him has he "forgot" to whom he speaks thus, and he answers

> No, by the rood, not so:
> You are the Queen, your husband's brother's wife;
> And—would it were not so!—you are my mother.

She has been false to her husband and to herself. But she has also been false to him, to his faith in her.

The relation between any mother and son rests primarily on instinct; and in Hamlet's unbalanced state, at that enkindled moment more particularly, instinct has full play. For all his self-awareness he will not be intellectually aware of the mixture of motives in him; he has not been of the process by which he is brought to this passionate crisis. But we have seen that, with faith in his mother's virtue, his faith in all womanhood has vanished; his own sense of moral health too—for is he not her son, her very flesh and blood? That side of life has been poisoned for him; the taint is betrayed in his treatment of Ophelia. He has been warned to leave his mother's punishment to heaven, but the excitements of the play-scene are too much for him. By what he says when he is summoned to her he means to scourge her to repentance; he will "speak" daggers to her, will wring her heart

> If it be made of penetrable stuff. . .

But beneath this purpose surges—be it known to him or no—an embittered idealist's lust to be avenged upon this traitor to his ideal; and in its sating will be the sense that he is thus ridding himself too of some of the poison in him.

Ophelia is also our witness to Hamlet's unspoiled attitude towards women. His love for her, as we hear of it, was still only in its imaginative phase, finding expression in such pleasant foolishness as

> Doubt thou the stars are fire;
> Doubt that the sun doth move;
> Doubt truth to be a liar . . . .
> Thine evermore, most dear lady, whilst this machine is to him. . . .

and given countenance

> With almost all the holy vows of heaven.

But there exist—though they may be rare—these essentially chaste natures, whose manhood's love will be the son's devout love for his mother, rededicate, little changed, to a wife. They are not lacking in passion. Far from it; there are no stronger passions than these pure ones, set on some ideal. And Hamlet's is such a nature, and his love for his mother was just such a passionate love.

He still instinctively feels himself, moreover, so much a partaker of her life that her degradingly hasty marriage to his uncle disgusts him with life itself, brings him to wishing that his own

> too too solid flesh would melt. . .[23]

---

[23] A point which Dover Wilson's reading of "sullied" does most temptingly underline.

Morbidly sensitive in this (the grief for his father's death telling
on him too) though he may already be, he has, up to this point,
his trouble more or less in hand; he can hold it at arm's length,
even, with the wry humor of a

> Thrift, thrift, Horatio! the funeral baked meats
> Did coldly furnish forth the marriage tables. . . .

It is the Ghost's revelation of the murder, and of the baser fact of
her adultery with its all too obvious bearing upon the murder,
which turns him, as by a sort of balefully miraculous conversion,
into a man possessed. Inevitably the shock tells hardest upon the
wound already there, a wound which is intellectually so poorly
protected too. And thus it is that the grief for her frailty is turned
to rage in him, and that the sense of her corruption infects him
and all womanly beauty in his eyes. Such moral ignorance and
wantonness, he cries, make a man mad. The cleavage between
the two of them has significance for Hamlet alone. In his
mother's eyes he is, to begin with, simply unreasonable and un-
kind. His moral indictment, when he launches it, bewilders her.
And of the obscure play of thought and feeling within him she
has no idea.

But the attack on her, despite its rancor, is his effort to heal the
breach between them. Its initial passion—not quelled even by the
shock of the calamity to Polonius; it surges up again the moment
after—comes in sharp contrast to the cold reasoning that has
spared the King. Claudius is damned, and cannot be too deeply
damned; but she may still be saved. And he loves her still; it is
with a kind of exasperated love that he rages at her. He means to
be cruel,

> cruel, only to be kind. . .

and is doubtless crueler than he means to be; for the sensitive
nature, set to the harsh task, becomes more cruel than another.
By the Ghost's intervention his passionate anger is quelled, and
he is kept from inflicting worse cruelty on her. But this link of
past love between them proves to be none now. The little cloud of
tenderness soon dissolves; and he is left (his pulse as hers tem-
perately keeping time) to see her with a terrible clarity as to his
steeled intellect she is, no renewal of virtue in her possible, nor in
himself of any faith in such virtue. His anger had hope in it. But

its "damned custom" has now sardonically become the "monster,"
to whom he commits her for as much salvation as she is likely to
earn. This is the tepid end to many a moral crusade.

He is remorseful for his overrighteous wrath. His queer

> Forgive me this my virtue. . . .

is not all irony. Forgive me—is the impulse of it—even though
the fault be yours, for whatever in me parts me from you. And if
it will comfort her he will beg a mother's blessing of her again.

But this is playing round realities. And when, about to leave
her, he surveys her there, crushed, yet—he is certain—infatuate
still, the cold

> One word more, good lady.

unmasks the uncompromising mind.[24] What shall she do? That
she can still ask such a question! And in the sarcasm of the

> Not this, by no means, that I bid you do. . .

sounds his despair of her; even as the nausea of

> Let the bloat king tempt you again to bed;
> Pinch wanton on your cheek; call you his mouse;
> And let him, for a pair of reechy kisses. . .

tells us that the poison in himself is by no means purged. Plead
as he might, she will relapse, he feels, to this. So she will act, for
so at heart she is. And when at last he does leave her it is to the
accustomed mockery of

> Mother, good night. . . . Good night, mother!

—a very refrain it has become.

Throughout the play, from that first quiet, ironic

> 'Tis not alone my inky cloak, good mother. . .

what changes of grief and bitterness, love and anger has not
Shakespeare set his Hamlet to ring on that one word! Nor are
these the last hereabouts. He insinuates a yet bitter farewell to
her into the cryptic parting with Claudius:

---

[24] It is not easy to distinguish the significance of Hamlet's varying forms of
address to his mother. "Madam" in public would be but a natural term of respect
both for mother and Queen; in private there may be some estrangement in it. We
have noted the play he makes with Guildenstern's slightly impertinent "your
mother's commandment." This present "good lady" is without doubt harshly
ironical, if only because it preludes a passage of the very harshest irony.

> Farewell, dear mother.
> Thy loving father, Hamlet.
> My mother. Father and mother is man and wife; man and wife
> is one flesh; and so, my mother.

—which is as much as to say that, at last, he surrenders his share
in her to his enemy, to the man who has degraded her in flesh
and soul to what she is.

He troubles no more about her, makes no contact with her
when he returns from his adventurous voyage, his "madness"
shed. He ignores her at the graveside. His one reference to her
is the cursory, brutal

> He that hath killed my king and whored my mother. . .

And when, in a breathing-space of the fight, she approaches him
reconcilingly with the pretty, motherly

> Here, Hamlet, take my napkin, rub thy brows. . . .

the coquettish

> The Queen carouses to thy fortune, Hamlet.

a coldly courteous

> Good madam.

is all his response.

In his cry as he kills the King, in the

> Follow my mother!

there is a last echo of the old afflicted love. But, stricken himself,
he has no kinder farewell for her than a

> Wretched queen, adieu!

as she lies there dying or dead.

The story of Hamlet and his mother is of a second and spiritual
parturition. Every mother is prepared for such a wrench. But this
is a morbid one; and it is the child that suffers and resents.

HAMLET AND OPHELIA

We have, to begin and end with, two explicit indications of
Hamlet's uncorrupted feelings for Ophelia; the first, her account
to her father of his wooing her "in honourable fashion," of his
giving

> countenance to his speech . . .
> With almost all the holy vows of heaven.

the second, his own cry when he learns that she is dead:

> I lov'd Ophelia. . . .

—and, from their very nature, they are meant to be believed. In the interval the two are at cross-purposes, and people and circumstances and they themselves conspire to make matters worse. It would be a common tale enough of two lovers, were the circumstances not so terrible and Hamlet other than he is.

We see them alone together only once, and then every element of mischief is distilled into the situation. They have been parted for long (but for that single, strange, silent incursion on her which she describes); he has lost faith in life itself, and she, no more than obediently faithless to him till now, must now be as obediently false—for they are not, in fact, even alone together, as she knows.[25]

But from the beginning of the play the whole pernicious process has been in train. Laertes warns his sister to beware of the "trifling" of her lover's favor, and of opening her "chaste treasure . . . to his unmastered importunity," and her father sullies him to her still more by telling her that his "holy vows" are

> mere implorators of unholy suits,
> Breathing like sanctified and pious bawds,
> The better to beguile.

Plainly this is a slander upon the Hamlet we have just seen; the young idealist, with his

> Frailty, thy name is woman!

heartbroken by the one betrayal of his ideal. He is to learn within a little that the betrayal is far worse than he thought it, and coincidently to find his own love for Ophelia treated as just such a matter of lust as his uncle's for his mother. What must be the effect on him?

One index to it is given us, pretty promptly, when Polonius "boards" him; and out of that picture of natural corruption:

---

[25] "for long." Once again we must remember how arbitrarily Shakespeare turns time to his account. We are not told, nor allowed to calculate, how long the separation has been. Ophelia speaks of "this many a day," and of remembrances which she has "longed long to re-deliver." That is evidence enough.

> For if the sun breed maggots in a dead dog, being a god kissing
> carrion . . .

springs the sudden, irrelevant enquiry:

> Have you a daughter?

(but it *is* a relevant question, surely, since you have been shutting
her away from me for so long) to be followed by:

> Let her not walk i' the sun; conception is a blessing, but not
> as your daughter may conceive:—friend, look to 't.

Ironic tribute to paternal worldly wisdom! It is most prudent of
you, my good sir, to be treating me as a common seducer[26] and
your daughter as a potential harlot. For so, doubtless, all women
are.

Later comes another gibe:

> Oh, Jephthah, judge of Israel, what a treasure hadst thou! . . .
> *One fair daughter, and no more,*
> *The which he loved passing well.*

—for he also "sent her away for two months; and she . . . be-
wailed her virginity."[27] But *does* it follow that this is how best to
show you love your daughter "passing well"; or even—hints the
mischievous mockery of

> Why,
> *As by lot, God wot,*
> And then, you know,
> *It came to pass, as most like it was* . . .

—that you *will* have kept her so safe after all? What is most like
to come to pass if man and maid should get together? A few
months more may show.

From which opprobrious levity we may gather what Hamlet
thinks of Polonius' part in the matter. And the matter itself,

---

[26] But Hamlet's faith in his own untried virtue has disintegrated too:

> We are arrant knaves all, believe none of us.

[27] Judges 11: 38. The coincidence of the two months (in Hamlet's first soliloquy
his father has been dead "but two months . . ," and in the now imminent play-
scene Ophelia is to say he has been dead "twice two months"; therefore it is for
two months that he and she have been parted) is more interesting as an indication
of the working of Shakespeare's mind—and Hamlet's—than important as another
solid spot in the fluidity of the play's scheme of time. For even in days when men
knew their Bible far better, not many among his audience will have known it
so well as this.

amidst grimmer troubles, might well be meaning no more to him, supine beneath those as he seems to be. But in another scale is the Hamlet of the strange incursion on Ophelia; a man spiritually stricken, whom we divine too in some reflexive twists to his sarcasms and behind the parade of pessimism, whom we hear railing at his "unpregnant" counterpart, whom we finally see for ourselves—Ophelia now set in his path—with his self-questionings sternly harvested into a questioning of life's very title to be endured; "the pangs of disprized love" but one item in its catalogue of ills. And suddenly he sees her there, a creature from the world of faith he has left behind.

His exclamation; that oddly ruthful

> Nymph, in thy orisons
> Be all my sins remembered.

reflects, I think, in its meaning and music together, as far as a single phrase may, the complex of the effect on him; an emotion at the sight of her which is like the vibrating of a frayed, neglected string; regret for the loss of her, and of his faith in all that the love for her nourished in him—and he half whimsically, a little wistfully, commends his present impiety to her prayers. But there is too a shrinking in the tenor of it (this the keynote of the coming scene) from any risk of a renewed desire for her.[28]

He can never have thought of confiding his secret to her; to her father's daughter, or, his mother's treachery haunting him, to any woman. But for him love and trust go together; and some fear that he might betray it will have been among the other feelings working in him when, as she tells us, after the long perusal of her face

> he lets me go,
> And, with his head over his shoulder turn'd,
> He seem'd to find his way without his eyes;

[28] Dowden says, "There is estrangement in the word 'Nymph,' " and other good authorities agree with him. I accept this gladly enough, though I wish I knew more precisely what its emotional significance for Shakespeare's audience was. But when Dover Wilson adds that "The touch of affectation in 'nymph' and 'orisons' (both pretentious words) and of sarcasm in 'all my sins' shows that Hamlet speaks ironically. . . ." I cannot but protest. Hamlet, for one thing, is not apt to be sarcastic about his own sins, and he is, at this moment, in his least sarcastic mood. And how the word "orisons"—in the face of Juliet's earlier and Imogen's later use of it—can be called affected and pretentious I really do not see.

> For out o' doors he went without their help,
> And to the last bended their light on me.

—when he let her go indeed, with that symbolically silent good-
bye. And we see that, in touch with her again, at the first provocation he begins riddling with the truth. And a little later, in his
frenzied excitement, it nearly escapes him.

But, dedicate to his task, what has he to do with love? Nor is he
the man that loved her. Nor is this world of wickedness the world
in which they loved. Her approach to return his gifts stirs his
senses. It is with the violence of self-distrust that he repels her.
Her distress at it touches his pity. Then he will lesson her—all
the kindness he can show her—in the realities of life as he has
learned them. Is she honest as well as fair? Her beauty will corrupt her honesty. He is himself "indifferent honest," yet it were
better his mother had not borne him. In the days of his foolish
innocence he thought that he loved her. He made her believe so.
She should not have believed him. That was not love, and men
are "arrant knaves all." Her father was wise to part them; and
here is sounder counsel still:

> Get thee to a nunnery: why wouldst thou be a breeder of sin-
> ners? . . . Go thy ways to a nunnery. . . .

—and have no share in perpetuating the wickedness of the world.
The menace in his sudden, searching

> Where's your father?

terrifies her into a lie. He cannot be sure, of course, that it is one;
and in that "thou shalt not escape calumny" he is giving her some
benefit of the doubt. But whether, having been kept from him
lest he should debauch her, it is wittingly or unwittingly that she
now lends her purity to his enemies as a bait for him, she is—so
much is certain—a part of their machinery of evil; and his compassion turns to insensate rage. In such a rage the objects of it are
less themselves than typical fuel for its fury. And Ophelia is no
more Ophelia to him, but womankind, the matrix of this evil
which has corrupted the world for him, which has made him mad.
Yet through his wrath we still hear the Hamlet that loved her
pleading with her—in the reiterated

> Get thee to a nunnery. . . . To a nunnery. . . .

—to save herself from the miserable guilt of the giving of life, for such ends as this. It is his second anguished farewell to her. And thus is completed—and dissipated in anguish—the stern reasoning of

> To be, or not to be . . .

Among the gay assemblage for the play he sees her yet more patently—in his tense excitement—as a part of this machinery of evil which surrounds and threatens him. Kept from Court for so long, and now so demurely presented to him; can he doubt, then, that she is but another spy and decoy? His enemies' cue has been to

> drive his purpose on to these delights.

and his is to play the allotted part—to another purpose. Therefore, with a

> No, good mother, here's metal more attractive.

he ostentatiously yields to the pretty magnet. But he can at the same time, as usual, from behind the mask of his madness, take a gratifying toll of verbal revenge on them. They maligned his honorable love for her; he will better the dishonor in which she returns to him, will show his uncle-father and aunt-mother, the old bawd her father, the wretched, compliant girl herself, and all the Court, just what a vile thing it is they are making of her. He will let his mother see, too, how she has taught him to treat women. And even as the gentle nature, given merciless work to do, seeks force for it in cruelty, so is this grossness, with which he now spatters and defames Ophelia, the likely product of a romantically idealist imagination turned the wrong side out. Moreover, his "celestial" Ophelia having failed him, and he having no more use for her, his mind, set only on its task, now needs one that it can, without compunction, reject and forget. And here, in the worthless little trull of his treatment of her, she is.

She is swept out of the way with the rest in the excitement to follow. And he does, it would seem, forget her; until, returning from exile cured of his "madness," and stopping to sentimentalize over that expectant grave, he finds that it is for her they have dug it.

The past echoes back in his agonized

> I lov'd Ophelia; forty thousand brothers
> Could not, with all their quantity of love,
> Make up my sum. . .

But his mockery of Laertes' ranting is only a bitterer mockery of himself. For, with the quenching of his madness, the Hamlet that felt and imagined and suffered and could love is no more. The passions, whose conflict left him impotent, are burned out of him; he is fitted at last for his task. He can rant about her with the best; but he, at heart, is as dead as she. This is, indeed, the last pang he is to suffer.

THE INTRINSIC HAMLET

His troubles apart, what sort of a man is Hamlet? The course of the action gives us three different views of him: in his disillusioned grief; under the strain of his madness; and returning, hardened, to quit his account with the King. But they are all abnormal views. And, while we discount without much difficulty the antic disposition and even the moments of sore distraction, there would be no measuring the depth of the moral tragedy did not Shakespeare contrive to give us also some refracted glimpses of a more normal man.

The Players are put to this use. The imaginative Hamlet finds forgetfulness in that unreal world, and in the noble music of Æneas' tale to Dido, though his thoughts soon drift back.[29]

Here is the man of fastidious taste, who prefers a play that "pleased not the million" and had "no sallets in the lines to make the matter savoury"—upon which small point alone he will be at odds with his surroundings, with the reveling Claudius, and with that man of the world Polonius, who is

> for a jig or a tale of bawdry, or he sleeps.

Here is a Hamlet, too, as princely in welcoming a common Player as his friend, as (from another standpoint) in his frank mockery of Polonius, and (from yet another) in his curt warning to the favored Player not to follow his example. The famous advice to the Players throws light on the intrinsic Hamlet too. It is like

---

[29] I do not think that he is meant to *choose* the subject of Priam's slaughter with his father in his mind; but it must very soon suggest his father to him.

him, at such a crisis, to trouble with it at all. Upon *what* he has
written for them to act his whole project may depend; but that
they might mouth it, or saw the air with their hands, or o'erstep
the modesty of nature cannot matter in the least. But this is
Hamlet ingrain; delighting in the thing that does not matter, and
delighting in it for its own sake; and only the more because it is
a fictive thing. The imaginative man prefers the unreal to the
real; he can have his will of it.

But the chief use of these glimpses of a sounder Hamlet is for
a counterpoise to the soliloquies—where, at first blush, we might
expect to see him as he most unfeignedly is. But we do not. In
a tragedy of spiritual struggle, discord will be at its worst when
a man is left alone with his thoughts. When we see Hamlet alone
he is either lapsed in self-conscious grief, or savagely self-reproach-
ful, wrought to murderous excitement, or in suicidal despair. And
when, in the calm of defeat, he deliberately questions himself, he
has to admit that he knows nothing of himself at all.

But, this moral turmoil apart, it is not from his self-communings
that we should best learn the simple truth about him. He is too
imaginative a man for that. When he says to his mother:

> you shall not budge;
> You go not till I set you up a glass
> Where you may see the inmost part of you.

it is his own disposition that prompts the image. He is always
looking at himself in the glass of his conscience. He tells the
Players "to hold, as 'twere, the mirror up to nature"; and there is,
indeed, more than a little of the actor in him.[80]

It is not that he is crudely self-conscious.[81] But he is ever trying
to see himself, with his mind's eye, as he is; never, in the nature
of things, succeeding; never satisfied of the truth of what he sees.
Before such a mirror so constantly and provokingly held up, a
man inevitably falls to attitudinizing, and to distorting the truth

---

[80] It is, of course, a very obvious image, and Shakespeare employs it again and
again. But its use comes most naturally to the consciously imaginative man. And
Hamlet's cousin-german Richard II, it will be remembered, at a most poignant
moment actually sends for a looking-glass and moralizes upon it.

[81] Nor, for that matter, will the good actor be. The actor's necessary consciousness of himself, not as himself but as somebody else, is a very different and a far
more complicated thing.

about himself. Till suffering has flogged all self-consciousness out
of him, Hamlet is ever a little apt to be striking spiritual attitudes.

Such morbidly introspective characters are neither truest to
themselves in solitude nor very likely to be happy in the intimacy
of love—when their egoism may be either overfed, if they are the
more loved, or if they are the more loving, starved. But they may
find relief from the obscure and warping tyranny of self in the
generosities of friendship. With their friends they can be confidently and forgetfully and·transparently themselves. And while
the play may seem to be but one long opportunity for Hamlet to
express himself, the simple truth about him is rather that which
is reflected from the few moments' self-forgetful praise of his
friend. Here he is free of all antic disposition, assumed or innate.
Such moments are very revealing; they outweigh in their vividness
many wordy apologies, protests and explanations. And the dramatist can, through the undeniable personality of the actor, make
them vivid and convincing indeed.

We learn much about a man when we learn what qualities in
other men or women he unaffectedly admires. Hamlet's is a con-
tinued tale of disillusion about others and about himself. Horatio
is the one human being brought into close touch with him, whom
he does not look on either with contempt or reprobation. So there
is heart of grace in the very music of that

> Horatio, thou art e'en as just a man
> As e'er my conversation coped withal. . . .

and what follows rings out like a true confession of faith:

> Dost thou hear?
> Since my dear soul was mistress of her choice
> And could of men distinguish, her election
> Hath seal'd thee for herself; for thou hast been
> As one, in suffering all, that suffers nothing,
> A man that fortune's buffets and rewards
> Hast ta'en with equal thanks. . . .

This is what he finds best in a man; these are the saving virtues.
There is, then, sounder self-judgment in the wistful

> and bless'd are those
> Whose blood and judgment are so well commingled

> That they are not a pipe for fortune's finger
> To sound what stop she please.

—in that merely implicit confession of his own contrasted weakness—than in all the self-scoldings of the soliloquies. We shall discount these a little in any case. He did not—it was then and there plain—really envy the Player his facile emotion; that was only a stick with which to beat himself. He knows he is no coward. He does not in the least wish that he were Fortinbras; his only interest in the sight of him, "with divine ambition puffed," being that it is an "occasion" which informs against him—and which he can improve. He teems with intellectual pride; and his self-depreciation—the commonest of traits in the sensitively proud —is only a token of it. But when he exclaims to Horatio:

> Give me that man
> That is not passion's slave, and I will wear him
> In my heart's core, ay, in my heart of heart,
> As I do thee. . . .

he is, by the humble title of his love for him, asking the aid and comfort of qualities in his friend which, past the need of protest or excuse, he knows himself to lack.

This spontaneous revelation does not contradict what he says about himself; there is, of course, much actual and more potential truth in that. But it simplifies and clarifies it; helps us winnow the grain of it from the chaff. We see him here with his friend, and the gentle spirit and good mind shine out. But we see too that had his mother lived spotless and his father died of old age, he would still have been the man whose blood and judgment are so ill-commingled that he will always be his "passion's slave." That "vicious mole of nature" in him is rooted deep. Misfortunes do not change a character, they but bring out its weakness or its strength.

THE INNER STRIFE

Hamlet's task would at best be a hard one. He is to kill an anointed king, his uncle and his mother's husband; and, after, he will have to justify his deed to her and to the world—for while he may take the Ghost's word for a thousand pound, will they his mere report of it? Shakespeare does not develop this political and practical aspect of the business. It will have been implicitly clearer

to his Renaissance-minded audience than it is to us. The Queen
is brought within sight of the vindicative truth. We see the King
belatedly protected by his courtiers and Switzers. The protagonist
of that potential drama would need all his wits about him.

But Hamlet, from the very outset, is inwardly divided and
weakened. The finer the nature, the nicer its balances; his can ill
afford such strife. His spirit is in revolt against his natural affections; and the supernatural shock to come makes yet worse work,
the unhappy mind alone being poorly armed against it. Thereafter
he is triply at odds within himself; affections, faith and reason,
warring each with the other; the harvest of it his questioning

> Whether 'tis nobler in the mind to suffer
> The slings and arrows of outrageous fortune,
> Or to take arms against a sea of troubles,
> And by opposing end them? . . .

—end them by killing, not his enemy, but himself? To some such
cross-purposes does war within a man fatally lead.

But even were he at one with himself, it will be (he is to find)
another sort of self that the task needs. And what we watch in
him is the dire process of the conversion. His finer traits must be
blunted. Gentleness, simplicity, generosity; of what use are they?
In the unexacted courtesy towards Marcellus and Bernardo and
the Players is the old Hamlet; in the mockery of Polonius, the
overt contempt for Osric, is the new. Of impulsive, trustful affection Rosencrantz and Guildenstern cure him; and they teach him
to pay men back in their own coin. He must learn to be callous.

> What a piece of work is a man!

—but after his wanton destruction of a piece of such work, it is

> I'll lug the guts into the neighbour room.

He must learn to be cruel. He has already fleshed his tongue on
the helpless Ophelia when, summoned to his mother, he goes,
praying only that he may

> speak daggers to her, but use none.

Now a man is always a little ridiculous when he strives to be
other than he is; and Hamlet is so, if tragically so. He is conscious
of it, for he is conscious of everything concerning him; and the
riddling talk and antic disposition, besides being an ambush, are

an outward travesty of this ineptitude, behind which the humiliating reality is obscured. It is another source of discord within him. The incongruity between "the soul of Nero" and his own is brought home to him when, for all his arrogated callousness, he suddenly "weeps for what is done."[32] And this effort to be what he is not only increases his self-distrust. He spurs himself from backsliding. Having spoken daggers, and (he hears her cry) cleft his mother's heart in twain, he has relapsed—the Ghost intervening—into pity for her also. That will not do; so he stirs himself to a few more quite superfluously brutal strokes before he leaves her.

His reiterated "Let me be cruel," "I must be cruel. . . ." shows him well aware, in fact, that he is not replacing his weakness and melancholy by confidence and strength, only disguising them as in ill-fitting armor, giving them a weapon—to be so ineptly used that it will prove more dangerous to the innocent than the guilty. By sheer reckless inadvertence he kills Polonius, after he has deliberately spared the guilty King at his prayers, because he must needs catch him

> about some act
> That has no relish of salvation in 't . . .

and trip him so

> that his heels may kick at heaven,
> And that his soul may be as damned and black
> As hell, whereto it goes.

Into such a devil's labyrinth is he led!

And when he departs in custody to England, it is not so much that Claudius has defeated him as that within himself he is still a baffled man; his own primary problem is still unsolved. His

---

[32] Gertrude tells Claudius that he did so; and while she may wish to soften him towards Hamlet, there is nothing to show that she is inventing. The moment is indicated by

> For this same lord,
> I do repent . . . .

But Shakespeare evidently wishes to emphasize this bent in him; for later by the graveside Gertrude assures Laertes that though

> thus awhile the fit will work on him;
> Anon, as patient as the female dove,
> When that her golden couplets are disclosed,
> His silence will sit drooping.

affections are poisoned, his will is self-destructive, and the ever-questing mind, playing so curiously around his purposes, has but betrayed them. Upon which his verdict is:

> from this time forth,
> My thoughts be bloody, or be nothing worth!

And what bitterer contempt could the intellectual Hamlet find to pour upon his "paragon of animals," so "infinite in faculty," and upon "capability and god-like reason," with all that it has done for him so far?

When he returns he is "sane" again; the inner strife is ended. Upon what terms? They show in his placid philosophizings beside the forgotten Ophelia's grave. His power to suffer for his mother's sin has thinned out to the sentiment of "Alas, poor Yorick!" And when we hear of the lethal trick he has played upon his one-time comrades, his enemy's ignorant instruments, and that it comes not near his conscience, plainly he no longer lacks nerve to deal with that enemy himself. The King's doom sounds in his coldly confident answer to Horatio's warning:

> the interim is mine;
> And a man's life's no more than to say 'One.'

So here is a Hamlet fit at last for his task. But in the conversion much that seemed lovely in his nature has perished, failing under the test to which he had to put it. Yet though the physical man issues from the trial sorely strained, and the mind is hardened, the spirit is still not debased. Its nobility shines through the apology to Laertes for the "madness" which has been "poor Hamlet's enemy." Let the terrible task be but fulfilled, there is promise of a Hamlet at peace, and the better a man for his ordeal. But that cannot be. The penalty of things done in that "sore distraction" must be paid.

THE FRUSTRATE MIND

Were Shakespeare not a dramatist but a preacher, or had he confused the two callings, he might well have presented Hamlet to us as a warning of the dangers of thinking for oneself. Beneath the shocks of the action this quiet disintegrant is ever at work. And among the half-dozen passages which outdo, by their poignancy or weight, the rest of the self-revealing, there are two bearing particular witness to it.[88] Midway through his ordeal, and for fruit of his deepest meditation, we have:

> Thus conscience does make cowards of us all,
> And thus the native hue of resolution
> Is sicklied o'er with the pale cast of thought,
> And enterprises of great pitch and moment
> With this regard their currents turn awry
> And lose the name of action. . . .

—and the blunders that follow are proof of it. (This "conscience," needless to say, is not the good or bad conscience of the moralist; it stands for knowledge of himself.[84]) Then, with the consequences of the blunders to be faced, comes the exasperated

> Sure he that made us with such large discourse,
> Looking before and after, gave us not
> That capability and god-like reason
> To fust in us unused. . . .

Yet his use of it has paralyzed his actions, his thought being

> but one part wisdom
> And ever three parts coward. . .

and, what is worse, he remains essentially ignorant still. He breaks off his arguing with the cry:

> I do not know
> Why yet I live to say 'This thing's to do,'
> Sith I have cause and will and strength and means
> To do 't. . . .

For beside that failure his blunders hardly seem to count. His weakness and melancholy and his fits of "madness" are depressions and storms which will pass; the "honesty" of the Ghost, even,

---

[88] Key-passages; those which are given, by one dramatic means or another, an uncommon emphasis. For example:

> O, that this too too solid flesh would melt . . .

> The time is out of joint! O cursed spite,
> That ever I was born to set it right!

> Give me that man
> That is not passion's slave. . . .

and the two I am about to quote. The interpretative value of such lines is to be measured by their immediately salient effect.

[84] The O.E.D. quotes Swift: "The word Conscience properly signifies, that knowledge which a man hath within himself of his own thoughts and actions."

is a side issue. But here is fundamental frustration. He faces it with the calm which belongs to the morrow of a defeat. He puts his case at its best; he has "cause and will and strength and means." But the keystone of the arch is out. Of what avail a capability and god-like reason, which offers you all knowledge except the knowledge of yourself, without which you cannot put the rest to any certain use? Was ever such mockery? Here, therefore, we have the last of the introspective Hamlet; and the practical man, back from banishment, will mock at reason as reason once mocked at him:

> Rashly—
> And praised be rashness for it!—let us know,
> Our indiscretion sometimes serves us well
> When our deep plots do pall; and that should learn us
> There's a divinity that shapes our ends,
> Rough-hew them how we will.

A Fortinbras could never find himself so frustrated. But Hamlet, the philosopher forced to action, must needs ask *why* he does what he does, must pause, "looking before and after," thinking precisely—much "too precisely on the event."

Disillusion will force from him an ironical good word for "that monster custom." But in the very first emphatic thing he said, in that

> Seems, madam? Nay, it is. I know not 'seems.' . . .

we could recognize the discriminating mind, and the contempt for all

> actions that a man might play . . .

He was for truth in word and deed. The flaw in the position was that, feeling he had

> that within which passeth show . . .

he assumed that he had there too a paramount judge of what the truth must be. It is such a mind, set impersonally to work, that delights to

> trace the noble dust of Alexander till he find it stopping a
> bunghole . . .

and it may happen upon many interesting facts by the way. But its hairsplitting sensitiveness is only too likely to convert an impulsive

> Haste me to know't, that I, with wings as swift
> As meditation or the thoughts of love,
> May sweep to my revenge.

more swiftly still into a

> The time is out of joint! O cursed spite,
> That ever I was born to set it right!

and, overindulged, as we are let see, it can bring a man, sword poised above his enemy, to the tragi-comic futility of

> Now might I do it pat, now he is praying;
> And now I'll do 't; and so he goes to heaven,
> And so am I revenged. That would be scanned:
> . . . and am I then revenged?

Would Fortinbras have paused, and thought so precisely, and looked before and after—and let that consummate moment pass?

Such deadlocked impotence, when it is of the mind only, makes a comic rather than a tragic spectacle; we laugh at mere cleverness self-defeated. It becomes tragic when things beyond the mind's mastery are at stake; and when, affections disabled and spiritual security gone, only "god-like reason" is left a man for guide. Hamlet's is a human soul adrift. And all the wisdom which his rash and lonely mind can teach him is that Denmark is a prison, and the world one, the goodly frame of the earth a sterile promontory, and man—the beauty of the world, the paragon of animals—a quintessence of dust. No better than a beast if he does not use his reason; yet, using it, this is what he finds. Small wonder if a consciousness of such anarchy make him an impotent coward and lead him to the despair which, but for "the dread of something after death," would have him done with it all! Yet to what less barren conclusion is unmitigated reason likely to lead? For is it not by our unreasoning impulses and affections, by our faith in life, that we chiefly live and act? In Hamlet this native faith has been stunned. And he never recovers from the blow.

He never regains a natural spiritual health, nor does he reach self-understanding. His loathing of life only hardens to indifference. The baffled "I do not know. . . ." is his last word on the matter, except for that riddling recognition of a mad Hamlet in him and a sane, the one that did not do the things he willed (so

much for sanity!), the other that did the things he did not will
to do. The dying

> Had I but time—as this fell sergeant, death,
> Is strict in his arrest—O! I could tell you...

may hint at belated light breaking in. But Shakespeare leaves the
matter there; and he is, of course, dramatically right to do so. For
if Hamlet understood himself the spiritual tragedy would disappear again in the tragedy of action; and if anyone else explained
him to us he would become a merely interesting "case." While
we know no more of him than he knows himself he holds our
sympathy. And, in a double sense, his trouble is very much our
own.

A SOUL ADRIFT

His heresies, worn by three centuries currency, no longer shock
us. But they are grave enough—and gravest when he faces suicide
—for him to have good cause to wish that his sins may be remembered in Ophelia's prayers.[85] Shakespeare (with his play's licens-
ing to consider) cannot, if he would, meddle with theology. But
he has managed before now to deal with much belonging to it;
and, in this case, the problem of the Ghost brings him as near to
the kernel of the matter as he needs to go.

Hamlet's heart tells him that it is his father's ghost, but his
mind as promptly questions whether it be

> a spirit of health or goblin damned ...

While he listens he believes; but when, on its vanishing, he in-
vokes the host of heaven, he adds

> And shall I couple hell?

And later, at his calmest, he thinks it well may be

> a damned ghost that we have seen ...

In this again, then, his native faith is flawed; and the rift but
opens deeper doubts. Insoluble doubts; for if man's mind cannot
master the mortal world, what chance has it against mysteries
beyond? Yet if they can touch him so nearly as this, and since

---

[85] This question of the sin of suicide is amply canvassed; by Hamlet himself
more than once, and from more than one standpoint in Ophelia's case.

death is the common door to them, bring himself to braving them
he must. Hamlet, the intellectual hero, very certainly must be
allowed to face them. It is the crown to his dignity that he should.
Subtract these reckonings from his account, indeterminate though
they are, and by how much would not his dramatic stature be
diminished?

Little explicit argument emerges; in this, as in the struggle for
self-understanding, no more than the play's action can be brought
to engender. But that central soliloquy questions eternity itself:

> To be or not to be . . .

not simply here—a dagger thrust will settle that—but hereafter.
And the

> consummation
> Devoutly to be wished . . .

is not merely the body's death, but the soul's. The proud faith
that could still brave the Ghost with

> And for my soul, what can it do to that,
> Being a thing immortal as itself?

is gone, and doubt and dread replace it. The infection, which his
mother's treachery to his faith in her sowed in his heart, has
spread and deepened. The disillusioned mind now asks: may not
this seeming spirit of my father be even as treacherous, be abusing
me to damn me? And out of such doubt he builds a dreadfully
imagined limbo around him, where evil is still potent and the
departed soul as helpless as in a dream.

The Ghost is proved to be an honest ghost, but this does not
give Hamlet back the old confident possession of his soul. He has
let himself be made an instrument of these supernatural powers.
No blind instrument; the enfranchised mind rebels against the
indignity of that, against working for mere "bait and salary." He
is lending his mind to their work to better the occasion offered
him when he spares for a worse fate the kneeling, guilty King.
A minute later he has involuntarily killed Polonius. These powers
he serves—who have tricked him into that—are truly not nice in
their dealings:

> but heaven hath pleased it so,
> To punish me with this and this with me,
> That I must be their scourge and minister. . . .

To punish him with this indeed; a lonely soul seeking its right and wrong amidst such anarchy!

The strange little scene of the Ghost's return opens sadder uncertainties. The armored figure of the battlements is now:

My father, in his habit as he liv'd!

—here in a fleeting happiness with wife and son. Commands to vengeance have become "this piteous action"; the majestic, memorable farewell turns to a stealing-away out at the portal; and his mother is blind and deaf to what he must still believe he sees. Evil which no vengeance can expiate; the helpless suffering of the dead, the irremediable estrangement of these three that once were one. Matter, indeed, far more for tears than blood.

Hamlet, after this, talks no more of the Ghost, nor of the soul.[36] As to the hereafter:

To what base uses we may return, Horatio! . . . Alexander died, Alexander was buried, Alexander returneth into dust; the dust is earth, of earth we make loam; and why of that loam, whereto he was converted, might they not stop a beer barrel?

And when he comes to die, his hope is simply that the rest will be silence.

SHAKESPEARE'S PROPHETIC SOUL

To the more perceptive of Shakespeare's audience the most interesting thing about *Hamlet* must have been that in the old story retold an old issue was dealt with afresh. There must always be interest in this. To every age the same problems recur, differently decked out; and men have to decide whether to attack them as their fathers did, obey habit and authority, or seek and take their own conscientious way. And in that age of the breaking-up of creeds which was Shakespeare's, this, under one guise or another, was a dilemma with which many men were faced.

Hamlet is a man adrift from old faiths and not yet anchored in new; a man of his time in that, more particularly. The theologians had been busy, patching and repatching. But formulas, which the mind may accept, are one thing; and the lively faith, by which we live in unconscious harmony with our surroundings, is

---

[36] Such statistics are not necessarily significant; but the word is in very ample use up to this point in the play, and by Hamlet himself is not once used after.

very much another. This faith extends to secular everyday things.
Let it be flawed here and there, it will be weakened everywhere.
Put it then to some extraordinary test, and we at once find that
its integrity is broken. Reason, brought to the rescue, cannot help,
for it works by other means; it cannot even tell us what is wrong.
Act we must, if action is what is asked of us, for the world will
not stand still. But with crippled faith and enfranchised reason
at odds in us we do self-defeating things, and may lapse into
impotence and despair. That is Hamlet's case. And while none of
those first spectators may have stood, as he did, with

> a father killed, a mother stained . . .

and under ghostly command to avenge the crime, not a few of
them must have seen in his spiritual troubles only a more vivid
shadowing-forth of their own.

He is of an intellectual generation to whom the word has been
let penetrate: Prove all things; for only so can one learn to hold
fast that which is good. Could he simply have been set to prove
the theory of a carefully selected few—he and his fellow-student
Horatio—in the shelter of that Protestant Wittenberg to which he
so longed to return, all might have been well. But he has to face
an urgent, practical problem, which is colored for him, moreover,
by his own most intimate concern with it. How can a man treat
such a matter dispassionately and trust to his own isolated judgment of the right and the wrong of it? And if it is a question, as
this is, of life and death, and even worse, of salvation or damnation—let him go arguing such issues as these forth and back and
back and forth again in terms of his own doubts and griefs and
fears, into what dark and vertiginous places may not the lonely
mind be lured?

> What if it tempt you toward the flood, my lord,
> Or to the dreadful summit of the cliff
> That beetles o'er his base into the sea,
> And there assume some other horrible form,
> Which might deprive your sovereignty of reason
> And draw you into madness?

Such is Horatio's poetic picture of what does, in fact, occur.

Some men manage, seemingly, to reduce these high issues to
their own measure, and will emerge from such an ordeal with

their God in their pocket, as it were, justifying whatever they may now choose to do. Some will stay lost in the moral anarchy, which is all they have found. Many retreat baffled from the adventure, and the readier to act thereafter as habit or authority or the formulas of their dead faith dictate. Many a man, then, can find touches of himself in the later Hamlet at least, who returns weary of questioning, hardened (by a sea-fight and some ruthless practice upon his jailers) to his deadly task, and looking back to the old self-torture as "madness."

Yet his soul's adventure, which seemed but to lead him to defeat, was heroic too. For if men shirk such perils, how are these high matters to be brought home to spiritual freedmen? Nor will mere intellectual venturing suffice, if lively faith, in its health and strength, is to be found and enjoyed again. Hamlet, being called upon, flings his whole being—mind and affections both, the best and the worst of him, weakness no less than strength—into the trial. And he widens the issue till he sees eternal life and death, his own and his enemy's, at stake. He will reconcile himself, as he is and in all he is, with these now unveiled verities of this world and the next, if that may be. In which Promethean struggle towards the light he is beaten—as who has not been?—with havoc wrought, not in him only, but by him, even to his own despite. It is none the less a heroic struggle.

Here, for me, is the master-clue to Hamlet's "mystery." The "sane" world around him has naturally no sense of it, nor the too sane spectator of the play. He does not pluck out the heart of it himself. Neither are we meant to. For his trouble is rooted in the fact that it is a mystery. Shakespeare, for his part, must order his play in terms of action (even as Hamlet is called on to act); the tragedy of thwarted thought and tortured spirit is the rich soil in which he replants his borrowings. Yet while the action keeps us interested, it is this tragedy and the mystery of it, which is enthralling.

If we are at one with Polonius in thinking that

to expostulate
> What majesty should be, what duty is,
> Why day is day, night night, and time is time,
> Were nothing but to waste night, day and time . . .

and that, as to Hamlet,

> to define true madness,
> What is't but to be nothing else but mad?

why, Shakespeare will not, so to say, have spoiled our Kyd for us.
The play is attractively alive on the surface; the riches of its
underworkings of emotion and thought fall to those whose own
are a touchstone for them. And it fulfills, in this, the double
demand of drama, which is not for action alone nor the revelation
of character only, but for character in action. Pertinently so; since
the character-revealing problems of life present themselves as
problems of action, which men attack even as Hamlet does, imagi-
natively, thoughtfully, passionately too. And the play's progress,
like a stream in flood, here flowing deeply and evenly, here eddy-
ing and spreading, there rushing down some steep channel—it is
thus, and not to any clocklike measure, that human affairs do
move.

In England, for the best part of a century before *Hamlet* was
written, and for sixty years after, the finer issues of the spiritual
revolution which the Renaissance had begun were obscured by
secular discord, persecution and civil war; and the ensuing peace
left them hardened into formula. To the popular mind thus distressed and coarsened the finer issues implicit either in play or
character might well make small appeal. Nor would they be
likelier to touch the conscience of the positive eighteenth century.[37]
Not till it was waning, and many men had come to find their set
creeds unsatisfying, till they began to ask the old essential questions once again, to have a better answer if they might, did the
Hamlet of spiritual tragedy come by his own; then to become,
indeed, the typical hero of a new "age of doubt." It was as if
Shakespeare, so alive to the spirit of his own time, had been in this
mysteriously attuned besides to some

> prophetic soul
> Of the wide world dreaming on things to come.

While our age of doubt endures, and men still cry despairingly,

---

[37] See Johnson's note to the play. He praises the conduct and, in particular, the
"variety" of the action. But "of the feigned madness of Hamlet there appears no
adequate cause, for he does nothing which he might not have done with the
reputation of sanity."

"I do not know. . . ," and must go on uncomforted, the play will keep, I should suppose, its hold on us. If a new age of faith or reason should succeed, or one for a while too crushed by brute reality to value either, Hamlet may then be seen again simply as the good Polonius saw him.